Costa Rica

WORLD BIBLIOGRAPHICAL SERIES

General Editors:
Robert G. Neville (Executive Editor)
John J. Horton

Robert A. Myers   Ian Wallace
Hans H. Wellisch   Ralph Lee Woodward, Jr.

John J. Horton is Deputy Librarian of the University of Bradford and currently Chairman of its Academic Board of Studies in Social Sciences. He has maintained a longstanding interest in the discipline of area studies and its associated bibliographical problems, with special reference to European Studies. In particular he has published in the field of Icelandic and of Yugoslav studies, including the two relevant volumes in the World Bibliographical Series.

Robert A. Myers is Associate Professor of Anthropology in the Division of Social Sciences and Director of Study Abroad Programs at Alfred University, Alfred, New York. He has studied post-colonial island nations of the Caribbean and has spent two years in Nigeria on a Fulbright Lectureship. His interests include international public health, historical anthropology and developing societies. In addition to *Amerindians of the Lesser Antilles: a bibliography* (1981), *A Resource Guide to Dominica, 1493–1986* (1987) and numerous articles, he has compiled the World Bibliographical Series volumes on *Dominica* (1987) and *Nigeria* (1989).

Ian Wallace is Professor of Modern Languages at Loughborough University of Technology. A graduate of Oxford in French and German, he also studied in Tübingen, Heidelberg and Lausanne before taking teaching posts at universities in the USA, Scotland and England. He specializes in East German affairs, especially literature and culture, on which he has published numerous articles and books. In 1979 he founded the journal *GDR Monitor*, which he continues to edit.

Hans H. Wellisch is Professor emeritus at the College of Library and Information Services, University of Maryland. He was President of the American Society of Indexers and was a member of the International Federation for Documentation. He is the author of numerous articles and several books on indexing and abstracting, and has published *The Conversion of Scripts* and *Indexing and Abstracting: an International Bibliography*. He also contributes frequently to *Journal of the American Society for Information Science, The Indexer* and other professional journals.

Ralph Lee Woodward, Jr. is Chairman of the Department of History at Tulane University, New Orleans, where he has been Professor of History since 1970. He is the author of *Central America, a Nation Divided*, 2nd ed. (1985), as well as several monographs and more than sixty scholarly articles on modern Latin America. He has also compiled volumes in the World Bibliographical Series on *Belize* (1980), *Nicaragua* (1983), and *El Salvador* (1988). Dr. Woodward edited the Central American section of the *Research Guide to Central America and the Caribbean* (1985) and is currently editor of the Central American history section of the *Handbook of Latin American Studies*.

VOLUME 126

Costa Rica

Charles L. Stansifer

Compiler

CLIO PRESS

OXFORD, ENGLAND · SANTA BARBARA, CALIFORNIA
DENVER, COLORADO

British Library Cataloguing in Publication Data

Stansifer, Charles L.
Costa Rica – (World bibliographical series v. 126)
I. Title   II. Series
016.97286

ISBN 1–85109–027–4

Clio Press Ltd.,
55 St. Thomas' Street,
Oxford OX1 1JG, England.

ABC-CLIO,
130 Cremona Drive,
Santa Barbara,
CA 9311.', USA.

972·0866016

Designed by Bernard Crossland.
Typeset by Columns Design and Production Services, Reading, England.
Printed and bound in Great Britain by
Billing and Sons Ltd., Worcester.

THE WORLD BIBLIOGRAPHICAL SERIES

This series, which is principally designed for the English speaker, will eventually cover every country in the world, each in a separate volume comprising annotated entries on works dealing with its history, geography, economy and politics; and with its people, their culture, customs, religion and social organization. Attention will also be paid to current living conditions – housing, education, newspapers, clothing, etc.– that are all too often ignored in standard bibliographies; and to those particular aspects relevant to individual countries. Each volume seeks to achieve, by use of careful selectivity and critical assessment of the literature, an expression of the country and an appreciation of its nature and national aspirations, to guide the reader towards an understanding of its importance. The keynote of the series is to provide, in a uniform format, an interpretation of each country that will express its culture, its place in the world, and the qualities and background that make it unique. The views expressed in individual volumes, however, are not necessarily those of the publisher.

VOLUMES IN THE SERIES

To all students of Costa Rica

Contents

Contents

Contents

Introduction

Costa Rica is a young country. The indigenous inhabitants left no enduring monuments compared to those left by the Mayas in Guatemala and Mexico and the Incas in Peru. During the colonial period Costa Rica was a small, poor province of the Kingdom of Guatemala, of little interest to the masters of the Spanish Empire or, for that matter, to the Empire's rivals. Upon independence, achieved in 1821 virtually without Spanish resistance, it became the weakest member of the Central American confederation, and only when the confederation broke up in 1838 did Costa Rica launch its independent life.

One hundred and fifty years ago Costa Rica was an isolated backwater, with fewer than 100,000 inhabitants and scarcely any dependable transport connections to any other country. San José, the capital, had fewer than 20,000 inhabitants. In the capital there was no pharmacy, no professional doctor, and only a primitive hospital. There was no theatre and no bookstore. The first printing press had been brought to Costa Rica in 1833 and the first university, the Universidad de Santo Tomás, opened its doors only in 1844. When Carl Scherzer visited the university in 1853 the university's library consisted of only four or five bookcases. Adequate information about Costa Rica, its people, its history, and its natural resources was unavailable in any language in any library.

However, two forces were already in motion in the mid-nineteenth century which were to change Costa Rica drastically. These ultimately attracted the attention of many foreign observers and scholars and led Costa Ricans themselves to self-examination. The first was the coffee revolution, which had begun earlier in the nineteenth century when coffee was introduced into the country by a far-sighted local governor. By 1850 coffee was the country's most important export and the principal reason for the breakdown of Costa Rica's isolation. The coffee revolution brought foreign exchange and outside contacts and thus provided both the pressure and the wherewithal to improve transport connections with Europe and the United States. The modernization process was under way.

The second force, a magnetic one, was the evolving political economic model which began to accentuate the differences between Costa Rica and its Central American neighbours. As early as the middle of the nineteenth century Costa Rica's commitment to education, its relatively equal distribution of income, and the humaneness of the Costa Rican political process were noticed by a few foreign travellers. These characteristics became even more pronounced with the coffee prosperity of the late nineteenth century. By the 1950s, with no army, an advanced social security system, and a passionate commitment to regular elections, Costa Rica's reputation was secure as one of Latin America's most democratic countries. Today, Costa Rica, although not without its flaws, is generally considered the most democratic country of Latin America.

Interest in the Central American isthmus as a transport route between the East and West coasts of the United States, characteristic of the 1850s, was another factor which began to draw the world's attention to the Central American republics. Panama to the south and Nicaragua to the north naturally drew the bulk of attention because of narrower and more convenient transit routes, but a spillover of visitors did reach Costa Rica. Subsequently, Costa Rica's varied wildlife and evolving political system made it an attractive target for visitors, immigrants, investors, and scholars.

In the second half of the nineteenth century it was Costa Rica's natural wonders which especially contributed to breaking down the country's isolation and to attracting the attention of natural scientists. Intrigued by the variety of wildlife in Costa Rica's many life zones within a small area, European and North American biologists, geographers and others began intensively to explore Costa Rica. Between 1850 and 1914 Costa Rica emerged from scientific obscurity to become one of the best-known centres in the western hemisphere for biological collectors. Although this process was interrupted by the world wars of the twentieth century it was renewed in the 1960s, stimulated by the work of the Organization for Tropical Studies, a consortium of North American and Costa Rican universities, and by a small corps of Costa Rican scientists. Now, it is safe to say that a sizeable number of the world's tropical biologists have been trained or worked in Costa Rica. Few environmentalists today are unaware of Costa Rica's strides in the environmentalist movement.

These forces and characteristics have helped to shape this bibliography, resulting in few entries under some headings and many under others. Because of the absence of large numbers of sedentary Indian civilizations and monumental indigenous cities, such as those found elsewhere in Latin America, the number of archaeological investigations is modest. Unlike many Latin American countries, there are relatively few Costa Rican studies of the colonial period, given the poverty and isolation of that time. With no army since 1948 it is not surprising that there should be only three entries under 'Military', and Costa Rica's excellent record in the field of human rights results in a scarcity of bibliographical entries under that topic.

In contrast, there are many studies of agriculture, especially coffee and bananas, on environment and flora and fauna, and on Costa Rica's political economic model. The attractiveness of the political system, plus the openness of the society, the availability of documentation, and in general the ease of working in Costa Rica, has resulted in hundreds of investigations in the fields of history and political science. Many of these had their origins in PhD dissertations. For many of the same reasons economists, who had tended to ignore Costa Rica before, hurried to Costa Rica to analyse the economic crisis of the mid-1980s. Costa Rica's heavy commitment to environmental protection has led to scores of monographs on flora and fauna and to general environmental studies.

Other factors too have helped to dictate the contents of this bibliography. Because of the proliferation of studies of all kinds in the past decade the compiler has had to be highly selective. Readers will find that English-language titles are favoured over Spanish, books over articles, more recent titles over older ones, and the social sciences over the natural and physical sciences. Among specific disciplines political science is favoured over sociology, biology over geology, geology over medicine, and the visual arts over music. These choices were made in the belief that the favoured disciplines provided more literature of interest to the general reader, but they are also influenced by *what has been written* since, by its very nature, this bibliography cannot report what has not been written. It appears, for example, that political scientists have been more active in attempting to understand the Costa Rican political system than sociologists have been in analysing the social structure. Similarly, more studies have been made of Costa Rican visual arts than of music.

The primary purpose of the bibliography is to assist English-language readers to locate material on Costa Rica. This results in an extraordinary selectivity of titles in Spanish in certain fields, such as in history and law. Many Spanish-language titles in history are included (although for reasons of space many more had to be excluded) since any serious student of Costa Rican history knows that he or she must control the Spanish-language titles in order to perfect his or her knowledge of this field. History titles included tend toward the general, but students will find many specific periods and topics covered in specialized Costa Rican periodicals such as the *Revista de los Archivos Nacionales* or the *Revista de Historia*. As for law, the fact is that few English-language students of law have attempted to fathom the inner workings of the Costa Rican legal system, and Costa Rican legal scholars themselves have done the bulk of the legal analysis. Users of this bibliography will note a considerable number of Costa Rican biographies in contrast to other Latin American bibliographies in this series. One of the reasons for this is the strong commitment of the Editorial Costa Rica in San José to promoting the publication of studies of famous Costa Ricans.

One additional explanation of the contents is in order. The bibliography contains many articles on Costa Rica in edited books about Central America or Latin America. Only chapter articles specifically on Costa Rica were selected from these publications, and no attempt was made to select general syntheses of Central America which include or touch on Costa Rica. Many of these have been admirably annotated by R. Lee Woodward's *Nicaragua* (Oxford: Clio Press, 1983) and there seems little justification in duplicating his annotations. Incidentally, for the reader who wants a general orientation on the history of Central America he or she can do no better than consult Woodward's *Central America: A Nation Divided* (New York: Oxford University Press, 1985).

Under the Farmington Plan of Library Acquisitions the University of Kansas Libraries made a commitment in 1958 to collect everything published on Costa Rica. That commitment has been scrupulously adhered to from that time to the present. The result is that, as a University of Kansas professor, I have had at my fingertips the largest collection of Costa Ricana in the United States. Although I have of necessity occasionally relied on other libraries in the United States and of course on the libraries of Costa Rica, the University of Kansas Libraries have provided me with most of the items mentioned in this bibliography (and with many other items that were left out for reasons of space). Needless to say, I am grateful to those who made that important decision on collections policy in the first place and to those who had the wisdom to continue it.

Many people have assisted me in the preparation of this bibliography. My greatest debt is to Rachel Miller, Acquisitions Librarian at the University of Kansas Libraries, and to Javier Gaínza, Professor of Computer Science at the Universidad de Costa Rica:

gingerly yet determinedly they moved me from the three-by-five card age to the computer era, thus hastening the completion of the project. Several specialists in Latin American acquisitions at the University of Kansas Libraries, particularly Ellen Brow, Shelley Miller and Rhonda Neugebauer, have been particularly helpful. Nancy Chaison of the Center of Latin American Studies of the University of Kansas, and Marcia Quirós, of the University of Kansas Department of History, were faithful supporters when the project threatened to be shelved by administrative commitments. My historian colleagues, Carlos Meléndez of the Universidad de Costa Rica and Larry K. Laird of the United States Agency for International Development, deserve credit for inspiring me many years ago to begin not only a collection of publications about Costa Rica but also of titles on Costa Rica. My wife, Mary Ellen Stansifer, has helped in ways too numerous to mention. To all of them I express my most sincere gratitude. When the printed bibliography is in their hands they will be, I hope, as delighted as I am to see the finished product. They of course need feel no responsibility for errors – those are mine alone.

Charles L. Stansifer
Lawrence, Kansas
January 1991

Dissertations on Costa Rica

Justo Jacobo Aguilar. 'Technological change and governmental policies in the industrial sector of Costa Rica', University of Connecticut, 1985. 142p. (DES86-04924.)

D. Craig Anderson. 'Overview and analysis of agricultural programs in higher education in Costa Rica', Iowa State University, 1983. 144p. (PSN83-23263.)

Marcelino Avila. 'An economic evaluation of alternative annual cropping systems in two regions of Costa Rica', Columbia University, 1979. 204p. (BTK80-02338.)

Tatyana Basok. 'Local settlement of Salvadoran refugees in Costa Rica', York University (Canada), 1988.

Lee Bourgoin. 'Economic and public policy implications of energy pricing in Costa Rica', Harvard University, 1986. 376p. (DES86-09723.)

Arthur August Breitsprecher. 'Stem-growth periodicity of trees in a tropical wet forest of Costa Rica', University of Washington, 1987. 175p. (DA8802197.)

Chalmers Sherfey Brumbaugh. 'Costa Rica: the making of a livable society', University of Wisconsin, Madison, 1985. 492p. (DES86-01529.)

Paterno Reyes Castillo. 'Geology and geochemistry of Cocos Island, Costa Rica: implications for the evolution of the aseismic Cocos ridge', Washington University, 1987. 318p. (DA8729918.)

Colin Austin Chapman. 'Foraging strategies, patch use, and constraints on group size in three species of Costa Rican primates', University of Alberta (Canada), 1986.

Winifred Creamer. 'Production and exchange on two islands in the

Gulf of Nicoya, Costa Rica, A. D. 1200-1500', Tulane University, 1983. 390p. (PSN83-22093.)

Christopher Phillip Daniel. 'Public housing and potable water policy in Costa Rica: administrative decision making in a developing society', University of Florida, 1979. 258p. (BTK79-21921.)

Marilyn April Dorn. 'The administrative partitioning of Costa Rica: politics and planners', University of Chicago, 1985.

Eduardo Doryan-Garrón. 'Explaining development strategy choice by state elites', Harvard University, 1988. 311p. (DA8901675.)

Carmen María Fallas Santana. 'Business and politics in Costa Rica, 1849–1860: consensus and conflict within the coffee planter and merchant elite during the Mora years', University of California, Los Angeles, 1988. 178p. (DA8906404.)

Gerardo Enrique Fonseca Retana. 'A systematic cross cultural replication of the "class" program in Costa Rica', University of Oregon, 1981. 70p. (PSN82-09664.)

Hector Ricardo Gertel. 'Economic fluctuations, the state, and educational reform movements: the case of Costa Rica, 1850–1900', Stanford University, 1982. 203p. (PSN82-20463.)

Thomas Henry Gindling, Jr. 'An investigation of labor market segmentation in San José, Costa Rica', Cornell University, 1988. 170p. (DA8804545.)

Victor M. Gómez. 'Fertility change in Costa Rica: 1964–1986', University of Wisconsin, Madison, 1989. 300p. (DA8906520.)

Mark M. Graham. 'The stone sculpture of Costa Rica: the production of ideologies of dominance in prehistoric rank societies', University of California, Los Angeles, 1985. 506p. (DEV87-23213.)

Dianne Wilner Green. 'Some effects of social security programs on the distribution of income in Costa Rica', University of Pittsburgh, 1977. 121p. (BTK78-01861.)

Federico David Guendel. 'Seismotectonics of Costa Rica: an analytical view of the southern terminus of the Middle America trench', University of California, Santa Cruz, 1986. 174p. (DA8709129.)

John Wilton Hoopes, II. 'Early ceramics and the origins of village life in lower Central America', Harvard University, 1987. 779p.

Sally Peterson Horn. 'Fire and paramo vegetation in the Cordillera de Talamanca, Costa Rica', University of California, Berkeley, 1986. 160p. (DET86-24793.)

Michael Alan Huston. 'The effect of soil nutrients and light on tree growth and interactions during tropical forest succession: experiments in Costa Rica', University of Michigan, 1982. 292p. (PSN82-24971.)

Moisés Guillermo León Azofeifa. 'Chinese immigrants on the

Atlantic coast of Costa Rica: the economic adaptation of an Asian minority in a pluralistic society', Tulane University, 1987. 440p. (DA8817293.)

Douglas John Levey. 'Fruit–frugivore interactions in a Costa Rican rain forest', University of Wisconsin, Madison, 1986. 288p. (DA8701857.)

Lawrence Reed Lew. 'The geology of the Santa Elena Peninsula, Costa Rica, and its implications for the tectonic evolution of the Central America–Caribbean region', Pennsylvania State University, 1985. 509p. (DES85-24824.)

Eugenia López-Casas. 'Social and biological reproduction of lower-income groups on the Meseta Central in Costa Rica', University of Durham (United Kingdom), 1988. 354p. (Available from UMI in association with The British Library.)

Lorena Madrigal-Díaz. 'Hemoglobin genotype and fertility in a malarial environment: Limón, Costa Rica', University of Kansas, 1988. 132p. (DA8918393.)

Haydée María Mendiola. 'The impact of higher education expansion on social stratification and labour markets: the case of Costa Rica', Stanford University, 1988. 182p. (DA8826200.)

Louis Fernando Miron. 'The national plan for educational development in Costa Rica: theoretical and historical perspective', Tulane University, 1986. 245p. (DET86-24423.)

John Charles Morgan. 'The Partido Liberación Nacional of Costa Rica: a case study on political myth and political culture', Louisiana State University, 1979. 236p. (BTK79-27538.)

Samuel Apollo Musisi-Nkwambwe. 'Transportation networks as agent and index of modernisation in Costa Rica', University of Kansas, 1974. 220p. (DAH75-30069.)

Suzanne M. O'Connor. 'Costa Rica in the world community of nations, 1919–1939: a case study in Latin American internationalism', Loyola University of Chicago, 1976. 202p. (DAH76–24451.)

Aurora Pal Montano. 'The utilization of health care services in two Costa Rican communities', Michigan State University, 1983. 178p. (PSN83-24757.)

Carlos German Paniagua. 'The state and higher education in Costa Rica', Stanford University, 1988. 269p. (DA8815035.)

Maurice Jerome Picard. 'Development and structural change in Costa Rica: a study of the effect of economic linkages and macrosociological variables on welfare', New School for Social Research, 1987. 199p. (DEV87-26442.)

Boris Jacob Popov. 'American retirement abroad: the Costa Rican experience', University of Massachusetts, 1979. 231p. (BTK80-04976.)

Trevor W. Purcell. 'Conformity and dissension: social inequality, values and mobility among West Indian migrants in Limón, Costa Rica', Johns Hopkins University, 1982. 416p. (PSN82-19572.)

Jorge Arturo Quesada Pacheco. 'Types and functions of repetition in American and Costa Rican newspaper editorials', Georgetown University, 1989. 196p. (DA9004746.)

Noel Ernesto Ramírez Sánchez. 'The causes of inflation in small developing economies with a fixed rate of exchange: a comparative analysis of Costa Rica and Nicaragua', Yale University, 1982. 318p. (PSN83-10579.)

William Rickard. 'Environment and densities of population in Costa Rica: a preliminary investigation on the northern zone', University of Kansas, 1974. 275p. (75-17671.)

Peggy Orme Roberts. 'The composition of the Costa Rican population: some evidence from history, genetics, and morphology', University of Colorado, 1978. 160p. (BTK78-20551.)

Ralph Henry Russomando. 'Structures of integration and labor relations in Costa Rica: democratic participation or authoritarian control', University of Massachusetts, 1982. 364p. (PSN82-19846.)

Steven Alan Sader. 'Remote sensing data applications for the inventory and monitoring of renewable natural resources in Costa Rica', University of Idaho, 1981. 172p. (PSN81-19889.)

Mario Samper. 'Generations of settlers: a study of rural households and their markets on the Costa Rican frontier, 1850–1935', University of California, Berkeley, 1988. 462p. (DA8902259.)

Eugenio Sancho Riba. 'Merchant-planters and modernization: an early liberal experiment in Costa Rica, 1849–1870', University of California, San Diego, 1982. 191p. (PSN82-19213.)

Rita Margarethe Schneider-Sliwa. 'Rural nonfarm employment and migration: the case of Costa Rica', Ohio State University, 1982. 204p. (PSN83-05390.)

Stephen Grove Sellers. 'The farmers of Tucurrique', Brandeis University, 1980. 430p. (BTK80-13638.)

Rama Seth. 'Optimal foreign borrowing: the case of Costa Rica', Columbia University, 1986. 224p. (DET86-23608.)

Gail M. Shields. 'Family migration and household production: the Costa Rican experience', University of Utah, 1985. 229p. (DES85-27096.)

Esther R. Skirboll. 'The transitional period in the central highlands of Costa Rica: an analysis of pottery from the Curridabat and Concepción sites', University of Pittsburgh, 1981. 252p. (PSN82-13114.)

Carlos L. Solera-Ruiz. 'Assessment of the goals and the policies of the national development plan 1979–1982 for beef cattle in Costa

Rica', Iowa State University, 1981. 303p. (PSN81-22565.)

Ralph Edward Sullivan. 'Anatomy of a national teachers' strike: a case study of the strike by La Asociación de Profesores de Segunda Enseñañza, republic of Costa Rica, 1977', University of North Dakota, 1978. 245p. (BTK79-04712.)

Oscar Byrne Tinney, Jr. 'Social criticism in the novels of Quince Duncan', University of North Carolina, Chapel Hill, 1988. 185p. (DA8823482.)

Ana Cecilia Torres. 'Barriers to library cooperation in Costa Rica', Texas Woman's University, 1985. 162p. (DES86-08502.)

Joann Myer Valenti. 'An environmental attitude survey: Costa Rica', University of Michigan, 1983. 133p. (PSN93-14372.)

Claudia María Vargas. 'Decentralization of the educational system of Costa Rica', University of Southern California, 1989. (Available exclusively from Micrographics Department, Doheny Library, USC, Los Angeles, California 90089-0182.)

Beatriz Villareal. 'An analysis of the special education services for children and youth in Costa Rica', University of San Diego, 1989. 256p. (DA8918195.)

Anke Maria Neumann Wells. 'Evolution of a humid tropical landscape, in northcentral Costa Rica as deduced from geomorphic and pedogenic evidence', University of Kansas, 1979. 285p. (BTK80-02762.)

Antonio Ybarra-Rojas. 'A typology of agrarian production systems by relations of reproduction in the Pacífico Sur region of Costa Rica', Iowa State University, 1989. 567p. (DA8920200.)

The Country and Its People

1 **Anatomía patriótica.** (A patriotic anatomy.)
   Luis Barahona Jiménez.   Ciudad Universitaria Rodrigo Facio:
   Universidad de Costa Rica, 1970. 97p. (Publicaciones de la Universidad
   de Costa Rica, Serie Filosofía, no. 33).

A philosophical-historical essay in the tradition of the Latin American *pensadores*, the book is an attempt to explain the development of Costa Rican individualism, pragmatism, and conservatism. From this base the author then attempts to fit in the Costa Rican style of leadership and Christianity, and the Costa Rican passion for political and human rights. He ends with a plea for politicians to respect Costa Rica's religious, family, and educational institutions and to develop its ties with Central America and Latin America.

2 **La patria esencial.** (The essence of the country.)
   Luis Barahona Jiménez.   San José: Litografía Impr. LIL, 1980. 120p.

After writing several books touching on the theme of the national character of Costa Rica Barahona offers this summation of his views on essential aspects of Costa Rica. He gives his opinions on literary production, historiography, and social science output within the framework of Costa Rica's system of education and economic limitations. As in other works, he is particularly critical of Costa Rica's failure to develop its own body of political thought and unique political parties. The last fifth of the book is dedicated to religion, which the author believes has a special responsibility in providing the country with a moral compass.

3 **Costa Rica: a country guide.**
   Tom Barry.   Albuquerque, New Mexico: Inter-Hemispheric Education
   Resource Center, 1990. 2nd ed. 108p. bibliog.

Unlike the other guides listed in this bibliography this volume provides, in the main text, a critical analysis of politics, economics, the environment, and foreign policy. It is not a guide to hotels and tourist attractions. The author, while admiring certain virtues of the Costa Rican political economic model, does not hesitate to criticize the apparent

1

complacency of politicians, violations of human rights, and the widening gap between the rich and poor. The book provides details on the increasing number of non-governmental organizations, refugees, and foreign business interests in Costa Rica. Statistical data and a chronology are included in the appendices.

4 Costa Rican life.
John Berry Biesanz, Mavis Biesanz. Westport, Connecticut: Greenwood Press, 1979. 272p. bibliog.

Chapters on class and everyday living, courtship and marriage, family life, education, work, play, religion, and democracy give a clear indication of the effort of the two United States sociologists to present the lives of ordinary people in Costa Rica. The authors spent ten months in the town of Heredia and six months in San José making the observations leading to this book. *Costa Rican life* is a reprint of a book first published under the same title by Columbia University Press of New York in 1944. It was translated and published in San José in Spanish in 1975 by the Ministry of Culture, Youth and Sports.

5 Los costarricenses. (The Costa Ricans.)
Mavis Hiltunen de Biesanz, Richard Biesanz, Karen Zubris de Biesanz. San José: Editorial Universidad Estatal a Distancia, 1979. 730p. bibliog.

Almost everything you might want to know about Costa Rica's social and economic life is touched upon in this book. Descriptive rather than analytical, it contains detailed chapters on communities, the economy, social classes, housing and daily life, family life, education, religion, recreation, and politics. Introductory chapters place these details in geographical and historical perspective. It is based primarily on observations and informal interviews by Karen and Richard Biesanz between 1968 and 1979 and is a massive extension of *Costa Rican life* (New York: Columbia University Press, 1944) by John and Mavis Biesanz. The commentary resulting from the observations and interviews is more informal than scientific but it is buttressed by a solid reading of the social science literature on Costa Rica and spiced by occasional reflective comments on aspects of the Costa Rican national character. Numerous excellent photographs add another valuable dimension to the work. Unfortunately, it has no index.

6 The Costa Ricans.
Richard Biesanz, Karen Zubris Biesanz, Mavis Hiltunen Biesanz. Englewood Cliffs, New Jersey: Prentice-Hall, 1982. 246p. bibliog.

The reader of this work will find many generalizations, too many, probably, for the social science purist. But the authors' observations, while they may not conform to the highest social science methodological standards, were done systematically, and over a long period of time, roughly during the decade of the 1970s. In that period the authors interviewed approximately 1,000 Costa Ricans. In addition, the bibliography is extensive and the latest scientific research is incorporated in the narrative. Chapter headings tell the prospective reader that this is a truly comprehensive view of Costa Rica: land and people, history, community, class and race, housing and health, the family and the life-cycle, education, religion, leisure and the arts, politics and government, and change *a la tica* [Costa Rican style].

7 **Costa Rica and her future.**
Paul Biolley.   Washington, DC: Judd and Detweiler, 1889. 96p. map.
Written approximately one year after Biolley, a Swiss botanist, had immigrated to
Costa Rica, the purpose of this book is to dispel certain erroneous notions about the
country and to encourage immigration from Europe. The narrative covers what one
would expect in an emigrant-oriented publication – description of the topography,
nature of the population, economic conditions, and the like – but it should be noted
that it is an excellent example of the genre. Even though it is approximately 100 years
old it provides a clear idea of the differences between Costa Rica and its neighbours.
Originally written in French, it was translated into English by Cecil Charles. It was also
published in German in 1890.

8 **The Republic of Costa Rica.**
Joaquín Bernardo Calvo Mora, translated from the original Spanish.
Chicago, Illinois: Rand, McNally, 1890. 292p. maps.
Submitted as a report to the Minister of Public Works and first printed in Spanish in
1887 the Calvo volume contains a wealth of detailed information on commerce,
transport, population, and social conditions. Much of the statistical material appears to
be derived from government censuses and reports but the author also accumulated
data on the flora and fauna of Costa Rica as well as on contemporary cultural
characteristics. The author had in mind a guide for investors and immigrants, but for
later generations of students he left a comprehensive picture of Costa Rica when it was
just beginning to consolidate its unique political system.

9 **The Costa Rica reader.**
Edited by Marc Edelman, Joanne Kenen.   New York: Grove Press,
1989. 396p.
English-language readers will benefit from this compilation of articles and excerpts
from books, many of them translated from Spanish and published in English for the
first time. Well-known Costa Rican historians like Carlos Monge Alfaro and Carlos
Meléndez Chaverri and other contemporary Costa Rican social scientists are
represented in the selections. The editors provide careful historical introductions to
each of the seven chapters which are organized on a chronological basis. Many
periodical articles not abstracted for this bibliography because of their brevity are
included in this anthology. A strong commitment to Costa Rican anti-militarism and
the Arias Peace Plan is evident in the selection of the articles for the last two chapters
which focus on Costa Rica and the Nicaraguan Revolution of 1979 and on the Arias
Plan.

10 **Costa Rica and civilization in the Caribbean.**
Chester Lloyd Jones.   Madison, Wisconsin: University of Wisconsin,
1935. 175p. bibliog. (University of Wisconsin Studies in the Social
Sciences and History, no. 23).
In this pioneering general survey of Costa Rica there are chapters on population,
health, education, government, foreign trade, export crops, international relations,
and social conditions. While the author admires Costa Rica's institutions he is sharply
critical of personalism in politics and of voter apathy. Jones was a professor of
economics and political science at the University of Wisconsin. A second edition was
published in 1941 by Borrasé of San José.

11 **Costa Rica, a country study.**
Harold D. Nelson. Washington, DC: United States Government
Printing Office, 1984. 2nd ed. 336p. maps. bibliog. (Area Handbook
Series).

One of a series of handbooks prepared by the American University, Washington DC,
for United States personnel assigned overseas. It furnishes the 'basic facts about the
social, economic, political, and military institutions and practices' of Costa Rica. For
example, in the chapter on 'Education, Public Information, Artistic and Intellectual
Expression' all major newspapers and periodicals published in Costa Rica are listed. A
unique feature is a chapter on national security (p. 241-76), which includes a
description of Costa Rica's Public Security Forces, Civil Guard, and Rural Assistance
Guard. The bibliography (p. 296-315) is especially strong in English-language titles.

12 **The Republic of Costa Rica.**
Gustavo Niederlein. Philadelphia, Pennsylvania: Philadelphia
Commercial Museum, 1898. 127p.

Niederlein, chief of the scientific department of the Philadelphia Commercial Museum,
collected the data for this book on a seven-month trip to Costa Rica in 1897-98.
Although sketchy on history and interpretation it succeeds in covering every aspect of
life in Costa Rica, usually in statistical fashion. The purpose appears to be to stimulate
commercial exchange with Costa Rica.

13 **Costa Rica ayer y hoy, 1800-1939.** (Costa Rica yesterday and today,
1800-1939.)
Alberto Quijano Quesada. San José: Editorial Borrasé Hermanos,
1939. 771p. bibliog.

An encyclopaedic collection of articles and photographs of Costa Rica, its government,
industry, agriculture and education. Articles deal with specific industries, such as the
banana and coffee industries, and with specific banks and business firms. Other articles
cover towns and regions of Costa Rica, international boundaries, and specific aspects
of the country's history. It is not a guide for the 1990s, but it does give the flavour of
the 1930s and is good background for understanding contemporary Costa Rica.

14 **Costa Rica: su historia, tierra y gentes.** (Costa Rica: its history, land and
people.)
Edited by Jorge Luis Rojas Ramírez. Barcelona, Spain: Océano, 1988.
2 vols. bibliog.

There are two principal attractions of this work. First, it is a competent,
comprehensive introduction to Costa Rica. The first volume (p. 1-184) covers
geography, economics, population, institutions, and culture, with a special section on
precolumbian Costa Rica. Volume two (p. 185-368) covers history from the conquest
to the contemporary period and includes a summary of all Costa Rica's presidents. The
second attraction is the illustrations, which are numerous and carefully selected to
highlight the narrative. The work of a team of experts, the book lacks interpretation
and a consistent theme but of course its object is coverage not controversy.

15 **Nobel Costa Rica: a timely report on our peaceful pro-Yankee, Central American neighbor.**
Seth Rolbein.   New York: St. Martin's Press, 1989. 253p.

The award of the Nobel Peace Prize to President Oscar Arias in 1987 seems to have been the inspiration for this book. It is a book of praise of Costa Rica, for its civility, its commitment to democracy, and its resistance to the efforts of the United States to involve the country in the war against the Sandinistas in Nicaragua. In the process Rolbein makes comments about several Costa Rican landmarks such as the National Theatre, Santa Rosa National Park, and the Quaker colony at Monteverde. He also gives considerable space to John Hull, the North American who, from his ranch in northern Costa Rica, supported the anti-Sandinista cause, and of course to President Arias.

16 **Costa Rica: immigration pamphlet with two maps, a guide for the agricultural class coming from other countries to make Costa Rica its home.**
John Schroeder.   San José: Tipografía Nacional, 1893. 173p.

Despite the title, this is a bit more than a pamphlet. It is a work of twenty-three chapters covering all aspects of Costa Rica, including climate, geography, and principal products. As Schroeder practised farming in Costa Rica and served as United States consul for eight years, he provides first-hand details on agricultural and commercial activities.

The new key to Costa Rica.
See item no. 52.

Costa Rica: the gem of American republics. The land, its resources and its people.
See item no. 58.

Costa Rica contemporánea. (Contemporary Costa Rica.)
See item no. 237.

El gran incógnito: visión interna del campesino costarricense.
See item no. 280.

El costarricense. (The Costa Rican.)
See item no. 283.

Datos y cifras de Costa Rica. (Facts and statistics about Costa Rica.)
See item no. 741.

Geography and Geology

General

17 **Costa Rica: transition to land hunger and potential instability.**
John P. Augelli. In: *1984 yearbook, Conference of Latin Americanist Geographers*, edited by Katherine M. Kvale. Muncie, Indiana: Conference of Latin Americanist Geographers, 1984, p. 48-61. bibliog.

This is an interpretative essay covering such subjects as the land frontier, coffee and banana cultivation, large landownership, peasants, agrarian reform, the problem of squatters, internal migration, and the contemporary economic crisis.

18 **Costa Rica's frontier legacy.**
John P. Augelli. *Geographical Review*, vol. 77, no. 1 (Jan. 1987), p. 1-16. maps.

Professor Augelli traces the history of the emergence, movement, and finally the disappearance of the land frontier in Costa Rica. Although there is no more land for settlement, the perception of land abundance, based on historical experience, persists. The author worries that this conflict between reality and perception may give rise to political and economic instability in the future.

19 **Reseña geográfica del cantón central de San José.** (A geographical review of the central canton of San José.)
Mario Barrantes Ferrero. San José: Instituto Geográfico de Costa Rica, 1964. 12p. maps. bibliog.

In the absence of a geographical or historical monograph on San José this brief geographical sketch of Costa Rica's capital is useful, as it contains essential data on canton and district boundaries, population distribution, climate, and altitude.

20 **Costa Rica.**
Gary S. Elbow. In: *Middle America: its lands and peoples*, edited by
John P. Augelli, Robert C. West. Englewood Cliffs, New Jersey:
Prentice-Hall, 1989, p. 443-56. 3rd ed. maps.

The distinguishing feature of this excellent survey of the geographical characteristics of
Costa Rica is its attention to cultural matters. In addition to describing the physical
features, regions, climate, transportation, agriculture, and industry Elbow gives
considerable attention to the racial composition of the people and the historical spread
of settlement. Special attention is also given to the banana plantation zones of the
Pacific Coast and to tourism.

21 **Geografía de Costa Rica.** (The geography of Costa Rica.)
Eusebio Flores Silva. San José: Editorial Universidad Estatal a
Distancia, 1982. 2nd ed. 473p. maps. bibliog.

Described by the author as an 'optimistic geography', the book emphasizes
opportunities for development of Costa Rica's natural resources. Designed as a text for
high school or beginning college students, it includes end-of-chapter questions and
exercises. The first edition was published by the same publisher in 1979.

22 **Costa Rica: a geographical interpretation in historical perspective.**
Carolyn Hall. Boulder, Colorado: Westview Press, 1985. 348p. maps.
bibliog.

First published in Spanish by the Editorial Costa Rica in 1984, this book is an
excellent, scholarly, one-volume introduction to Costa Rica. It is comprehensive,
thoroughly supported by statistics and maps, and is solidly based on other scholarly
literature. Historical and geographical topics are covered equally well. Among the best
chapters are those on agricultural production, population growth, industry, and
regional planning.

23 **Le Costa Rica.** (Costa Rica.)
Guy Lassere. *Revista Geográfica*, no. 66 (June 1967), p. 107-33. maps.
bibliog.

Lassere, a professional geographer, covers the principal geographical features of Costa
Rica in this article: physical features, vegetation, climate, population distribution,
colonization, geographical regions, agriculture, and industry. The strength of the
article is in the description of the three regions which Lassere identifies, namely the
high central uplands, the Caribbean plains, and the Pacific coastal area. A three-page
English summary of the original French is appended.

24 **Human responses and adjustments in the 1963-65 ashfalls of Irazu**
Volcano, Costa Rica: a geographical study of environmental perception.
Gilles Hector Lemieux. *Revista Geográfica*, nos 86-87 (July 1977-June
1978), p. 227-74. bibliog.

Lemieux provides a lengthy introduction on the concept of environmental perception
and on the history of eruptions of Irazú volcano. Maps showing the extent and
intensity of the ashfalls of 1963-65 are helpful. Questionnaires and interviews provided
the data for the study, which concludes that peasants are both fatalistic about national
hazards and yet expect to receive government assistance. On the basis of his findings

the author makes suggestions about public decision-making in Costa Rica in case of other similar emergencies.

25 **Nueva geografía de Costa Rica.** (A new geography of Costa Rica.)
Jorge León. San José: Librería la Española, 1952. 170p. maps. bibliog.
All but two of the seventy-one bibliographical references were published before 1940.
The first edition was published in 1942. Although statistics and other material are out of date, the regional descriptions, which emphasize towns and natural features rather than resources, are informative and clearly written.

26 **The Huetar Atlantica region of Costa Rica.**
John Tillman Lyle. In: *Design for human ecosystems*, John Tillman Lyle. New York: Van Nostrand Reinhold, 1985, p. 54-68. maps.
Following the guidelines of a report prepared by a landscape planner, a regional planner, an agricultural economist, a transportation planner, and a demographic planner, the author makes concrete suggestions on land and resource use in the Huetar Atlántica region, or the city of Limón and its hinterland.

27 **Regiones periféricas y ciudades intermedias en Costa Rica.** (Peripheral regions and intermediate cities in Costa Rica.)
Edited by Miguel Morales, Gerhard Sandner. San José: Universidad Nacional in association with University of Hamburg, Germany, 1982. 322p. maps. bibliog.
This detailed study, the product of several years of effort by a group of scholars, principally geographers and economists from Costa Rica's National University and the University of Hamburg, is written especially for specialists in geography and planning. First, there is a lengthy discussion of the theoretical considerations of the interrelations among the processes of urbanization, industrialization, and regional development. Then, these processes are placed in the general Costa Rican context. At this juncture of the study plentiful detail is supplied concerning such national problems as land use, land tenure, agricultural production, and development policies. Finally, the principal authors and their collaborators focus on regions peripheral to the main development centre of Costa Rica, the Central Valley. Specifically, they treat the cases of the following cities and their surrounding regions: Ciudad Quesada, San Isidro del General, and Liberia. It does not purport to be a blueprint for the regional development of Costa Rica but it provides a scientific base and points to development possibilities that must be valuable to decision makers and regional planners.

28 **Estudio geográfico regional de la zona atlántico norte de Costa Rica.**
(A regional geographical study of the North Atlantic zone of Costa Rica.)
Helmut Nuhn, S. Pérez R. (et al.). San José: Instituto de Tierras y Colonización, 1967. 368p. maps. bibliog.
The result of a technical assistance agreement with the Federal Republic of Germany, this study was commissioned by ITCO (Costa Rica's Land and Colonization Institute) in the hope of stimulating colonization in the lightly populated North Atlantic zone. This zone extends from the city of Limón to Barra Colorado on the border of Nicaragua. Nuhn, Pérez, and their collaborators provide extensive data in narrative and graphic form on soils, climate, geology, vegetation, subregions, population, means

of transport, land use, agricultural production, and social services. Finally they offer recommendations on the potential for specific kinds of agricultural development. Eleven fold-out maps accompany the book. The study lays a firm scientific base for economic development planning in this region.

29 **La base funcional de ciudades pequeñas: ejemplo costarricense.**
(The functional base of small cities: a Costa Rican example.)
Jane E. Ratcliffe. *Anuario de Estudios Centroamericanos*, no. 2
(1976), p. 345-68. maps. bibliog.

Gives special attention to thirty-seven Costa Rican towns with populations of between 300 and 25,000. The purpose is to test geography's 'central place theory' by comparing data with the results of similar studies carried out in Wales, Iowa, and Illinois. Data were collected on commercial and non-commercial establishments in each of the towns and then plotted according to town size. The results not only validated central place theory as a useful approach to the study of small towns; they also identify characteristics of small towns in Costa Rica, useful information for community and regional planners and politicians alike.

30 **Revista de la Universidad de Costa Rica.** (Costa Rica University Review.)
San José: Universidad de Costa Rica. no. 38 (July 1974), 220p. bibliog.

Number 38 of the *Revista de la Universidad de Costa Rica* contains twelve valuable articles on the Guanacaste region of Costa Rica. Articles cover geographical, historical, literary, and other topics. Perhaps the most useful article for the researcher on Guanacaste is an annotated bibliography of books on the region by Mireya Hernández F. de Jáen (q.v.).

31 **Revista Geográfica.** (Geographical Review.)
Rio de Janeiro: Pan American Institute of Geography. July 1977–June 1978, p. 11-358.

This issue of *Revista Geográfica* is a special edition almost entirely dedicated to Costa Rica. Of the seventeen articles on Costa Rica two are in English (see separate entries under Carolyn Hall and Gilles H. Lemieux), one is in French, and the rest are in Spanish. English summaries are provided. The articles deal with such diverse topics as integrated regional planning, urban–regional planning, planning and migration, cattle ranching, the Irazú ashfall, previous mining cycles, population prospects in the year 2000, internal migration, volcanic eruption risk and zoning, disadvantages of high humidity for urban sites, characteristics of urban poverty, and the national park system.

32 **Densities of population in Holdridge life zones in Costa Rica: an empirical approach.**
William Rickard. In: *Graduate Studies on Latin America at the University of Kansas*, edited by Charles L. Stansifer. Lawrence, Kansas: Center of Latin American Studies, University of Kansas, 1980. vol. 4, p. 19-30.

This article is a summary of Rickard's dissertation (University of Kansas, 1974), which is one of the rare attempts to apply theoretical principles of the effects of the physical environment on human populations to a specific place, in this case the northern zone of

Costa Rica. Rickard is successful in demonstrating the predictability of Holdridge's 'life zone' theories in northern Costa Rica.

33 **Ríos, playas y montañas.** (Rivers, beaches and mountains.)
Miguel Salguero. San José: Editorial Costa Rica, 1984. 174p.

The purpose of this book is to provide a description of the most important rivers, beaches, mountains, lakes, and islands of Costa Rica. Hundreds of excellent colour and black-and-white photographs provide a visual dimension to the descriptions. Along with the descriptions the author provides a running narrative of his exploration of Costa Rica.

34 **La colonización agrícola de Costa Rica.** (The agricultural colonization of Costa Rica.)
Gerhard Sandner. San José: Instituto Geográfico de Costa Rica, Ministerio de Obras Públicas, 1962-64. 2 vols. 357p. bibliog.

Professor Sandner, a geographer of the University of Kiel, did the research for this comprehensive study during 1958-59. It was first published in German as *Agrarkolonisation in Costa Rica* (Kiel: Schmidt & Klaunig, 1961) and translated by Federico Latorre into Spanish for the present edition. It is an outstanding example of the insights provided by the perspective of a cultural geographer with a strong historical background. It is, in effect, a thorough analysis of the process of the extension of the Costa Rican agricultural frontier by transnational corporations, government-directed expansion, and squatters. Maps and photographs are used extensively to illustrate the expansion.

35 **Investigaciones geográficas en la sección oriental de la península de Nicoya, Costa Rica.** (Geographical investigations in the eastern section of the Nicoya Peninsula, Costa Rica.)
Gerhard Sandner. *Revista Geográfica*, vol. 28, no. 54 (Jan.-June 1961), p. 5-27. maps.

This article describes the eastern zone of the Nicoya Peninsula, which the author visited three times in 1958 and 1959. After a technical geographical description of the terrain the author describes the towns and villages of the region, particularly the town of Nicoya. Nicoya's economic development appeared to Sandner to be growing at a slower pace than other similar regions of Costa Rica. Excellent maps accompany the narrative.

36 **Population pressure upon resources in Costa Rica.**
Gerhard Sandner. In: *Geography and a crowding world*, edited by Wilbur Zelinsky, Leszek A. Kosínski, R. Mansell Prothero. New York: Oxford University Press, 1970, p. 535-55. maps. bibliog.

Sandner, a geographer with years of field experience in Central America, presents in this article a clear picture of the interrelationships between population distribution, internal migration, population growth rates, colonization, minifundism, food production, and government policy in Costa Rica. His analysis is supported by his own special studies and appropriate secondary sources.

37 **The treasure of Cocos Island.**
   Frank J. Thomas. *Américas*, vol. 48, no. 4 (May 1960), p. 31-4.
Costa Rica's Cocos Island, some 400 miles offshore in the Pacific Ocean, has intrigued
scientists, treasure hunters, and adventurers for many years. This is a readable,
satisfactory account of all reported visitors to the island, including Franklin D.
Roosevelt who was there three times on fishing cruises.

38 **Nicoya, a cultural geography.**
   Philip Laurence Wagner. Berkeley, California: University of California
   Press, 1958. 250p. bibliog. (University of California Publications in
   Geography, vol. 12, no. 3).
The result of a visit to Nicoya during 1951-52, this book contains the detailed
observations of a cultural geographer on the daily life of the residents of Nicoya,
including diet, house furnishings, handicrafts, tools, crop practices, land use, and
animal husbandry. Although generally reliable the book contains some comments
based on impressions rather than scientific investigation. Wagner notes that although
recent immigrants from the Central Valley have tended to modernize farming
methods, practices dating from the pre-colonial period are still evident.

Geology and natural resources

39 **Geology and soils of comparative ecosystem study areas, Costa Rica.**
   W. W. Bourgeois (et al.). Seattle, Washington: College of Forest
   Resources, University of Washington, 1972. 41p. maps. (Tropical
   Forestry Series, no. 11).
This is a comparative study, with eight maps, of the climate and soils of two distinct
areas of Costa Rica: Finca La Selva in the Atlantic Lowlands (tropical wet forest) and
of Hacienda Comelco in Guanacaste (tropical dry forest).

40 **Geología de Costa Rica: una sinopsis.** (The geology of Costa Rica: a
   synopsis.)
   Rolando Castillo M. San José: Editorial Universidad de Costa Rica,
   1984. 182p.
As the title suggests, this book is a synopsis. It covers the main subfields of geology:
physical geography, stratigraphy, vulcanism (with a brief review of eruptions of the
principal volcanoes of Costa Rica), structure, tectonic history, and seismic activity.
There is a separate chapter on the glacial age and the final chapter covers mineral
resources. In the appendix Castillo adds a chronology of Costa Rica's contracts with
petroleum companies and the resulting explorations. The book is carefully written and
amply supported by maps, charts, and photographs.

Geography and Geology. Geology and natural resources

41 **An introduction to the study of Volcano Irazu.**
Elliott Coen. *Geophysical Magazine*, vol. 32, no. 2 (1964), p. 131-51.
maps. bibliog.
Coen studied Irazú volcano while it was erupting in 1963-64, gathering data about the intensity of eruptions and the extent and severity of the ashfall. His principal purpose is to examine the effect of rainfall and atmospheric pressure on the volcano's activity.

42 **Estudio geológico de la región de Guanacaste, Costa Rica.** (A geological study of the region of Guanacaste, Costa Rica.)
Gabriel Dengo. San José: Imprenta del Instituto Geográfico, 1962.
112p. maps. bibliog.
The author, who made his first research visit to Guanacaste in 1942, bases this comprehensive monograph on his own field research, on numerous scientific studies of the region, and on unpublished reports of the Petroleum Company of Costa Rica. He does not discuss mineral deposits. Maps, charts, and photographs are included.

43 **Recursos naturales.** (Natural resources.)
Luis Fournier Origgi. San José: Editorial Universidad Estatal a Distancia. 1983. 216p. bibliog.
Recursos naturales is a carefully written textbook for correspondence students. After a general explanation of ecosystems and natural resources the author, with the liberal use of statistical charts, describes land use, resource exploitation, and the evolution of the national park system. Lastly, he describes the economic development of Costa Rica under current practices and suggests an alternative plan of development.

44 **Temblores, terremotos, inundaciones y erupciones volcánicas en Costa Rica 1608-1910.** (Tremors, earthquakes, floods and volcanic eruptions in Costa Rica 1608-1910.)
Cleto González Víquez. San José: Tipografía de A. Alsina, 1910.
200p.
Not a work of historical analysis but rather a careful collection of data and accounts of natural disasters in Costa Rica, including the disastrous Cartago earthquake of 1910.

45 **Conocimiento de sismicidad en Costa Rica.** (Knowledge of seismic activity in Costa Rica.)
Setsumi Miyamura. San José: Editorial Universidad de Costa Rica, 1980. 190p. maps. bibliog.
This is one of the few professional books on seismic activity in Costa Rica. The first three chapters offer an introduction and detailed study of specific earthquakes of the 1970s. Chapter four (p. 121-46), which, unlike the other chapters, is in English, is a provisional chronological catalogue of earthquakes occurring in and near Costa Rica from 1904 to 1963. Data on the intensity of each earthquake is included. Chapter five includes headlines of Costa Rican newspapers reporting earthquakes from 1890 to 1966.

46 **Costa Rica: Vulcan's smithy.**
Henri F. Pittier. *National Geographic Magazine*, vol. 21, no. 6
(June 1910), p. 494-525.

As founder of the National Geographic Institute of Costa Rica in 1888 and its director for fifteen years, Pittier was well qualified to write this description of Costa Rica's volcanic belt and review of the history of volcanic eruptions and earthquakes in Costa Rica. Of particular interest because of its immediacy is the acocunt, with photographs, of the great earthquake which struck Cartago in 1910. Pittier's observations on Costa Rican national character are also of interest.

47 **Volcanes de Costa Rica.** (The volcanoes of Costa Rica.)
Miguel Salguero. San José: Editorial Costa Rica, 1982. 4th ed. 42p.

Stretching from the Central Valley of Costa Rica to the Nicaraguan border are ten volcanoes. All of these are described by the author, who adds information gleaned from the studies of previous explorers and scientists. Excellent colour photographs accompany the text.

48 **Volcanic history of the Meseta Central Occidental, Costa Rica.**
Howell Williams. *Bulletin*, Geological Sciences, University of
California, vol. 29, no. 4 (1952), p. 145-79.

Both from the point of view of historical research and of geological field research this study is outstanding. The author is thoroughly familiar with the work of geologists and natural scientists who have worked in the region in the past, and the field research, done in 1949, is equally thorough. Although a chronology of volcanic activity is included, the principal contribution is an explanation of the geological origins of the eastern section of the Central Valley (Meseta Central) of Costa Rica.

Maps, atlases and gazetteers

49 **Atlas cantonal de Costa Rica.** (Atlas of Costa Rica's cantons.)
Eduardo Chinchilla Valenciano. San José: Instituto de Fomento y
Asesoría Municipal, 1987. 395p. maps. bibliog.

This extraordinary publication is the work of two public agencies, the Municipal Assistance and Development Institute and the National Geographic Institute. Detailed colour maps of each of the seven provinces and each of the eighty-one cantons, or counties, are the principal feature of the publication. The narrative accompanying each map follows a uniform model, with basic information on territorial divisions, population statistics, geology, altitudes, hydrography, precipitation, land use, and history. The atlas is a monumental contribution to basic knowledge about Costa Rica, and will be of use to researchers and casual students as well as tourists and investors.

50 **Costa Rica: evolución territorial y principales censos de población.**
(Costa Rica: territorial evolution and principal population censuses.)
Hermógenes Hernández. San José: Editorial Universidad Nacional,
1985. 183p. maps. bibliog.

This remarkable atlas aims to show every recorded territorial division and its
population in Costa Rican history. Boundaries and population are shown for
provinces, cantons, and districts for all of Costa Rica. Bernardo Augusto Thiel's
population studies are the source of data for the colonial period and the national
censuses for the independent republic. Forty-four excellent maps are included.

51 **Maps of Costa Rica: an annotated cartobibliography.**
Albert Earl Palmerlee. Lawrence, Kansas: University of Kansas
Libraries, 1965. 358p. maps. bibliog. (University of Kansas Publications,
Library Series, no. 19).

An exhaustive bibliography of 1,600 published and unpublished maps of Costa Rica.
Descriptive notes indicate technical data such as scale and dimensions, type of data,
and the location of each map. It is well indexed. Although many maps of Costa Rica
have been printed since 1965 this cartobibliography remains an invaluable research
tool.

Tourism and travel guides

52 **The new key to Costa Rica.**
Beatrice Blake, Anne Beecher. San José: Publications in English,
S. A., 1989. 9th expanded and updated ed. 252p. bibliog.

Blake and Beecher update a guidebook first published in 1978 by Jean Wallace. Except
for shopping, which is somewhat neglected, this is a traditional, comprehensive
guidebook. Entries on hotels and restaurants tend to be succinct. Coverage of schools,
including language schools, property agencies, and churches is aimed at the long-term
visitor, as is the guide to Costa Rican fruits and vegetables. A ten-page section called
'The Ecological Picture' features a list of environmental agencies interested in Costa
Rica. Regional chapters also highlight national parks and environmental points of
interest.

53 **The national parks of Costa Rica.**
Mario A. Boza, Rolando Mendoza, Ronald Cháves. Madrid: Instituto
de la Caza Fotográfica y Ciencias de la Naturaleza, 1981. 310p. map.
bibliog.

A translation of the long version of Boza's *Los parques nacionales de Costa Rica*,
which was published by the same publisher in two versions in 1978 (the long version
contains 224 pages and the short 80 pages). It presents scientific information about
each of the twelve national parks or reservations in a fashion understandable to the
layperson. Mario Boza founded Costa Rica's National Park Service in 1970 and as its
first director had much to do with the astounding growth of the Costa Rican national
park system in the subsequent eight years. This growth is discussed in the text, which is

accompanied by an excellent map and scores of brilliant photographs of Costa Rican flora and fauna.

54 The lost treasure of Cocos Island.
Ralph Hancock, Julian A. Weston. New York: Thomas Nelson & Sons, 1960. 325p.

Costa Rica's small island of Cocos lies nearly 400 miles from the nearest Costa Rican port, Puntarenas, and has occasionally attracted scientists, adventurers, and treasure seekers. This book is an account of the stories of buried treasure and the people who have searched for it. Considerable space is given to August Gissler, who lived alone on the island for several years in the early 20th century.

55 Adventure in Costa Rica.
Donald E. Lundberg. Tallahassee, Florida: Dixie Publishers, 1968. 2nd revd. ed. 224p. maps.

Adventure in Costa Rica is a guide to living conditions in Costa Rica. It appears to be aimed more at the prospective North American retiree or investor than the casual visitor. Readers may find the comments on Costa Rican national character controversial, but the sections on investment climate, North Americans living in Costa Rica, travel, and others are thorough and accurate. The first edition was published by the same publisher in 1960. The second edition was revised by Juan Mora.

56 The Costa Rican traveler: getting around in Costa Rica.
Ellen Searby. Juneau, Alaska: Windham Bay Press, 1988. 2nd ed. 251p. maps. bibliog.

A basic guide for visitors to Costa Rica. The emphasis falls heavily on the country's national parks and other environmental attractions but hotels, restaurants, transport, shopping, sports, and other tourist necessities are also covered. The author personally inspected over 200 of the country's 300 hotels for this edition. The comments, however, tend to be exuberant rather than critical. Sections on retirement in Costa Rica, learning Spanish, and investment are of benefit to the prospective long-term resident, but treatment of Costa Rica's historical and cultural background is sparse. Out-of-the-way regions are covered well, better than the cities. The second edition has been expanded from the first, 205-page edition, published by the same press in 1985.

57 Costa Rica: a natural destination.
Ree Strange Sheck. Santa Fe, New Mexico: John Muir Publications, 1990. 270p. maps. bibliog.

The special appeal of this guidebook is the extensive coverage of Costa Rica's national parks, biological reserves, and wildlife refuges. For a small country these are numerous and they are quite well covered in this book, in terms both of the natural attractions and of nearby tourist accommodation. An additional appeal are the occasional inserts on agricultural products, specific fauna such as sea turtles or resplendent quetzals, and the like. Information about museums, restaurants, banks, shopping and transport tends to be basic.

58   **Costa Rica: the gem of American republics. The land, its resources and its people.**
Richard Villafranca.   New York: Sackett and Wilhelms, 1895. 139p.
As indicated by the title of the first chapter, 'Why it is desirable to live in Costa Rica', and the last, 'Costa Rica's greatest want – emigration', this is an emigration tract covering climate, commerce, natural resources, and agriculture. It was done especially for the Costa Rican exhibit at the Cotton States and International Exposition at Atlanta in 1895.

59   **The new key to Costa Rica: all you need to know.**
Jean Wallace.   San José: Editorial Texto, 1983. 146p. maps. bibliog.
Written by a North American resident of Costa Rica, this guidebook is especially useful for prospective foreign residents. It covers language schools, churches, banks, information about property, and local food customs as well as hotels, restaurants, and tourist attractions. Information on hotels and restaurants is sketchy. This guide was originally published in San José by Publicaciones en Inglés in 1977.

60   **Costa Rica: nature, prosperity, and peace on the rich coast.**
Allen M. Young.   Milwaukee, Wisconsin: Interamerican Research Corporation, 1984. 66p. maps.
More than a travel guide, this is a reflective, somewhat personal account of Costa Rica, especially its natural phenomena, by a North American biologist who has done extensive research in Costa Rica. Excellent photographs illustrate the regions described.

Costa Rica and her future.
See item no. 7.

The Republic of Costa Rica.
See item no. 8.

The Republic of Costa Rica.
See item no. 12.

Costa Rican natural history.
See item no. 71.

Historia y geografía del Cantón de San Ramón. (The history and geography of the Canton of San Ramon.)
See item no. 177.

The distribution of population in Costa Rica.
See item no. 246.

An ethnic geography of Costa Rica's Atlantic zone.
See item no. 264.

Les migrations intérieures à Costa Rica: une approche régionales [*sic*] au problème. (Costa Rican internal migration: a regional approach to the problem.)
See item no. 278.

Emigrantes a la conquista de la selva: estudio de un caso de colonización en Costa Rica, San Vito de Java. (Emigrants conquering the jungle: study of a colonization case in Costa Rica, San Vito de Java.)
See item no. 279.

Rural development in Costa Rica.
See item no. 303.

Análisis electoral de una democracia: estudio del comportamiento político costarricense durante el período 1953-1974. (The electoral analysis of a democracy: a study of Costa Rican political behaviour during 1953-74.)
See item no. 376.

Costa Rica–Panama arbitration: report submitted to the representative of Costa Rica by Luis Matamoros, consulting engineer of the government of Costa Rica.
See item no. 435.

Un área rural en desarrollo: sus problemas económicos y sociales en Costa Rica. (A rural area in development: its economic and social problems in Costa Rica.)
See item no. 545.

Structural determinants of the location of rural development institutions in Costa Rica.
See item no. 546.

Vegetación y clima de Costa Rica. (Vegetation and climate of Costa Rica.)
See item no. 597.

Field guide to the natural history of Costa Rica.
See item no. 607.

Bibliografía agrícola de Costa Rica. (Agricultural bibliography of Costa Rica.)
See item no. 751.

Bibliografía de la geología de Costa Rica. (A bibliography of Costa Rican geology.)
See item no. 752.

Travellers' Accounts

61 **A ride across a continent: a personal narrative of wanderings through Nicaragua and Costa Rica.**
Frederick Boyle.   London: R. Bentley, 1868. 2 vols.
Although the book deals principally with Nicaragua, the last two chapters provide a detailed account of Boyle's trip through Costa Rica in 1866. He crossed from Puntarenas to the Central Valley and on to the Atlantic coast, travelling via the Sarápiqui and San Juan rivers. Despite a general approach to Central America right out of the anti-Spanish Black Legend, Boyle praises the Costa Ricans for their industry and prosperity.

62 **The windward road: adventures of a naturalist on remote Caribbean shores.**
Archie Fairly Carr.   New York: Alfred A. Knopf, 1956. 258p.
The principal topic is the migratory green turtle which once flourished in great herds or fleets in the Caribbean Sea. Their numbers have rapidly diminished as a result of increasingly sophisticated harvesting and the growing population of the Caribbean. One of the last breeding grounds is at Tortuguero, on the Atlantic coast of Costa Rica. Carr describes Tortuguero and its turtle-oriented residents as well as the habits of the green turtle, and makes a plea for conservation.

63 **Los viajes de Cockburn por Costa Rica.** (Cockburn's trips through Costa Rica.)
John Cockburn.   San José: Editorial Costa Rica, 1976. 2nd ed. 100p. maps. bibliog.
The narrative of John Cockburn, a Scottish seaman who traversed the isthmus of Central America in 1731 from the Bay of Honduras to Panama, including the length of the Pacific coast of Costa Rica. In addition there is a commentary by Franz Termer on the ethnographical and geographical importance of Cockburn's observations, and notes by Costa Rican historian Carlos Meléndez Chaverri. The first Editorial Costa Rica edition was published in 1962.

64 **Costa Rica en el siglo XIX.** (Costa Rica in the 19th century.)
Ricardo Fernández Guardia. San José: Editorial Universitaria
Centroamericana, 1982. 4th ed. 585p. bibliog. (Colección Viajeros).

Provides glimpses into the social, political, and economic life of Costa Ricans as
observed by foreign travellers or residents such as John Hale, John L. Stephens, R. G.
Dunlop, E. George Squier, Wilhelm Marr, Francisco Solano Astaburuaga, Thomas
Francis Meagher, and Felix Belly. The translator, Ricardo Fernández Guardia, Costa
Rican archivist and historian, also provides explanatory notes.

65 **Talamanca, el espacio y los hombres.** (Talamanca, space and man.)
William M. Gabb. San José: Editorial Universidad Estatal a Distancia,
1981. 2nd ed. 167p. map. bibliog.

Includes two works. The first was originally published as: *Informe sobre la exploración
de Talamanca* (San José: Tipografía Nacional, 1894). Gabb (1838-78), a geologist,
came to Costa Rica in 1873 to look for transportation routes and settlement sites. But
his 30-month exploration of the Talamanca region left far more than a geographical
report. His *Informe* is a complete scientific account of his explorations. The second
work was originally published as: *On the Indian tribes and languages of Costa Rica*
(Philadelphia, Pennsylvania: McCalla & Stavely, 1875). It was the first ethnographical
account of Costa Rican Indians. Luis Ferrero provides a thorough introduction to
Gabb's life and work and an account of other explorations of the Talamanca region.

66 **Vacaciones en Costa Rica.** (Vacation in Costa Rica.)
Thomas Francis Meagher, translated by Ricardo Fernández Guardia.
San José: Tipografía Trejos Hermanos, 1923. 138p. bibliog.
(Publicaciones, Liceo de Costa Rica, Serie A, no. 10).

Thomas F. Meagher was born in 1823 in Ireland and migrated to the United States in
1849. Because of the interest in Central America aroused by the William Walker
expeditions in Nicaragua, Meagher became determined to visit the Central American
isthmus. He arrived in Puntarenas in March 1858 and visited San José and Cartago for
the next two months. He left Costa Rica by way of the Turrialba volcano, Sarápiqui
river, and San Juan del Norte, Nicaragua. *Vacaciones de Costa Rica*, first published in
English in the *New Monthly Magazine* (New York) in 1858-59, is a report of his
observations while on this trip. His remarks, although brief, provide one of the most
complete accounts that we have of Costa Rican society in the 1850s.

67 **Viajeros por Guanacaste.** (Travellers in Guanacaste.)
Carlos Meléndez Chaverri. San José: Ministerio de Cultura, Juventud
y Deportes, 1974. 557p. (Serie Nos Ven, no. 4).

Expertly annotated by Carlos Meléndez, Costa Rica's leading historian, this book
contains selections from twenty-eight travellers to Guanacaste. Several colonial
explorers are included. Foreign naturalists of the 19th and early 20th centuries, such as
Henri Pittier, Karl Sapper, and Philip Calvert, are included along with Costa Rican
scientists and explorers such as José Fidel Tristán and Alberto M. Brenes.

68 **Treasure cruise: the voyage of the "Vigilant" to Cocos Island.**
James Plumpton. London: H. F. and G. Witherby, 1935. 191p.

Cocos Island is a Costa Rican possession lying some 400 miles offshore in the Pacific Ocean. Plumpton, a retired British naval officer, and a few others of like mind, sailed the *Vigilant* to Cocos Island in 1931-32 to look for buried treasure. This book relates the story of their adventures getting to the island and their six-month search. Like others before and after them, they found no treasure.

69 **La república de Costa Rica en Centro América.** (The republic of Costa Rica in Central America.)
Moritz Wagner, Carl Scherzer. San José: Ministerio de Cultura, Juventud y Deportes, 1974. 2 vols. map. (Serie Nos Ven, no. 2).

For an understanding and appreciation of mid-19th-century Costa Rica this classic travel account is a necessity. Wagner, the primary author, was interested in natural history, and Scherzer's interest lay in what we would now call the social sciences, especially ethnology. The two travellers were in Costa Rica for ten months during 1853. They prepared chapters on geography, geology, meteorology, natural history, population, means of communication, public finances, and commerce. The book was first published in German in 1856 and first published in Spanish (San José: Biblioteca Yorusti) in 1944.

Flora and Fauna

General

70   A year of Costa Rican natural history.
Amelia Catherine Smith Calvert, Philip Powell Calvert.   New York:
Macmillan, 1917. 577p. maps.

As a yardstick for understanding what was known about Costa Rican flora and fauna in
1910, the Calvert volume is indispensable. Philip Calvert, an entomologist, and his wife
Amelia, a biologist, spent a year – from April 1909 to May 1910 – based in Cartago,
Costa Rica. They travelled often, observed with scientific devotion, and meticulously
preserved their observations. The result is a classic: it is the first thorough,
scientifically sound and yet popular account of Costa Rica's natural riches.

71   Costa Rican natural history.
Edited by Daniel H. Janzen.   Chicago, Illinois: University of Chicago
Press, 1983. 816p. maps. bibliog.

Janzen's idea was to put together an introductory but comprehensive volume for the
student or scientist interested in field biology in Costa Rica. The book is divided into
sections on agriculture, plants, reptiles and amphibians, mammals, birds, and insects.
Each of these sections consists of an introduction, a checklist of species, and many
species accounts which discuss the scientific studies and current understanding of a
particular species. Both the introductions and species accounts are followed by
pertinent bibliographies. One hundred and seventy-four authors contributed. Publication of this monumental volume, which contains chapters on the history of field biology
in Costa Rica, biotic history and palaeogeography, climate, geology, and soils, was in
itself a major event in the study of nature in Costa Rica.

72 **Guanacaste National Park: tropical ecological and cultural restoration.**
Daniel H. Janzen. San José: Tinker Foundation, Fundación de
Parques Nacionales, Editorial Universidad Estatal a Distancia, 1986.
104p. maps. bibliog.

In this book Professor Janzen describes an ambitious attempt to preserve physically
what little remains of the dry forest in Guanacaste and more broadly to urge Costa
Ricans to undertake similar such preservation projects.

73 **Clave preliminar de las familias de los árboles en Costa Rica.**
(Preliminary key to the families of trees in Costa Rica.)
Elbert L. Little, Jr. *Turrialba*, vol. 15, no. 2 (1965), p. 119-29.

The layperson without a botanical background but interested in trees in Costa Rica can
use this key to identify native and exotic trees found there. There is an English
summary.

74 **A naturalist on a tropical farm.**
Alexander F. Skutch. Berkeley, California: University of California
Press, 1971. 397p.

When he wrote this book Alexander Skutch had lived on a small farm near San Isidro
del General for approximately forty years. It is a personal account of his life as a
farmer combined with his scientific observations of nature, especially birdlife. Among
the many excellent sensitive accounts of nature and man's relationship to nature are his
brilliant vignettes of the changing seasons and their impact on him. This book was
reprinted by the University of California Press in both paperback and hardbound
editions in 1980.

75 **A naturalist in Costa Rica.**
Alexander F. Skutch. Gainesville, Florida: University Press of Florida,
1971. 378p. bibliog.

Many foreign naturalists have been attracted to the variety of flora and fauna in Costa
Rica but few can match the continuing dedication to scientific observation of tropical
plants and wildlife of Alexander Skutch. This book reflects forty years of such
observation, primarily in southern Costa Rica near San Isidro del General. His
numerous scientific publications indicate his interest in the life-cycles of birds and
nidification. In this book he writes on these subjects but comments as well on other
animal life, plant life (he received a PhD degree in botany from Johns Hopkins
University in 1928) and farming. His book approaches the ideal among the writings of
naturalists in Latin America. He is a recognized scientist and his commentary is based
on a lifetime of disciplined observations and experience.

76 **Parque Nacional Corcovado: plan de manejo y desarrollo.** (Corcovado
National Park: a plan of management and development.)
Christopher Vaughan. Heredia, Costa Rica: Editorial de la
Universidad Nacional, 1981. 351p. maps. bibliog. (Colección Zurquí,
Serie Ecología, Subserie Areas Silvestres).

Corcovado National Park consists of 34,346 hectares of humid tropical forest on the
Peninsula of Osa, in the South Pacific region of Costa Rica. It was set aside under
national protection in 1975. The Vaughan study is an effort to provide a basic

inventory of the natural resources in the park and a plan for their management and preservation. In the appendices there are lists of various wildlife species known to be in the park. One appendix even lists the names of the park's human residents.

77 **Animales y plantas comunes de las costas de Costa Rica.** (Common animals and plants of the coasts of Costa Rica.)
Carlos Villalobos Solé.   San José: Editorial Universidad Estatal a Distancia (EUNED), 1982. 147p. bibliog. (Serie Educación Ambiental, no. 6).

The purpose of this book is to give an idea of the principal plants and animals of both coasts of Costa Rica and to identify their place in the different coastal ecosystems. The author is a professor of marine science at the University of Costa Rica. The book is part of a EUNED series emphasizing education of the general public about Costa Rica's natural environment.

Flora

78 **Costa Rican mosses collected by Paul C. Standley in 1924-26.**
Edwin Bunting Bartram.   In: *Contributions from the United States National Herbarium.* Washington, DC: United States Government Printing Office, 1928.
vol. 26, part 3, p. 51-114.

Paul Standley collected mosses at over thirty sites not previously explored by bryologists. These sites are listed, along with 272 species of Costa Rican mosses, a third of which were new to Costa Rica at the time of publication. The author believes that Costa Rican mosses are more closely related to South American mosses than to Mexican.

79 **Plantas acuáticas y anfibias de Costa Rica y Centroamérica.** (Aquatic and amphibious plants of Costa Rica and Central America.)
Luis Diego Gómez.   San José: Editorial Universidad Estatal a Distancia, 1984. 430p.

This is the first in a projected two-volume work on aquatic plants in Central America, with emphasis on Costa Rica. The first volume covers Liliopsida and the second is to cover dicotyledons. According to the author, former director of the National Museum of Costa Rica, this is the first book to treat Central American aquatic plants.

80 **Arboles de Costa Rica.** (Trees of Costa Rica.)
L. R. Holdridge, Luis J. Poveda A.   San José: Centro Científico Tropical, 1975. 546p. bibliog.

The purpose of this manual is to provide a guide so that the non-specialist can identify the species of an unknown tree by checking the shape and size of the leaves against the data provided. The authors emphasize that many species of trees in Costa Rica are still unidentified. Photographs are necessary to satisfy the authors' purpose and they are provided, although only in black and white. A glossary, bibliography, and index are appended. The present work is identified as volume one.

81 **Introducción a la flora de Costa Rica.** (Introduction to the flora of Costa Rica.)
Mayra Montiel. San José: Editorial Universidad de Costa Rica, 1980. 246p. bibliog.

In this introductory study there is a long section on the basic morphology of plants and taxonomic systems. The remaining part of the book is an attempt to cover the principal families of Costa Rican flora including scientific, economic, and ornamental information. A sketch of the plant geography of Costa Rica by Luis Fournier is included. The bibliography (p. 241-6) is excellent.

82 **El uso de algunas plantas medicinales en Costa Rica.** (The use of some medicinal plants in Costa Rica.)
Rafael Angel Ocampo S., Annabelle Maffioli. San José: Trejos Hnos, 1985. 95p. bibliog.

A compilation of descriptions, with drawings, of twenty-six medicinal plants of Costa Rica and their distribution, preparation, and use as remedies.

83 **Plantas usuales de Costa Rica.** (Common plants of Costa Rica.)
Henri F. Pittier. San José: Editorial Costa Rica, 1978. 3rd ed. 329p. bibliog. (Biblioteca Patria, no. 21).

This book, originally published in 1908 as *Ensayo sobre las plantas usuales de Costa Rica* (Essay on the common plants of Costa Rica), is essentially a detailed dictionary of the common names of plants found in Costa Rica, followed by an index of the scientific names. It also includes a review of plant distribution and an excellent account of early botanical exploration of Costa Rica in which the author, a prominent Swiss geographer and naturalist, played an important role. Rafael Lucas Rodríguez, a Costa Rican botanist, is the author of the prologue.

84 **Flora costaricensis, family 15, Gramineae.**
Richard Walter Pohl. Chicago, Illinois: Field Museum, 1980. 608p. Publication no. 1313. Series edited by William Burger. (Fieldiana Botany, new series, no. 4).

Not for the layperson, this book is a technical guide to the genera of grasses in Costa Rica. The author uses the classification system of grasses proposed by F. L. Stebbins and Beecher Crampton, with a few of his own modifications. There is no discussion of previous collectors or researchers. Details about range and the characteristics of grasses are contained in specific entries, arranged alphabetically. Most species are illustrated by drawings.

85 **The genera of the native bamboo of Costa Rica.**
Richard Walter Pohl. *Revista de Biología Tropical*, vol. 24 (1976),
p. 243-9.

The article contains taxonomic keys in English and Spanish for the seven native and the two introduced bamboos found in Costa Rica. Brief notes on the morphology and occurrence of each genus are included. The author pleads with field botanists to collect specimens and photographs of bamboo clumps; because of their size and rarity bamboos have received little attention from botanists.

86 **Keys to the genera of grasses of Costa Rica.**
Richard Walter Pohl. *Revista de Biología Tropical*, vol. 20, no. 2
(1972), p. 189-219.

In this article, which offers all data in Spanish as well as English, the author provides a master key and seven basic keys to the identification of grasses in Costa Rica. Keys to bamboos are not included because of insufficient information. (For information on Costa Rican bamboo see Pohl's later article, above.) A glossary is appended.

87 **Flora of Costa Rica.**
Paul Carpenter Standley. Chicago, Illinois: Field Museum of Natural
History, 1937-38. 2 vols. (Botanical Series).

For Standley this was obviously a labour of love. Preparation of the manuscript, he states in the preface, 'has been the most agreeable botanical work that the writer has ever undertaken'. The principal reason, as he explains, is that: 'No other area of equal size anywhere in America possesses so rich and varied a flora, and none in North America is at all comparable in these respects.' Essentially, the work is a systematic, annotated list of the plants of Costa Rica. For want of sufficient research, some areas of knowledge such as ferns are left out, but the work nonetheless is a monumental compilation that has stood the test of time. Not the least of the contributions is the excellent review of previous botanical explorations of Costa Rica. The specimens forming the basis of this work were collected in all parts of the country in the period 1923-26.

Fauna

88 **Batrachia and Reptilia of Costa Rica.**
Edward Drinker Cope. San José: Universidad de Costa Rica, 1967.
72p.

Without going to Costa Rica personally Cope, through friends of his who worked in the field, accumulated a sufficient number of specimens of Batrachia and Reptilia to write this seemingly definitive work. Originally published in Philadelphia in 1875 it was not superseded until the 1950s.

89 **The sea turtles of Santa Rosa National Park.**
Stephen E. Cornelius. San José: Tinker Foundation, Fundación de
Parques Nacionales, Editorial Universidad Estatal a Distancia, 1986.
65p. bibliog. maps.

Following an introductory section on taxonomy and sea turtle biology, characteristics
of the olive ridley, leatherback, Pacific green, and hawksbill turtles are treated in this
booklet. Santa Rosa National Park, where the research for the study was done, is on
Costa Rica's Pacific coast. In chapters on each turtle species the author, an
independent wildlife biologist, describes courtship, mating, nesting behaviour, and
migration. Numerous excellent photographs assist the reader in identifying characteristics of the turtles. Special emphasis is given to threats to their survival.

90 **Butterflies of Costa Rica and their natural history: Papilionidae, Pieridae,
Nymphalidae.**
Philip J. DeVries. Princeton, New Jersey: Princeton University Press,
1987. 327p. maps. bibliog.

This is a superb book. Although the author considers it primarily as a field guide to the
nearly 550 species of butterflies covered in the book, there is considerable material on
systematics, natural history, habitats, and ecology. It is thoroughly researched in the
field as well as in the museums and the literature. In view of the fact that sixty-six per
cent of all neotropical genera of butterflies occur in Costa Rica the study has a value
beyond the borders of the country. Appendices include a systematic checklist of Costa
Rican butterflies and a description of the major collecting localities. The fifty plates,
plus excellent maps and drawings, add to the book's usefulness and attractiveness.

91 **Introduction to the herpetofauna of Costa Rica.**
Jay M. Savage, Jaime Villa R. Athens, Ohio: Society for the Study of
Amphibians and Reptiles, 1986. 207p. maps. bibliog.

Professors Savage and Villa have collaborated to update and enlarge Savage's *A
Handlist with Preliminary Keys to the Herpetofauna of Costa Rica* (Los Angeles,
California: Allan Hancock Foundation, 1980), and the result is this publication which
describes 150 species of amphibians and 212 species of reptiles. According to the
authors, it is 'the richest and most diverse' herpetofauna in Central America, and, due
to the efforts of several individuals, it is the best known. The present edition is
bilingual in Spanish and English.

92 **Life history of the quetzal.**
Alexander F. Skutch. *Condor*, vol. 46, no. 5 (Sept.-Oct. 1944),
p. 213-35.

Many people assume that the famous, brilliantly plumed quetzal bird is found only in
Guatemala, but this is not true. Skutch spent nearly an entire year in the mountains
near Vara Blanca, Costa Rica in order to study and record the life history of the
quetzal at home in the forest. This is one of many articles by this great naturalist in a
series on the life histories of Central American birds.

93 **Life history of the Costa Rican tityra.**
Alexander F. Skutch. *Auk*, vol. 63, no. 3 (July 1946), p. 327-62.
The tityra referred to in the title is from the Cotingidae family and related to the
American flycatcher. The article in question is one of a series that Skutch, a classical
naturalist who lived for many years near San Isidro del General, Costa Rica, has done
on Central American birds. Detailed observations of the tityra and its social life and
territoriality are included.

94 **The birds of Costa Rica: distribution and ecology.**
Paul Slud. New York: American Museum of Natural History, 1964.
430p. maps. bibliog. (Bulletin, no. 128).
This is a major scientific study of Costa Rican birds by a North American ornithologist
who spent seven years (at various times between 1950 and 1962) studying birds in all
the life zones of Costa Rica. It contains descriptions of 758 species (compared to the
659 in Melbourne A. Carriker, Jr.'s work of 1910). His objective is to describe the
daily activities and areas of concentration of each species. The author considers Costa
Rica one of the richest areas of the world for biological study.

95 **A guide to the birds of Costa Rica.**
F. Gary Stiles, Alexander F. Skutch. New York: Comstock Publishing
Associates (a division of Cornell University Press), 1989. 511p. bibliog.
This book, according to the authors, 'is for people who want to know where a bird
lives, how it behaves, what it eats, and how it reproduces'. Actually, many more topics
are included, such as range, vocalization, and plumage. A full description of Costa
Rica's geography and climate, with specific reference to avian habitats, is also of value,
as is the section reporting on conservation efforts. Some 830 species of birds are found
in Costa Rica; all are described here and most are illustrated in the 52 colour plates
included in the book's mid-section. The illustrations are by Dana Gardner. An
authoritative, encyclopaedic, beautifully illustrated and organized volume by seasoned
professionals, this is not a coffee-table book; it will be a standard for ornithologists for
years to come.

96 **Additions to the known herpetological fauna of Costa Rica with comments
on other species.**
Edward H. Taylor. *University of Kansas Science Bulletin*, vols 36, 37,
39, nos 9, 13, 1 (1 June 1954, 15 Oct. 1955, 18 Nov. 1958), p. 597-639,
499-575, 3-40.
Professor Taylor, one of the pioneering students of Costa Rican herpetology, here
provides scientific data on snakes from all parts of Costa Rica.

97 **A brief review of the snakes of Costa Rica.**
Edward H. Taylor. *University of Kansas Science Bulletin*, vol. 34, no. 1
(1 Oct. 1951), p. 3-188.
A scientific review of all the known species of snakes in Costa Rica. The work is based
on collections made in Costa Rica during 1947. Fifty-six genera and 132 species and
subspecies are included.

98 **Further studies on the serpents of Costa Rica.**
Edward H. Taylor. *University of Kansas Science Bulletin*, vol. 36, no. 11 (15 July 1954), p. 673-800.
Three new collecting expeditions by herpetologist Taylor to Costa Rica after 1951 resulted in these additions to the herpetofauna of Costa Rica.

99 **A review of the lizards of Costa Rica.**
Edward H. Taylor. *University of Kansas Science Bulletin*, vol. 38, no. 1 (20 Dec. 1956), p. 3-322.
In four collecting trips to Costa Rica in the late 1940s and the early 1950s the indefatigable Professor Taylor collected 79 species and subspecies of lizards. They are listed and described scientifically in this treatise.

100 **A review of the frogs and toads of Costa Rica.**
Edward H. Taylor. *University of Kansas Science Bulletin*, vol. 35, no. 5 (1 July 1952), p. 577-942.
This is a scientific review of the frogs and toads of Costa Rica, with descriptions and illustrations.

101 **The salamanders and caecilians of Costa Rica.**
Edward H. Taylor. *University of Kansas Science Bulletin*, vol. 34, no. 12 (15 Feb. 1952), p. 695-791. bibliog.
In Professor Taylor's customary manner all of the salamanders and caecilians of Costa Rica (thirty species) are carefully listed and described. A bibliography and commentary complement the work.

102 **Los nombres vulgares en la fauna costarricense.** (The common names of Costa Rican fauna.)
Rómulo Valerio Rodríguez. San José: Imprenta Nacional, 1978. 3rd ed. 181p.
The author, a biology teacher and director of the National Museum from 1941 to 1949, prepared this volume as a handy guide to the best-known animals of Costa Rica. The first edition was published in 1944 by the Universidad de Costa Rica.

103 **A collection of birds from northern Guanacaste, Costa Rica.**
Alexander Wetmore. *Proceedings*, United States National Museum, vol. 45, no. 32179 (7 July 1944), p. 25-80.
Besides a description of thirty-seven species of birds this article contains a complete account of the circumstances of the author's collecting trip to Costa Rica and his collaboration with Costa Rican ornithologists. Wetmore was one of the leading ornithologists of his time to do research in Central America.

104 **Fruits and the ecology of resplendent quetzals.**
Nathaniel Thoreau Wheelwright. *Auk*, vol. 100, no. 2 (April 1983),
p. 286-301. bibliog.

Fruit-eating birds deserve special study because of their role as seed dispersers and the likelihood of co-evolution of birds and plants. Resplendent quetzals, according to this study of their dietary habits, depend mostly on berries of the laurel family and this dictates their movements. This study of the quetzal, which involved meticulous observation at Monteverde, Costa Rica during 1979-82, touches on many topics besides dietary habits. Among these are: nesting, habitat, and conservation prospects.

105 **Tropical fruit-eating birds and their food plants: a survey of a Costa Rican lower montane forest.**
Nathaniel Thoreau Wheelwright, William A. Haber, K. Greg Murray,
Carlos Guindon. *Biotropica*, vol. 16, no. 3 (Sept. 1984), p. 173-92.
bibliog.

Although written for professionals and published in a professional journal this article may attract the interest of laypersons. It surveys the fruit-eating birds (some seventy species) at one tropical Costa Rican site, Monteverde, which is readily accessible to bird-watchers and environmental enthusiasts. The data presented contribute to an understanding of the diversity of bird diets and in general to the important matter of the evolutionary relationship between birds and their habitat.

106 **The impact of seasonal flowering regimes on the biology of some tropical hummingbirds.**
Larry L. Wolf. *Condor*, vol. 72, no. 1 (Jan. 1970), p. 1-14.

Reports the results of a study of the feeding and territorial activities of nine species of hummingbirds. The study was carried out near Cañas between January and July 1967, thus including parts of both the dry and the rainy season. Each burst of flowering activity resulted in visits of different species of birds.

The Republic of Costa Rica.
See item no. 8.

Costa Rica: a natural destination.
See item no. 57.

The windward road: adventures of a naturalist on remote Caribbean shores.
See item no. 62.

The population of Costa Rica and its natural resources.
See item no. 253.

Plantas medicinales de Costa Rica y su folclore. (Medicinal plants of Costa Rica and their folklore.)
See item no. 285.

The rain forests of Golfo Dulce.
See item no. 559.

Flora and Fauna.

Biocultural restoration of a tropical forest.
See item no. 560.

Vegetación y clima de Costa Rica. (Vegetation and climate of Costa Rica.)
See item no. 597.

Costa Rica.
See item no. 599.

Primer Simposio de Parques Nacionales y Reservas Biológicas. (The first symposium on national parks and biological reserves.)
See item no. 601.

Corcovado: meditaciones de un biólogo. (Corcovado: meditations of a biologist.)
See item no. 606.

Field guide to the natural history of Costa Rica.
See item no. 607.

Serpientes venenosas de Costa Rica. (Poisonous snakes of Costa Rica.)
See item no. 623.

Prehistory and Archaeology

General

107 **Between continents/between seas: precolumbian art of Costa Rica.**
Edited by Suzanne Abel-Vidor.   New York: Harry Abrams; Detroit
Institute of Arts, 1981. 240p. bibliog.

This is a publication resulting from the first comprehensive exhibition of Costa Rican
archaeology to tour the United States. Organized principally by the Detroit Institute of
Arts, the exhibition toured the United States from 1981 to 1984. The book is both a
catalogue of the nearly 300 pieces exhibited and a collection of essays by leading
archaeologists, including Michael Snarskis, Oscar M. Fonseca Zamora, Elizabeth
Kennedy Easby, and Frederick W. Lange. The excellent photographs are by Dirk
Bakker. Articles on the history of the Costa Rican National Museum and on the
history of archaeological research in Costa Rica are also included.

108 **Colección de objetos indígenas de oro del Banco Central de Costa Rica.**
(A collection of indigenous gold objects in the Central Bank of Costa
Rica.)
Carlos H. Aguilar Piedra.   Ciudad Universitaria Rodrigo Facio:
Universidad de Costa Rica, 1972. 200p. bibliog. (Serie Historia y
Geografía, no. 13).

More than a catalogue of the Indian-made gold objects in the Banco Central
collection, the present work contains an account of the technological aspects of
indigenous gold-working, an analysis of the artistic styles represented, and a historico-
geographical explanation of the Indian groups who made the gold objects. It also
contains eighty-five illustrations. The gold museum of the Banco Central was
inaugurated in October 1966.

109 **El jade de Costa Rica: un album arqueológico con reproducciones en color.** (The jade of Costa Rica: an archaeological album with reproductions in colour.)
Carlos A. Balser. San José: Lehmann, 1974. 88p. bibliog.

According to Balser, jade amulets were produced in large numbers in two places in precolumbian Costa Rica: in Guanacaste and on the Atlantic watershed. Balser discusses the possible geological origin of the jade ornaments found in Costa Rica, their age, similarities with jade ornaments from Mexico and Guatemala, and how they were worked. The main part of the booklet, which is in English and Spanish, is a description and analysis (with photographs) of forty specific jade amulets.

110 **Jade precolombino de Costa Rica.** (The precolumbian jade of Costa Rica.)
Carlos A. Balser. San José: Instituto Nacional de Seguros, 1980. 130p. bibliog.

Most of the jade found in Costa Rica came from Nicoya in Guanacaste and Línea Vieja on the Caribbean coast. Balser explains the origins of jade work in Costa Rica, describes the technique of working in jade, and itemizes the kinds of jade work. The book is well illustrated.

111 **Metal and jade in lower central America.**
Carlos A. Balser. In: *International Congress of Americanists, XXXVII Mar del Plata, Argentina, 1966: actas y memorias*, vol. 4, p. 57-64.
Buenos Aires: International Congress of Americanists, 1968. bibliog.

A survey of interpretations of the origins of metal-working and jade-working in lower Central America. The author concludes that the artistic developments of gold-working were inventions of southern Costa Rica and northern Panama, but the techniques of metal-working were influenced by trans-Pacific contacts. Jade, he says, was probably introduced from the north.

112 **Cultural developments in lower Central America.**
Claude Baudez. In: *Aboriginal cultural development in Latin America: an interpretive review*, edited by Betty J. Meggers, Clifford Evans, item 159, p. 45-54. Washington, DC: Smithsonian Institution, 1963. maps. bibliog. (Smithsonian Miscellaneous Collections, vol. 146, no. 1).

This article summarizes the state of archaeological knowledge about lower Central America, including Costa Rica. Baudez, a French archaeologist who has conducted field research in Guanacaste, suggests an areal sequence divided into six time periods from 4850 BC to the Spanish Conquest.

113 **Los nicarao y los chorotega según las fuentes históricas.** (The Nicarao
and the Chorotega according to historical sources.)
Anne M. Chapman.   San José: Universidad de Costa Rica, 1974.
112p. map. bibliog. (Universidad de Costa Rica, Serie Historia y
Geografía, no. 4).

Los nicarao y los chorotega is an ethnohistorical study and comparison of the two
Indian cultures who lived near the Nicaraguan–Costa Rican border at the time of the
Spanish Conquest. The Nicarao, who spoke a Nahua dialect, dominated the Isthmus of
Rivas, and the Chorotega, who spoke a Chibcha dialect, dominated in the Costa Rican
province of Guanacaste. Based primarily on the accounts of Spanish chroniclers, the
work is based on the author's PhD dissertation at Columbia University. The 1974
edition is a reprint of the 1960 edition (same publisher) except that the last three
pages, containing bibliographical references, are unfortunately missing.

114 **Costa Rican archaeology and Mesoamerica.**
Michael D. Coe.   *Southwestern Journal of Anthropology*, vol. 18,
no. 2 (Summer 1962), p. 170-83. bibliog.

Reviewing recent archaeological work in Costa Rica, Coe provides a lucid explanation
of the concept of Costa Rica as a meeting ground between the cultures of North and
South America. The emphasis falls on evidence of Mesoamerican influence in the
Nicoya area. A chronological sequence for this and other areas of Costa Rica is also
presented.

115 **Pre-Columbian jade from Costa Rica.**
Elizabeth Kennedy Easby.   New York: André Emmerich, 1968. 103p.
maps. bibliog.

Sixty-eight illustrations highlight this excellent, comprehensive study of precolumbian
jade. After considering several possible sources of jade to the north and south of Costa
Rica and considering the quantities of jade found in Costa Rica, the author is
convinced that significant jade deposits were located in Costa Rica. The author also
discusses techniques of working with jade.

116 **Costa Rica precolombina: arqueología, etnología, tecnología, arte.**
(Precolumbian Costa Rica: archaeology, ethnology, technology, art.)
Luis Ferrero.   San José: Editorial Costa Rica, 1981. 4th ed. 492p.
bibliog. (Biblioteca Patria, no. 6).

This is a very thorough, and extremely well-illustrated synthesis of precolumbian Costa
Rica for the general reading public. Although there is adequate discussion of the
archaeological background the emphasis falls on the technical and aesthetic aspects of
indigenous art. An extensive bibliography (p. 425-34) and glossary (p. 389-424) add to
the book's value.

117 **The archaeology of lower Central America.**
Edited by Frederick W. Lange, Doriz Z. Stone. Albuquerque, New
Mexico: University of New Mexico Press, 1984. 476p. bibliog. (School
of American Research Advanced Seminar Series).

Lower Central America, defined archaeologically as a cultural periphery by the
authors, encompasses most of El Salvador and Honduras, and all of Nicaragua, Costa
Rica, and Panama. Several of the chapters in this book, presented first as scholarly
papers at the Advanced Seminar on Lower Central American Archaeology in April
1980, at the School of American Research, Santa Fe, New Mexico, deal specifically
with Costa Rica. Authoritative studies by Frederick W. Lange, Michael J. Snarskis,
Wolfgang Haberland, Robert P. Drolet, and Doris Z. Stone make this a valuable
contribution to Costa Rican archaeology.

118 **Prehistoric settlement patterns in Costa Rica.**
Edited by Frederick W. Lange, Lynette Norr. 439p. maps. bibliog.
(Special issue of *Journal of the Steward Anthropological Society*,
vol. 14, no. 1-2, Fall-Spring, 1982-83).

The present work is an excellent review of the status of archaeological knowledge of
Costa Rica in the early 1980s. Of the twenty-six articles, all by professional
archaeologists who have worked in Costa Rica, over half deal with 'macro' or regional
level surveys. Except for two ethnographical articles and two on Nicaragua the rest are
site-specific. The archaeological region which is best known and which receives the
most coverage in this volume is Greater Nicoya. Other articles deal with sites in
Guanacaste, the Central Valley, and the Boruca region. The Caribbean coastal region
is not covered. Despite the emphasis on certain regions the book is a valuable
benchmark study, pinpointing where extensive archaeological research has been done
and where additional research is needed.

119 **Jade and string sawing in Northeastern Costa Rica.**
Samuel K. Lothrop. *American Antiquity*, vol. 21, no. 1 (July 1955),
p. 43-51.

The author enumerates the several types of jade ornaments found in Guápiles and
discusses Northern and Southern influences on their design. He also comments on the
sawing technique used to produce the designs.

120 **Costa Rican stonework: the Minor C. Keith collection.**
John Alden Mason. New York: American Museum of Natural
History, 1945. 317p. bibliog. (Anthropological Papers of the American
Museum of Natural History, vol. 39, pt. 3).

The Keith collection consists of 16,308 specimens, mostly pottery, brought from Costa
Rica to the United States before 1914. Areas of Costa Rica best represented are the
Huetar region on the Atlantic slope and the Brunca region on the Pacific coast. Since
the provenance of most items is uncertain and excavation data are lacking, Mason
concentrates on a detailed factual description and comparison of the objects. The work
deals only with the stone objects in the collection. Forty-nine plates and forty-four
additional figures illustrate the text.

121 **Costa Rica: monumentos históricos y arqueológicos.** (Costa Rica: historical and archaeological monuments.)
María Molina de Lines, Jorge A. Lines.   San José: Instituto Panamericano de Geografía e Historia, Comisión de Historia, 1974. 221p. bibliog. (Monumentos Históricos y Arqueológicos de America, no. 13).

The chief contribution of this booklet, one of a series on historical and archaeological monuments published by the Pan American Institute of Geography and History, is a review of legislation providing protection to historical and archaeological sites. The narrative focuses on Costa Rican archaeological sites, artefacts, and previous archaeological studies, but Costa Rica's few architectural remnants of the colonial period are also covered. A shorter edition was published by the same publisher in 1967.

122 **Costa Rica: la frontera sur de Mesoamérica.** (Costa Rica: the southern border of Mesoamerica.)
Ricardo Quesada López-Calleja.   San José: Instituto Costarricense de Turismo, 1980. 2nd ed. 288p. maps. bibliog.

This is a book with the tourist in mind rather than a specialist in archaeology. Along with a discussion of Costa Rican prehistory and especially of the contacts between the indigenes of Costa Rica and their neighbours, there is a passionate plea to save for Costa Rica the country's archaeological artefacts and also a defence of Indian culture. It is generously illustrated with maps and photographs. The first edition was published in 1975.

123 **Inter-regional ties in Costa Rican prehistory: papers presented at a symposium at Carnegie Museum of Natural History, Pittsburgh, April 27, 1983.**
Esther Skirboll, Winifred Creamer.   Oxford, England: BAR, 1984. 276p. maps. bibliog. (BAR International Series, no. 226).

The symposium referred to in the title honoured Carl Vilhelm Hartman (1862-1941), considered the father of Costa Rican archaeology, on the seventy-fifth anniversary of Hartman's departure from the Carnegie Museum and return to his native Sweden. Of the fourteen papers presented, nine are in English and the rest in Spanish. As the symposium title indicates, most contributions treat relationships between indigenous inhabitants of Costa Rican regions and those living in regions bordering on Costa Rica. The whole volume provides a good summary of contemporary archaeological knowledge of Costa Rica.

124 **Aboriginal metalwork in lower Central America.**
Doris Z. Stone, Carlos A. Balser.   San José: Editorial Antonio Lehmann, 1967. 47p. bibliog.

The focus of this booklet is a collection of over a hundred metal objects, mostly gold, exhibited for the first time in the Costa Rican National Museum in 1958. Besides describing the objects, the authors explain where they were found, how they were made, and similarities with indigenous gold objects found to the north and south of Costa Rica. Among the objects are beads, earrings, awls, finger rings, bells, and needles. Photographs of all the objects are included.

125 **Introduction to the archaeology of Costa Rica.**

Doris Z. Stone. San José: Museo Nacional, 1958. 54p. map. bibliog.

According to the author, a leading student of Central American archaeology, rare and minute archaeological classifications have been avoided in this booklet. 'Instead, this is an attempt to present the interested with a clear preliminary picture of the prehistoric cultures of Costa Rica.' Nevertheless, details and figures are provided in order to illustrate different ceramic styles. The booklet was especially prepared for the 33rd Congress of Americanists which met in San José in 1958.

126 **Precolombian art of Costa Rica.**

Doris Z. Stone, Carlos A. Balser. San José: Museo Nacional de Costa Rica, 1964. 49p. map.

This booklet contains twenty colour reproductions and brief descriptions of highly selected artistic objects representing different Costa Rican archaeological zones. All are from the collections of the Costa Rican National Museum. The publication is in Spanish and English.

127 **Pre-Columbian man in Costa Rica.**

Doris Z. Stone. Cambridge, Massachusetts: Peabody Museum Press, 1977. 238p. bibliog.

Each of the three principal archaeological regions of Costa Rica – Nicoya, the Diquís Delta, and the Atlantic watershed – is described in separate chapters. The author depends heavily on ceramic details to reconstruct the prehistory of these regions. Details of burials, architecture, and artefacts are provided as each site is described but with little information on their social or religious significance. Even though it has these scholarly limitations it is still the best synthesis of the subject available in English.

128 **The stone sculpture of Costa Rica.**

Doris Z. Stone. In: *Essays in precolumbian art and archaeology*, edited by Samuel K. Lothrop (et al.). Cambridge, Massachusetts: Harvard University Press, 1961, p. 193-209.

In this essay Stone describes the three stylistic areas of stone sculpture in Costa Rica: the Nicoya region, the Atlantic watershed and Highland region, and the Diquís or South Pacific region. By showing stylistic connections with civilizations to the north and south, she emphasizes Costa Rica's importance as a meeting ground of cultures in pre-colonial times.

Regional

129 **Some Costa Rican jade motifs.**
Carlos A. Balser. In: *Essays on precolumbian art and archaeology*, edited by Samuel K. Lothrop (et al.). Cambridge, Massachusetts: Harvard University Press, 1961, p. 210-17.

Balser contrasts artistic motifs in jade work from the Atlantic watershed and the Nicoya Peninsula of Costa Rica and speculates on possible outside influences on this work.

130 **Recherches archéologiques dans la Vallée du Tempisque, Guanacaste, Costa Rica.** (Archaeological research in the Tempisque valley, Guanacaste, Costa Rica.)
Claude Baudez. Paris: Institut des Hautes Etudes de l'Amérique Latine, 1967. 401p. bibliog. (Travaux et mémoires, no. 18).

This report on excavations at four Costa Rican archaeological sites in the vicinity of the Tempisque river valley in Nicoya, contains the results of the first radiocarbon tests in Costa Rica. It is rich in detailed analysis of stratigraphy and ceramic types and is supported by photographs and charts. Baudez suggests five sequential cultural phases for the Tempisque area.

131 **The zoned bichrome period in northwestern Costa Rica.**
Michael D. Coe, Claude F. Baudez. *American Antiquity*, vol. 26, no. 4 (April 1961), p. 505-15.

Scholars realized the extent of precolumbian occupation of the Nicoya Peninsula in northwestern Costa Rica with the survey and excavation of many new archaeological sites in the 1950s. This article by archaeologists Coe and Baudez is an excellent survey of three phases of the Zoned Bichrome period, roughly from 100 BC to 300 AD, the period of the earliest pottery-making culture identified in Costa Rica. The authors explain 'zoned bichrome' and other ceramic styles found in the area, and compare these styles with those of other archaeological findings in Central and South America.

132 **La Gran Nicoya: vínculo cultural de América.** (Greater Nicoya: cultural link of America.)
Luis Ferrero. *Boletín Nicaragüense de Bibliografía y Documentación*, no. 27 (Jan.-Feb. 1979), p. 1-23. bibliog.

A chronological synthesis (600 BC–1200 AD) of the impact of neighbouring civilizations on the Nicoya Peninsula of Costa Rica. Ferrero gives special attention to Mexican and Mayan influence.

133 **Archaeological researches in Costa Rica.**
Carl Vilhelm Hartman. Stockholm: I. Haeggströms boktryckeri, 1901. 195p.

Carl V. Hartman of Sweden conducted an archaeological expedition to Costa Rica, 1896-99, and published his findings, principally a methodical listing of Atlantic slope grave sites and their contents, in this lavishly illustrated book. This was the first sustained, scientific archaeological work done in Costa Rica.

134 **Archaeological researches on the Pacific coast of Costa Rica.**
Carl Vilhelm Hartman. Pittsburgh, Pennsylvania: Carnegie Institute,
1907. 188p. (Memoirs of the Carnegie Museum, vol. 3, no. 1).
Hartman's 1907 volume is a sequel to his 1901 study of Costa Rican archaeology.
However, this time he worked on the Pacific side rather than the Caribbean side of
Costa Rica. The Carnegie publication describes grave sites and their contents from the
Nicoya Peninsula.

135 **Prehistory of the Reventazón river drainage area, Costa Rica.**
William J. Kennedy. *Vínculos*, vol. 2, no. 1 (1976), p. 87-100.
bibliog.
On the basis of tests at forty-eight archaeological sites in the Reventazón river
drainage area (Caribbean coast) the author draws conclusions on precolumbian
chronology and ceramic typology. A provisional regional chronology is presented in
tables. The principal contribution of the article is the analysis of ceramic ware and the
identification of ceramic types and subtypes with time and region.

136 **Ancient treasures of Costa Rica: art and archaeology of the rich coast.**
Edited by Frederick W. Lange. Boulder, Colorado: Johnson, 1990.
40p. maps. bibliog.
This catalogue of an exhibition of the art and archaeology of the Nicoya area of Costa
Rica is useful for several reasons. It admirably summarizes recent research on Costa
Rican archaeology. The maps and chronological chart are extremely well done and
helpful to the layperson attempting to understand the fundamentals of Costa Rican
archaeology. And also, the objects chosen for the exhibit, some of which are illustrated
in colour photographs and drawings, demonstrate that Costa Rican Indians were
skilled potters and metal-workers. Altogether the catalogue presents precolumbian
Costa Rica in a better light artistically than earlier publications on the subject. All
objects illustrated in the catalogue are from the Jan and Frederick R. Mayer collection
and were exhibited at the Denver Museum of Natural History in the summer of 1990.

137 **Costa Rican art and archaeology.**
Edited by Frederick W. Lange. Boulder, Colorado: University of
Colorado, 1988. 336p. bibliog.
An impressive collection of thirteen articles, which together form an indispensable
item for understanding the state of knowledge about Costa Rican archaeology. The
articles, all in English, represent the latest scientific research on a variety of
archaeological artefacts found previously in northwestern Costa Rica; these include
pottery, jade, mace heads, roller stamps, and gold objects. Some articles deal
specifically with artistic styles, symbols, chronology, and precolumbian trade and
exchange, while two offer overviews of the geographical and chronological setting. All
are well documented and carefully done. A separate bibliography (p. 303-30) is in itself
a useful research tool, demonstrating the extent of the recent explosion of knowledge
about Costa Rican archaeology. The principal limitation of the work is its sharp focus
on the area of Guanacaste in northwestern Costa Rica.

138 **The formative zoned bichrome period in northwestern Costa Rica, 800 B. C. to A. D. 500.**
Frederick W. Lange. *Vínculos*, vol. 6, nos 1-2 (1980), p. 33-42.
As a result of several excavations performed at the Vidor archaeological site in Guanacaste Professor Lange is able to clarify ceramic features of the Formative Zoned Bichrome period. Initially defined as running from 300 BC to AD 300, the period can be extended backward to 500 BC and forward to 800 AD. Further details are provided about cultural patterns and settlements during this period. Comparisons with similar archaeological research in Panama and Nicaragua help to complete the picture.

139 **Metallurgy in Costa Rica.**
Frederick W. Lange, Richard M. Accola. *Archaeology*, vol. 32, no. 5 (Sept.-Oct. 1979), p. 26-33. map.
The discovery of a copper bell and a mould fragment at archaeological sites in Guanacaste in northwestern Costa Rica enables Lange and Accola to reinterpret the prehistory of this region. Previously, it was thought that copper artefacts from this region were the result of trade. These new discoveries strongly suggest the existence of a local metallurgical industry. The authors also explore the relation of these discoveries and other ceramic evidence to previous speculation about precolumbian contact, trade, and influence.

140 **Mystery of the prehistoric balls.**
Eleanor B. Lothrop. *Natural History*, vol. 64, no. 7 (Sept. 1975), p. 372-7.
The article describes the efforts of the author and her husband, Samuel K. Lothrop, to explain the mystery of the prehistoric stone spheres found in the area of Palmar in southwestern Costa Rica.

141 **Archaeology of the Diquís Delta, Costa Rica.**
Samuel K. Lothrop. Cambridge, Massachusetts: Harvard University, Peabody Museum of Archaeology and Ethnology, 1963. 142p. maps. bibliog. (Papers, no. 51).
Without venturing into chronological generalizations, the author, an archaeologist, describes several sites near Palmar in southwestern Costa Rica. He also describes stone sculptures, pendants, and pottery, and gives particular attention to the mysterious stone balls of this area. Numerous maps, photographs, and figures illustrate the text. Sites were excavated on United Fruit Company farms in 1948.

142 **Mesoamerican influences among Talamanca and Western Guaymí Indians.**
Laura Laurencich Minelli. In: *Frontier adaptations in Lower Central America*, edited by Mary W. Helms, Franklin O. Loveland. Philadelphia, Pennsylvania: Institute for the Study of Human Issues, 1976, p. 55-65. maps. bibliog.
Minelli discusses traces of Mexican influence (names, myths, and the counting system) among the Guaymí Indians who live along the Costa Rican–Panamanian border on the Atlantic coast.

143 **Cult traits in southeastern Costa Rica and their significance.**
Doris Z. Stone. *American Antiquity*, vol. 28, no. 3 (Jan. 1963),
p. 339-59.

In this article Stone discusses the results of recent excavations in southern Costa Rica,
particularly around San Agustín, and suggests that the region was an important cultural
and trading centre between precolumbian peoples of Panama and Costa Rica.
Available in Spanish (translated by Alfonso Jiménez Muñoz) as a reprint (San José:
Museo Nacional, 1963).

144 **Date of maize in Talamanca, Costa Rica.**
Doris Z. Stone. *Journal de la Société des Américanistes*, vol. 45
(1956), p. 189-94.

This article discusses the principal foods of the Sigua Indians who lived in the Tarire
and Sixaola river valleys in Talamanca. They ate pejivalle nuts, yucca, and cacao until
corn was introduced by Indians of Mexican origin before the Spanish Conquest. Stone
refutes the thesis that corn was introduced into this region by the Spanish.

Specific sites

145 **El Molino: un sitio de la Fase Pavas en Cartago.** (El Molino: a Pavas
phase site in Cartago.)
Carlos H. Aguilar Piedra. *Vínculos*, vol. 1, no. 1 (1975), p. 18-56.
bibliog.

An illustrated description of an important site in Cartago Province in eastern Costa
Rica. Similarities with other carbon-14-dated phases indicate that the site was occupied
for several hundred years before 300 AD.

146 **Guayabo de Turrialba: arqueología de un sitio indígena prehispánico.**
(Guayabo de Turrialba: archaeology of a prehispanic indigenous site.)
Carlos H. Aguilar Piedra. San José: Editorial Costa Rica, 1972. 192p.
map. bibliog.

Guayabo is an archaeological site established as a national Archaeological Park near
the town of Turrialba. Professor Aguilar first visited it in 1954 and completed
excavation of the site in the late 1960s. His book describes the site and its environment
and provides a technical description of the objects found there. A map of the site and
illustrations of objects found at the site are included.

147 **Retes: un depósito arqueológico en las faldas del Irazú.** (Retes: an archaeological deposit on the lower slopes of Irazú.)
Carlos H. Aguilar Piedra. San José: Trejos Hermanos, 1953. 52p. map. bibliog. (Universidad de Costa Rica, Sección Tesis de Grado y Ensayos, no. 5).

Retes appears to be a cache where Costa Rican Indians hid sacred objects to save them from the Spanish conquerors. Canes, tables, drums, and stone sculptures were among the 187 objects found. Aguilar reproduces some of the designs on these objects and provides narrative detail. Photographs are included.

148 **South American and Mayan cultural contacts at the Las Huacas site, Costa Rica.**
Oscar M. Fonseca Zamora, James B. Richardson. *Annals of Carnegie Museum*, vol. 47, no. 13 (Sept. 1978), p. 299-317. map. bibliog.

The Las Huacas archaeological site is located in Nicoya, Guanacaste Province. It was first excavated by Carl V. Hartman in 1903. Analysis by Fonseca and Richardson of fourteen artefacts, including llama effigies, from the Hartman collection of the Carnegie Museum reveals cultural contacts with the Maya region and with South America.

149 **Stylistic analysis of stone pendants from Las Huacas burial ground, northwestern Costa Rica.**
Oscar M. Fonseca Zamora, Richard Scaglion. *Annals of Carnegie Museum*, vol. 47, no. 13 (Sept. 1978), p. 281-98. bibliog.

Stone pendants and maces from the Las Huacas burial site in Guanacaste Province show three distinct iconographical bird groups: harpy eagles, three-dimensional quetzals, and two-dimensional quetzals. The authors of this article provide an approximate ceramic chronology of the Las Huacas site (180 to 575 AD). They conclude that the artistic style was locally developed.

150 **A Middle Period lithic tool assemblage from the Atlantic watershed region, Costa Rica.**
William J. Kennedy. *Vínculos*, vol. 4, no. 1 (1978), p. 43-56.

Utilitarian stone tools found at the Monte Cristo archaeological site near the town of Orosi permit the author to provide the first stone tool classification for Costa Rican prehistory. Monte Cristo was a habitation site of the Middle Period (AD 850-1400).

151 **Stratigraphic excavations in the eastern lowlands of Costa Rica.**
Michael J. Snarskis. *American Antiquity*, vol. 41, no. 3 (July 1976), p. 343-53. map. bibliog.

Snarskis believes that the practice of dividing Costa Rica into zones of Mesoamerican and South American influence rests on insufficient ethnohistorical evidence. The author conducted test excavations in the Línea Vieja vicinity on the Caribbean coast and in this article submits archaeological evidence, particularly ceramics from the El Bosque archaeological site, that cultural patterns of the precolumbian inhabitants of eastern Costa Rica were part of a northern South American tropical forest pattern.

152 **Turrialba: a Paleo-Indian quarry and workshop site in eastern Costa Rica.**
Michael J. Snarskis. *American Antiquity*, vol. 44, no. 1 (Jan. 1979), p. 125-38. map. bibliog.

The recent discovery and excavation of a palaeo-Indian quarry and manufacturing site near Turrialba is described by archaeologist Michael J. Snarskis of the National Museum of Costa Rica. Discovery of eighteen fluted joints, preforms, and a variety of scrapers indicates that the Turrialba site, previously considered a single component ceramic site, can now be considered a multicomponent site 'with paleo-Indian occupation represented by a sophisticated percussion and pressure flaked lithic complex'.

Historia general de Costa Rica. (General history of Costa Rica.)
See item no. 160.

Ensayo geográfico histórico de la primera expedición de Juan Vázquez de Coronado al sur del país, enero 27 abril 18, 1563. (An historical geographical essay of the first expedition of Juan Vázquez de Coronado to the south of the country, 27 January to 18 April 1563.)
See item no. 186.

América Indígena.
See item no. 255.

The precolumbian art of Costa Rica.
See item no. 675.

History

General

153 **El desarrollo nacional en 150 años de vida independiente.** (National development during 150 years of independence.)
Edited by Oscar R. Aguilar Bulgarelli. San José: Universidad de Costa Rica, 1971. 401p. bibliog. (Publicaciones de la Universidad de Costa Rica, Serie Historia y Geografía, no. 12).
Sponsored by the National Commission for the 150th anniversary of Central American independence, the present volume is a collection of articles by different authors on the politics, economy, money and banking, letters, public education, newspapers, and arts of Costa Rica during its first 150 years. It is a documented, comprehensive review of independent Costa Rican history.

154 **Arqueología criminal americana.** (American criminal archaeology.)
Anastasio Alfaro González. San José: Editorial Costa Rica, 1961. 226p. (Biblioteca de Autores Costarricenses, vol. 3).
Originally published in 1906 by Imprenta Alsina of San José, the book surveys criminal cases from 1686 to 1850. There are separate chapters on specific categories of crimes and others on such subjects as contraband trade. Alfaro was archivist of Costa Rica at the time of his research in the criminal records of the National Archives.

155 **Costa Rica: the unarmed democracy.**
Leonard Bird. London: Sheppard Press, 1984. 224p.
Unfortunately, this first single-volume comprehensive history of Costa Rica in English turns out to have many defects. The author's lack of Spanish leads to many misspellings of names and places. Reference notes are scanty and unorderly. Although a history, the approach is 'presentist', and the book is unduly affected by the author's preoccupation with the economic crisis of 1983, when the book was written.

Nevertheless, the discussions of the revolution of 1948, the abolition of the army, the University for Peace, and the Quaker colony at Monteverde are useful.

156 **Una interpretación de la historia costarricense.** (An interpretation of Costa Rican history.)
Juan Bosch. San José: Editorial Juricentro, 1980. 2nd ed. 51p. (Colección Mundo de Ayer).

Juan Bosch, the political leader of the Dominican Republic, wrote this provocative essay on Costa Rican history while in exile in Costa Rica. He gives special attention to the formation of national character, the class struggle, and the revolution of 1948. First published as *Apuntes para una interpretación de la historia costarricense* (San José: Editorial 'Eloy Morua Carrillo', 1963, 38p.).

157 **La crisis de la democracia liberal en Costa Rica: interpretación y perspectiva.** (The crisis of liberal democracy in Costa Rica: interpretation and perspective.)
Rodolfo Cerdas Cruz. San José: Editorial Universitaria Centroamericana, 1978. 3rd ed. 191p. bibliog. (Colección Seis.)

To follow the unorthodox organization of this book, best described as an historical essay, the reader needs to have a good grasp of Costa Rican historical chronology beforehand. It was Braulio Carrillo, according to Cerdas, who moulded the inherited colonial institutions into a liberal government favouring coffee producers in the first years of independence. Thereafter, Costa Rica moved rapidly to create an agro-exporting economy, dependent on foreign commercial connections. A description of this process occupies the middle part of the book. The final section outlines the unpleasant political and economic structure Cerdas sees as a result of the solidification of this pattern of underdevelopment and dependency on international capitalism.

158 **Don Diego de la Haya Fernández.**
Luz Alba Chacón de Umaña. San José: Editorial Costa Rica, 1967. 276p. map. bibliog.

This book serves admirably for a glimpse of the low standard of living in colonial Costa Rica. It is based heavily on the frank reports and correspondence of Diego de la Haya Fernández, governor of the Province of Costa Rica from 1718 to 1727. Known as one of the most progressive and active of Costa Rica's colonial governors, he faced (in addition to lack of resources) piratical attacks, Miskito Indian raids, a volcanic eruption, illicit commerce, and legal conflicts among the small upper class. How he and the people of Costa Rica responded to these problems is spelled out in this book. The text is in Spanish.

159 **El ser de la nacionalidad costarricense.** (The essence of Costa Rican nationality.)
José Abdulio Cordero. San José: Editorial Universidad Estatal a Distancia, 1980. 129p.

An historical essay which examines the roots of Costa Rican nationality. Instead of giving primary attention to land distribution, as so many essayists do, Cordero focuses on Costa Rica's declaration of independence in 1821, the rise and fall of the Universidad de Santo Tomás, 1844-88, and the National War against William Walker as the most important factors in forging Costa Rican nationality. First published by Editorial Tridente (Madrid) in 1964.

160 **Historia general de Costa Rica.** (General history of Costa Rica.) Edited by Vladimir de la Cruz. San José: Euroamericana de Ediciones Costa Rica, 1988. 4 vols. bibliog.

Planned to be a monumental five-volume, quarto-size contribution to the history of Costa Rica, the project has turned out as four volumes and a documentary supplement. Volume one (459 pages) is divided into two parts, of which the first is a lavishly illustrated geographical introduction to Costa Rica. The principal contribution is the description of the physical characteristics of Costa Rica, including climate, soils, and life zones. The photographs and maps advance understanding but the explanation of basic geographical terms, meant presumably for beginner readers, is somewhat distracting. The second volume (487 pages) covers the Spanish exploration and conquest and the colonial period. Details are handled in such a way – with coloured insets on population, for example, and drawings – as to be attractive and supportive of the narrative. The biographical insets on colonial governors are helpful. The final section in this volume is on the archaeology of the colonial period, practically a new discipline for Costa Rica. Volume three (626 pages), which takes the history of Costa Rica through independence, the period of the federation (1821-38), up to 1870, and volume four (663 pages), which covers the period of the liberal republic (1870-1949), continue the pattern of the first two volumes. The 65-page supplement contains documents pertaining to the independence of Costa Rica. Biographical inserts on important historical figures are a contribution from the extensive biographical file of Rafael Obregón Loría. Lists of university rectors and public officials, pictures of national symbols and documents, and photographs of individuals and buildings add more to an appreciation of the atmosphere of a particular period than to its analysis or interpretation. Lists of newspapers and political party leaders, short descriptions of specific *cantones* or districts, and pictures of public works are informative but not well integrated with the text. Matter-of-fact narration, in general, triumphs over interpretation. The project directors, it seems, did not intend to contribute new knowledge to the history of Costa Rica: they intended to present the remarkable accumulation of information in the last few years about Costa Rica's past in an attractive new package, and they have certainly done that.

161 **Costa Rica: a democratic revolution.** Charles F. Denton. In: *Latin American politics and development,* edited by Howard J. Wiarda, Harvey F. Kline. Boulder, Colorado: Westview Press, 1985, p. 488-506. 2nd ed. map. bibliog.

The greatest appeal of this brief, general description of Costa Rica's political system is the explanation of how social, economic, and historical factors affected political development.

162 **Cartilla histórica de Costa Rica.** (An historical sketch of Costa Rica.) Ricardo Fernández Guardia. San José: Lehmann, 1976. 49th ed. 171p.

Ricardo Fernández Guardia (1867-1950) published the first edition of this outline of the political history of Costa Rica in 1909. Including its later corrected and enlarged editions, it has served as a secondary school textbook in Costa Rica for approximately 80 years.

163 **Cosas y gentes de antaño.** (Things and people of yesteryear.)
Ricardo Fernández Guardia. San José: Editorial Universidad Estatal
a Distancia, 1980. 250p. bibliog.

Historian Fernández Guardia relates forty-seven stories about Costa Rican cities and incidents of the 19th century. Most are based on documentary evidence from the National Archives of Costa Rica, which Fernández Guardia directed for a number of years. The 1980 edition is a reprint of the 2nd enlarged edition, which was published in San José by Editorial Trejos in 1939. The first edition was published in 1935.

164 **The expropriation of pious and corporate properties in Costa Rica, 1805-1860: patterns in the consolidation of a national elite.**
Lowell Gudmundson. *The Americas*, vol. 39, no. 3 (Jan. 1983), p. 281-303.

Gudmundson's contribution in this article is to show that in Costa Rica, unlike in the rest of Central America, Liberals and Conservatives alike pursued the 'liberal' policy of expropriation of Church wealth.

165 **The development of foreign trade and communication in Costa Rica to the construction of the first railway.**
Richard J. Houk. *The Americas*, vol. 10, no. 2 (Oct. 1953), p. 197-209.

This brief but informative article describes colonial Costa Rica's almost complete isolation and its breakdown in the early 19th century. The first governments after independence proclaimed free trade and worked to develop roads and seaports, but the major transformation in trade and communications was brought about by the beginning of coffee exports in the late 1830s.

166 **The origins of Costa Rican federalism.**
Thomas L. Karnes. *The Americas*, vol. 15, no. 3 (Jan. 1959), p. 249-69.

An excellent review of the economic and political connections between Costa Rica and the rest of Central America in the years just before and just after independence. Karnes points out that the intendency reforms of the Captaincy General of Guatemala during the 1780s tended to buttress Costa Rica's self-determination.

167 **Desarrollo de las ideas filosóficas en Costa Rica.** (The development of philosophical ideas in Costa Rica.)
Constantino Láscaris Comneno. San José: Universidad Autónoma de Centro América; Editorial Studium, 1983. 3rd ed. 514p. (Clásicos Costarricenses).

Philosophy for Constantino Láscaris (1923-79), a Spanish philosopher who taught for many years at the Universidad de Costa Rica, was very broad. In this book he does indeed cover the teaching of philosophy in Costa Rica, but he also gives space to politicians, educators, scientists, poets, artists, and intellectuals. In effect, the book is a well-organized intellectual history of Costa Rica from the time of the arrival of the Spaniards. In his discussion of the ideas of Costa Rican intellectuals Láscaris succinctly summarizes their points of view. In the process of the coverage of ideas he also contributes to an understanding of the evolution of Costa Rican institutions such as the Universidad de Costa Rica, the Catholic Church, and political parties. There is no other volume which so successfully reviews the history of ideas in Costa Rica. The 1983 edition was edited by Guillermo Malavassi, who offers a short sketch of Láscaris and a bibliography of Láscaris' writings. The first edition was published by the Editorial Costa Rica in 1964.

168 **Costa Rica: tierra y poblamiento en la colonia.** (Costa Rica: land and population in the colonial period.)
Carlos Meléndez Chaverri. San José: Editorial Costa Rica, 1977. 213p. bibliog.

Brings together eleven articles previously published by Professor Meléndez in various periodicals. Some deal with themes outside the Central Valley, such as the annexation of Nicoya, origins of the town of Liberia, development of the port of Puntarenas, and the Indians of Talamanca. The remaining articles treat topics of the Central Valley, such as the origins of Cartago, cultivation of wheat, and land tenure. Perhaps the most significant article, combining Meléndez' grasp of geographical features as well as historical trends, deals with the significant historical-geographical matter of the evolution of the hegemony of the Central Valley over the outlying areas.

169 **Historia de Costa Rica.** (A history of Costa Rica.)
Carlos Monge Alfaro. San José: Librería Trejos, 1980. 16th ed. 319p. maps. bibliog.

A standard textbook for high-school and college students for many years. Monge provides an outline of political history, but emphasizes social and economic history. Chronologically the focus falls on the colonial period and the 19th century, with only a sketch of a few pages dedicated to the period since 1921. The work was first published in 1947.

170 **El poder legislativo en Costa Rica.** (Legislative power in Costa Rica.)
Rafael Obregón Loría. San José: Imprenta Nacional, 1966. 538p.

Obregón is as interested in the legislators as he is in the legislature. He provides, in the first section, biographical sketches of principal figures in the history of the National Assembly, and in the second lists of deputies in the assembly. Documents relating to internal regulations, rules of parliamentary practice, and constitutional provisions concerning the assembly are included.

171 **Costa Rica: moderate democratization of a civil oligarchy.**
John A. Peeler. In: *Latin American democracies: Colombia, Costa Rica, Venezuela*, John A. Peeler. Chapel Hill, North Carolina: University of North Carolina Press, 1985, p. 59-76.

A skeletal knowledge of the political history of Costa Rica is all that is needed to profit from this excellent historical essay. Unlike many political explanations of Costa Rica's democracy, which tend to overemphasize developments since 1948, this essay accounts for the two significant democratic transitions – the liberalization of the coffee oligarchy in the 1880s and the break-up of the so-called Liberal republic in the 1940s. Peeler offers insight into political party developments in both the 19th and 20th centuries and he provides an even-handed interpretation of the Rafael Calderón Guardia period and the subsequent revolution of 1948.

172 **Biografía de Costa Rica.** (A biography of Costa Rica.)
Eugenio Rodríguez Vega. San José: Editorial Costa Rica, 1981.
2nd ed. 190p. bibliog.

Sociologist Rodríguez Vega, who has served as rector of the University of Costa Rica
and Minister of Education, informally traces the history of Costa Rica from the
discovery to the 1950s. He succeeds in showing the relationship among political, social,
economic, and cultural developments in each historical period.

173 **Política y reforma en Costa Rica, 1914-1958.** (Politics and reform in
Costa Rica, 1914-58.)
Jorge Mario Salazar Mora. San José: Editorial Porvenir, 1981. 253p.
bibliog. (Colección Debate).

In this book, which was originally the author's PhD dissertation at Tulane University
and is written in Spanish, Salazar challenges the conventional idea that liberalism as
a political force in Costa Rica withered after 1948. He connects the idea of reform with
liberalism and traces antecedents of this connection in the early years of the 20th
century. The focus of the book, however, is on the National Liberation Party's leaders
and on the 1940s and 1950s when the author believes reformism was in the ascendancy.
It is an exhaustively researched and carefully documented book which deserves the
close attention of anyone interested in the evolution of 20th-century Costa Rican
politics. The bibliography (p. 233-53) is a good starting place for the serious student of
Costa Rica.

174 **Orden y progreso, la formación del estado nacional en Costa Rica.**
(Order and progress, the formation of the national state in Costa Rica.)
José Luis Vega Carballo. San José: Instituto Centroamericano de
Administración Pública, 1981. 338p. bibliog.

Vega Carballo, a sociologist educated in universities in the United States, covers the
same terrain that many historians have written about in profusion: the weakness and
poverty of the late colonial period, the uncertainties of the independence movement,
the formation of the state apparatus, the promotion of coffee as an export crop, and
the evolution of a liberal oligarchy. But he approaches the period 1800-70 from a
different perspective, paying more attention to the theory of the state, and giving
greater weight to the economic and ideological bases of the Costa Rican state and less
to individual leadership. The result is a thoughtful synthesis of the old (predominantly
personal and narrow) political history and the new economic and social history.

175 **Antecedentes de la independencia de Costa Rica.** (Antecedents of the
independence of Costa Rica.)
Mario Zaragoza Aguado. *Anuario de Estudios Centroamericanos*,
no. 1 (1974), p. 227-62. bibliog.

Zaragoza argues that colonial Costa Rica, though poor, was not as poor as previous
historians would have us believe, and that, in contrast to Costa Rica's pacific
reputation at the time of independence, there were several significant revolutionary
incidents in the 1810-21 period.

Local and regional

176 **Guanacaste: libro conmemorativo del centenario de la incorporación del partido de Nicoya a Costa Rica, 1824-1924.** (Guanacaste: commemorative book on the centennial of the incorporation of Nicoya into Costa Rica, 1824-1924.)
Edited by Víctor Manuel Cabrera.   San José: Imprenta María v. de Lines, 1924. 86p. maps.

This publication, sponsored by the Costa Rican government to commemorate the acquisition of Guanacaste from Nicaragua, is an encyclopaedic collection of factual material on Guanacaste. It includes descriptions of its geographical features, lists of its governors, and articles on history, mines, agriculture, religious hierarchy, transportation, and the like. Maps, photographs, and reprinted articles from the press help to provide an image of what Guanacaste was like in 1924.

177 **Historia y geografía del Cantón de San Ramón.** (The history and geography of the Canton of San Ramón.)
Trino Echavarría Campos.   San José: Imprenta Nacional, 1966. 107p. bibliog.

A collection of basic information about schools, churches, hospitals, and other public buildings, and about events such as earthquakes occurring in San Ramón since the city was founded in the 1850s.

178 **Reseña histórica de Talamanca.** (An historical review of Talamanca.)
Ricardo Fernández Guardia.   San José: Editorial Costa Rica, 1975 [1976]. 3rd ed. 228p. bibliog. (Biblioteca Patria, no. 1).

The first part is a leisurely history of the efforts of various Spanish captains, priests, and entrepreneurs to colonize Talamanca, on Costa Rica's Caribbean coast. The Indians successfully resisted. The second part, which covers the 19th century, continues the story of the efforts of various outsiders to dominate Talamanca and the Indians' resistance. Colonial chroniclers and public documents furnish Fernández Guardia with enough information to piece the story together. The present work is the third edition and is bound with the author's *El descubrimiento y la conquista*. The first edition was published in San José by Alsina in 1918.

179 **El puerto de Puntarenas: (algo de su historia.)** (The port of Puntarenas: a little of its history.)
Cleto González Víquez.   San José: Imprenta Gutenberg, 1933. 124p. maps.

The approach is primarily a legal one, as laws and government reports on Puntarenas are transcribed and analysed. Since the Pacific port of Puntarenas has been the subject of relatively few studies this legal history is a particularly important source of information. The focus is on the 19th century.

180 **Reseña histórica de Limón.** (An historical review of Limón.)
Jaime Granados Chacón, Ligia María Estrada Molina. San José:
Asamblea Legislativa, 1967. 211p. bibliog.

In commemoration of the 100th anniversary of the decree declaring Limón a free port,
the Costa Rican legislature contracted with the authors to compile this work on Limón.
It contains considerable information on economic activity in the Limón area during the
colonial period and additional material on transportation problems, formation of
schools and hospitals, and legislative decrees relating to Limón, especially in the 20th
century, but it is unevenly documented and not analytical.

181 **Monografía de Cartago.** (A monograph of Cartago.)
Jesús Mata Gamboa. Cartago, Costa Rica: Imprenta El Heraldo,
1930. 631p.

Details of buildings, associations, and institutions of Cartago are the main feature.
Short biographies of famous citizens of Cartago are also included. Encyclopaedic in
scope, the book is a mine of information about Cartago, especially in the 1920s.

182 **Turrialba, su desarrollo histórico: recopilación y comentario de
documentos relativos a población y desarrollo del cantón de Turrialba,
publicado con motivo de su primer cincuentenario de vida cantonal.**
(Turrialba, its historical development: compilation and commentary on
documents relative to the population and development of the canton of
Turrialba, published for the 50th anniversary of canton life.)
Juvenal Valerio Rodríguez. San José: Editorial Tormo, 1953. 197p.
maps.

Valerio Rodríguez presents a narrative history of the town of Turrialba and its
surroundings from pre-colonial times to the present. Observers of Turrialba from the
colonial chroniclers to 19th-century travellers and 20th-century scientists are frequently
cited. Excellent maps provided by scholars connected with the Institute of
Interamerican Agricultural Sciences, which was founded in Turrialba in 1944, grace the
volume.

Colonial

183 **Historia económica del tabaco: época colonial.** (The economic history of
tobacco: colonial era.)
Víctor Hugo Acuña Ortega. *Anuario de Estudios Centroamericanos*,
no. 4 (1979), p. 279-392.

Unlike Marco Antonio Fallas' study of the tobacco monopoly of Costa Rica (q.v.),
which deals with government policy, Acuña's study focuses on the economic aspects of
tobacco production from the 1760s to 1821. Subsidiary topics covered include internal
commerce, external commerce, prices, and manpower. Technical aspects and
government regulations are also treated. It is a detailed study based on archival sources
and fully illustrated by graphs and charts.

184 **La esclavitud en Costa Rica durante el período colonial.** (Slavery in
Costa Rica during the colonial period.)
Oscar R. Aguilar Bulgarelli. *Estudios Sociales Centroamericanos*,
vol. 2, no. 5 (May-Aug. 1973), p. 187-99. bibliog.

A preliminary investigation in the National Archives of Costa Rica convinced Aguilar
that slavery was more important than had been previously thought and that further
research on the subject was badly needed. He concludes that there was definitely a
privileged class in colonial Costa Rica.

185 **Costa Rica en el contexto económico iberoamericano.** (Costa Rica in an
Ibero-American economic context.)
Carlos Araya Pochet. *Revista de Costa Rica*, no. 5 (1974), p. 9-38.
bibliog.

Araya argues on the basis of a re-examination of secondary sources that Costa Rica's
poverty during the colonial period was not as great as previously believed, but that
Spanish colonial policy and Costa Rica's isolation, according to Araya, had a
significant, negative impact on subsequent economic development.

186 **Ensayo geográfico histórico de la primera expedición de Juan Vázquez
de Coronado al sur del país, enero 27–abril 18, 1563.** (An historical-
geographical essay of the first expedition of Juan Vázquez de Coronado
to the south of the country, 27 January to 18 April 1563.)
Mario Barrantes Ferrero. San José: Instituto Geográfico de Costa
Rica, 1961. 46p. maps.

Based on research on indigenous place-names, archaeological sites, and the accounts of
chroniclers, the article fixes the route taken by Juan Vázquez de Coronado in the
conquest of Costa Rica in 1563.

187 **Progenitores de los costarricenses.** (Progenitors of the Costa Ricans.)
Mario Barrantes Ferrero. San José: Academia Costarricense de
Ciencias Genealógicas, 1973. 245p. bibliog.

A complete alphabetical list of the names which appear in the ten-volume collection
Documentos para la historia de Costa Rica, edited by León Fernández, with additional
information about Costa Rican personages of the colonial period and an appendix
listing Costa Rica's colonial governors.

188 **La población de la ciudad de Cartago en los siglos XVII y XVIII.** (The
population of the city of Cartago in the 17th and 18th centuries.)
Norberto de Castro y Tosi. *Revista de los Archivos Nacionales*, 2nd
semester, vol. 28, no. 7-12 (Jul.-Dec. 1964), p. 151-76.

Contains an excellent chart showing the castes and social classes of Cartago's colonial
population; explanatory notes on each of the twenty-five terms; and a narrative which
compares the nomenclature of Costa Rica's social system with others. The article is
based on archival research.

189 **La Costa Rica de don Tomás de Acosta.** (The Costa Rica of Tomás de Acosta.)
Ligia María Estrada Molina. San José: Editorial Costa Rica, 1965.
277p. maps. bibliog. (Biblioteca de Autores Costarricenses).

There are two parts to this book. The first and largest part is an excellent description of Costa Rica, its administration, commerce, cities, and population in the late colonial period. The second part is a biography of Tomás de Acosta, governor of Costa Rica, 1797-1810.

190 **La factoría de tabacos de Costa Rica.** (The state tobacco agency of Costa Rica.)
Marco Antonio Fallas. San José: Editorial Costa Rica, 1972. 249p. bibliog.

This is the most nearly complete account available of the state tobacco agency which functioned in Costa Rica between the years 1766 and 1813. Tobacco brought the Central Valley a degree of prosperity and assisted San José in outdistancing the other cities in the valley but it was also a contentious issue involving private versus public enterprise. Fallas covers these issues, as well as early tobacco experimentation, contraband, and administration of the monopoly.

191 **Colección de documentos para la historia de Costa Rica.** (A collection of documents on the history of Costa Rica.)
León Fernández. San José: Editorial Costa Rica, 1976. 2nd ed. 3 vols. bibliog. (Biblioteca Patria, nos 2-4).

The documents collected deal primarily with the conquest and settling of Costa Rica. Other topics covered are *encomiendas* [Indian grants], missionary activity, Indian relations in general, and colonial government. Fernández, founder of the Costa Rican National Archives in 1881, collected the documents in Spain. The collection was originally published in Barcelona between 1881 and 1907.

192 **Historia de Costa Rica durante la dominación española, 1502-1821.** (History of Costa Rica during the Spanish domination, 1502-1821.)
León Fernández. San José: Editorial Costa Rica, 1975. 2nd ed. 288p. bibliog. (Biblioteca Patria, no. 7).

Each chapter summarizes the activities of one of the conquerors or governors of the colonial province of Costa Rica. The author often quotes from documents which he studied in the Archives of the Indies in Sevilla, Spain. A posthumous publication, it was edited by the author's son, Ricardo Fernández Guardia, and first published in Madrid in 1889.

193 **Crónicas coloniales de Costa Rica.** (Colonial chronicles of Costa Rica.)
Ricardo Fernández Guardia. San José: Editorial Costa Rica, 1967. 221p.

Ricardo Fernández Guardia, historian and archivist, wrote these stories about colonial personalities of Costa Rica on the basis of archival resources. The present work is a luxury edition to commemorate the 100th anniversary of the author's birth. It was first published in 1921.

194   **El descubrimiento y la conquista.** (Discovery and conquest.)
Ricardo Fernández Guardia.   San José: Editorial Costa Rica, 1975.
5th ed. 228p. (Biblioteca Patria, no. 1).

Events from Columbus' sighting of Costa Rica in 1502 to the refounding of Cartago in 1572 are traced in this book. The author, reacting against the Black Legend of excessive Spanish cruelty and greed, uses Spanish chroniclers as his principal sources and the result is a book emphasizing the brave deeds of the early explorers. It was first published in 1905. This, the fifth edition, is bound with the author's *Reseña histórica de Talamanca* (q.v.).

195   **Costa Rica colonial: la tierra y el hombre.** (Colonial Costa Rica: man and the land.)
Elizabeth Fonseca Corrales.   San José: Editorial Universidad Centroamericano, 1983. 387p. maps. bibliog. (Colección Rueda del Tempo.)

The most comprehensive historical study yet undertaken to uncover the origins of Costa Rica's land-use patterns. The study was presented as a doctoral dissertation at the University of Paris under the direction of the noted Latin American agrarian historian François Chevalier. Based on research in land and village transactions in the Costa Rican archives, the study traces the land grants and *encomiendas* of the conquerors, the evolution of villages and towns, the conflict between individual and communal property, the development of the *hacienda* [estate], and the origins of small property holdings in the Central Valley. The study embraces land, production, types of property, and government in the colonial period.

196   **Conquistadores y pobladores: orígenes histórico-sociales de los costarricenses.** (Conquerors and settlers: the historical-social origins of the Costa Ricans.)
Carlos Meléndez Chaverri.   San José: Editorial Universidad Estatal a Distancia, 1982. 286p. bibliog.

The articles reprinted here are important, documented studies of the founding of settlements and cities in Costa Rica and of the origins of agriculture in Costa Rica in the colonial period. Carlos Meléndez Chaverri is Costa Rica's leading historian.

197   **De neustra historia patria: los gobernadores de la colonia.** (Our country's history: the colonial governors.)
Rafael Obregón Loría.   San José: Universidad de Costa Rica, 1979. 229p. bibliog.

In this book Obregón Loría, an indefatigable collector of data on individual Costa Rican personages, offers to students of colonial Costa Rica lists of colonial office-holders, from governors to city officials and *corregidores* [magistrates]. For the colonial governors he provides, in addition, basic genealogical data and a sketch of their lives and careers. Although a bibliography is included it is not always clear where the biographical data come from.

1821-1948

198 **Costa Rica y sus hechos políticos de 1948: problemática de una década.**
(Costa Rica and its political acts of 1948: problem of a decade.)
Oscar R. Aguilar Bulgarelli. San José: Editorial Costa Rica, 1978.
3rd ed. 674p. bibliog.

Primarily a political analysis, this study provides a detailed account of the major political events of the decade of the 1940s. The author's purpose is to be objective and he succeeds. His approach is to describe the political parties of major figures of the period – Rafael Calderón Guardia, Teodoro Picado, Manuel Mora, José Figueres, and many others – and to judge the extent of their support by means of newspaper reactions and electoral results. The revolution of 1948 actually occupies relatively little space in the narrative. Just as valuable as the section on the revolution itself is a section on the Centre for the Study of National Problems, considered a precursor of the National Liberation Party. The first edition was published in 1969.

199 **Historia económica de Costa Rica, 1821-1971.** (Economic history of
Costa Rica, 1821-1971.)
Carlos Araya Pochet. San José: Editorial Fernández-Arce, 1982.
4th ed. 230p. bibliog. (Colección Libros Universitarios).

This edition of Araya's economic history includes a slightly revised version of the material in his *Historia económica de Costa Rica, 1950-1970*, plus additional chapters on the origin and development of the agro-exporting economy, 1821-80, and the highpoint of the agro-exporting economy, 1880-1950. The chapter on the earlier period is based on primary research in Costa Rican archives and the chapter on the 1880-1950 period is a synthesis based on the works of Carolyn Hall, Samuel Z. Stone, Ciro F. Cardoso, and others.

200 **La minería en Costa Rica (1821-1843).** (Mining in Costa Rica, 1821-43.)
Carlos Araya Pochet. *Revista de Historia*, vol. 1, no. 2 (2nd semester
1976), p. 85-125.

A well-documented study of mining during the brief period when it was an important industry in Costa Rica. It contains details on specific mines, ownership, production, and export. The author believes that capital accumulated by mine owners was an important stimulus to the coffee industry in the early 19th century.

201 **La Trinchera y otras páginas históricas.** (La Trinchera and other
historical pages.)
Manuel Argüello Mora. San José: Editorial Costa Rica, 1975. 153p.
bibliog. (Colección 'Nuestros Clásicos', no. 6).

Argüello wrote these vignettes on presidential policies during the 1860s, some thirty years after the incidents took place. Consequently they are somewhat untrustworthy as a historical record but still useful in providing a picture of the period. José Marín Cañas and Carlos Meléndez Chaverri add clarifying notes to this edition. The articles were originally published in newspapers in 1898-99.

202 **Woodrow Wilson's use of the non-recognition policy in Costa Rica.**
George W. Baker, Jr. *The Americas*, vol. 22, no. 1 (July 1965),
p. 3-21.
Based almost entirely on United States diplomatic documents, this article explains the reasons for President Wilson's refusal to recognize the Federico Tinoco government in Costa Rica, 1917-19.

203 **Crisis in Costa Rica: the 1948 revolution.**
John Patrick Bell. Austin, Texas: Published for the Institute of Latin American Studies by the University of Texas Press, 1971. 192p. bibliog. (Latin American Monographs, no. 24).
A clear, succinct narrative of the political and social background of the revolution of 1948 and of the revolution itself. An epilogue briefly discusses actions taken by the Revolutionary Junta under José Figueres during the eighteen months of power, 1948-49. Frequently quoted, this book has come to be considered a standard source on the history of Costa Rica in the 1940s. It is based on over 200 interviews of participants and on primary sources.

204 **León Cortés y su época.** (León Cortés and his era.)
Carlos Calvo Gamboa. San José: Editorial Universidad Estatal a Distancia, 1982. 224p. bibliog.
After providing a panoramic description of Costa Rica in the decade of the 1930s and a biographical sketch of Cortés up to 1936, Calvo Gamboa focuses on Cortés as president (1936-40) and in political opposition until his death in 1946. Calvo Gamboa considers Cortés to be a transitional figure between liberalism and reformism and rejects accusations that Cortés admired nazism. This objective study is based on research in the Costa Rican National Archives, private papers, and official documents.

205 **La campaña nacional contra los filibusteros en 1856 y 1857: breve reseña histórica.** (The national campaign against the filibusters in 1856 and 1857: a brief historical review.)
Joaquín Bernardo Calvo Mora. San José: Asociación Nacional de Educadores, 1968. 326p. (ANDE, año 10, no. 26-29).
A re-publication of six pamphlets originally published during 1954-56 by the Commission for Historical Research on the Campaign of 1856-57. The pamphlets themselves are entitled 'The National Campaign', 'Juan Santamaría', 'Proclamations and Messages', 'The Battle of Santa Rosa', 'The Battle of Rivas', and 'The Second Campaign'. They consist almost exclusively of contemporary documents, mostly from Costa Rica but also a few from other countries, on the topics mentioned.

206 **La huelga de brazos caídos.** (The sitdown strike.)
Roberto Fernández Durán. San José: Editorial Costa Rica, 1983. 130p. (Ensayo Testimonio, no. 3).
This is the first in a series of testimonials of the Costa Rican revolution of 1948. It describes the strike of 1947 against the electoral policy of the Teodoro Picado administration. It was first published as a pamphlet in 1953 by the Editorial Liberación Nacional (San José).

207 **Morazán en Costa Rica.** (Morazán in Costa Rica.)
Ricardo Fernández Guardia. San José: Editorial Lehmann, 1943.
188p.

The distinguished historian and archivist Fernández Guardia gathers in this volume
many of his articles and essays dealing with Francisco Morazán's brief visit to Costa
Rica in 1834-35 and his final visit, ending in his death, in 1842. Although the focus is
indeed on Morazán, the book illuminates the political factions and regional rivalries of
Costa Rica at the time.

208 **Carrillo y Costa Rica ante la federación.** (Carrillo and Costa Rica
before the federation.)
Cleto González Víquez. *Revista de los Archivos Nacionales de Costa
Rica*, vol. 1, no. 1, 2 (Nov.-Dec. 1936), p. 492-521.

In this article, originally written in 1919, González Víquez defends the commitment to
Central American unionism of Braulio Carrillo and the people of Costa Rica. The
article is a response to an article by Nicaraguan historian José Dolores Gámez in which
Gámez states that Carrillo was a nationalist.

209 **Black into white in nineteenth century Spanish America: Afro-American
assimilation in Argentina and Costa Rica.**
Lowell Gudmundson. *Slavery and Abolition: A Journal of
Comparative Studies*, vol. 5, no. 1 (May 1984), p. 34-49.

According to the author, Afro-Costa Ricans and Afro-Argentines tended to disappear
as a part of a whitening process during the 19th century. This occurred despite vastly
different demographic circumstances – massive immigration combined with urbanization in Argentina and little immigration combined with ruralization in Costa Rica.

210 **Costa Rica before coffee: occupational distribution, wealth, inequality,
and elite society in the village economy of the 1840's.**
Lowell Gudmundson. *Journal of Latin American Studies*, vol. 15,
no. 2 (Nov. 1983), p. 427-52.

After a careful survey of census records of the 1840s and recent secondary accounts of
the economic history of the early 19th century, Gudmundson concludes that wealth
was more concentrated in the pre-coffee period than most scholars have believed. His
data show that San José was clearly wealthier than other Central Valley cities.
Additional details on the financial activities of specific wealthy families further dispel
the traditional vision of an egalitarian society before the expansion of coffee cultivation
in the mid-19th century.

211 **Peasant movements and the transition to agrarian capitalism:
freeholding versus hacienda peasantries and agrarian reform in
Guanacaste, Costa Rica, 1880-1935.**
Lowell Gudmundson. *Peasant Studies*, vol. 10, no. 3 (Spring 1983),
p. 146-62. map.

Gudmundson points out that even in one region of a small country like Costa Rica the
peasantry is not necessarily monolithic. He contrasts the subsistence-plus peasants who
settled the Guanacaste highlands in the 20th century from the more traditional

hacienda peasants of the Guanacaste lowlands. He then contrasts their varying responses to agrarian reform and agrarian capitalism, basing his conclusions on documentation of legal and political disputes over land policy.

212 **Urbanization and modernization in Costa Rica during the 1880s.**
Eduardo Hernández Alarcón. In: *Revolution in the Americas: proceedings of the Pacific Coast Council on Latin American Studies*, edited by Lewis A. Tambs. San Diego, California: San Diego State University, 1979, p. 139-51.

Hernández Alarcón relates the growth of the coffee industry of previous decades to the drive for modernization in the 1880s. As examples of modernization he stresses urbanization, the development of urban conveniences such as tramways, foreign influence, and the popularity of positivist ideology.

213 **Modernization and dependency in Costa Rica during the decade of the 1880's.**
Edward Dennis Hernández (Eduardo Hernández Alarcón). PhD dissertation, University of California, Los Angeles, 1975. 361p. bibliog. (Available from University Microfilms, Ann Arbor, Michigan, order no. 75-19,685).

Framed by opening and concluding remarks about modernization and dependency theories this dissertation contains factual information about most aspects of Costa Rican life in the 1880s. Foreign trade, foreign investment, demography, and immigration are some of the subjects treated. It is especially good in its analysis of liberal and positivist thinking, which the author believes was crucial in the modernization process.

214 **Documentos fundamentales del siglo XIX.** (Fundamental documents of the 19th century.)
Edited by Carlos Meléndez Chaverri. San José: Editorial Costa Rica, 1978. 507p. (Biblioteca Patria, no. 16).

In this monumental collection of 19th-century documents, Meléndez concentrates on borders, international relations, education, the economy, the campaign against William Walker, and pre-1850 internal politics. Basic documents on liberalism, suffrage, population, and the constitution are omitted here because other volumes in the Biblioteca Patria series deal with them. The result is a basic source for an understanding of the formation of the state of Costa Rica. Consulted along with others in the series the collection provides a comprehensive view of Costa Rica in the 19th century.

215 **Mensajes presidenciales.** (Presidential messages.)
Carlos Meléndez Chaverri. San José: Academia de Geografía e Historia de Costa Rica, 1981. 3 vols.

Historians of Costa Rica, particularly political historians, were handicapped for a long time by the absence of a collection of published presidential messages. This book fills the gap. A surprising number of the messages deal with foreign relations, particularly with the other republics of Central America. Professor Meléndez offers an introduction on changing executive power.

216 **La alborada del capitalismo agrario en Costa Rica.** (The dawn of capitalist agriculture in Costa Rica.)
Iván Molina Jiménez. San José: Editorial Universidad de Costa Rica, 1988. 190p. bibliog.

As exemplified in this excellent study of the 1824-50 era, Costa Rican historians in the decade of the 1980s were preoccupied with the birth of capitalism in their country. What is new about Molina's approach to this subject is his imaginative use of a source heretofore virtually unnoticed by historians: letters of power of attorney. Building on other similar studies and these letters Molina challenges two traditional interpretations of early Costa Rican history: that credit for agricultural development was virtually unavailable and that Costa Rican peasants meekly submitted to loss of their lands during the coffee expansion of the 1830s.

217 **Tinoco y los Estados Unidos: génesis y caída de un régimen.** (Tinoco and the United States: genesis and fall of a régime.)
Hugo Murillo Jiménez. San José: Editorial Universidad Estatal a Distancia, 1981. 191p. bibliog.

Originally presented in English as the author's doctoral dissertation in history at the University of California, San Diego, in 1978, this work is available from University Microfilms, Ann Arbor, Michigan (order no. 7813146). It is the most detailed study available of the Tinoco presidency and the reaction of the United States to it. A full explanation of the internal political situation leading to the 29 January 1917 coup of Federico Tinoco is offered as well as a discussion of the non-recognition policy of President Woodrow Wilson. Murillo concludes that Wilson's policy brought neither the stability nor the democracy that he desired.

218 **La campaña del tránsito, 1856-1857.** (The transit campaign, 1856-57).
Rafael Obregón Loría. San José: Universidad de Costa Rica, 1956. 383p. maps. bibliog. (Sección Historia, no. 2).

This is a detailed account of the military action of the Costa Rican army in its successful effort to drive William Walker and his filibuster army from the Nicaraguan transit road and from Costa Rican soil. An unusual but useful feature of the book is a geographical introduction providing details about places where military action took place. The focus of attention is on President Juan Rafael Mora and the Costa Rican forces, but diplomatic and Nicaraguan internal matters are also covered. A second edition, under the title *Costa Rica y la guerra del 56: la campaña del tránsito, 1856-1857*, was published by the Editorial Costa Rica (Biblioteca Patria series, no. 13, 250p.) in 1976.

219 **De nuestra historia patria: Costa Rica en la federación.** (Our country's history: Costa Rica in the federation.)
Rafael Obregón Loría. San José: Universidad de Costa Rica, 1974. 195p. bibliog. (Serie Historia y Geografía, no. 20).

This is the most nearly complete account available of the attitude of Costa Rica's leaders and the actions of its representatives while Costa Rica was a member of the federation called the United Provinces of Central America (1821-38). Costa Rica's opposition to becoming a part of the Mexican empire, and its hesitancy about handing over significant power to the central government of the federation in Guatemala, are obvious as one reads instructions from Costa Rican delegates in Guatemala and their instructions from Costa Rican leaders. The narrative holds close to the documents and offers minimal interpretation. This book was republished in 1977 by the Editorial Costa Rica (San José: Biblioteca Patria series, no. 8).

220 **De nuestra historia patria: los primeros días de independencia.** (Our country's history: the first days of independence.)
Rafael Obregón Loría. San José: Universidad de Costa Rica, 1971. 237p. (Serie Historia y Geografía, no. 10).
This is a detailed account of how the citizens of the principal cities of Central America received the news of the independence of Mexico and the declaration of independence of Guatemala of 15 September 1821. As for Costa Rica, Obregón provides a step-by-step account of the reaction of Costa Rican cities and of their representatives at various meetings held in 1821 and 1822. The principal relevant documents are appended. This book was republished in 1977 by the Editorial Costa Rica (San José: Biblioteca Patria series, no. 8).

221 **Alfredo González Flores, estadista incomprendido.** (Alfredo González Flores, a misunderstood statesman.)
Eduardo Oconitrillo García. San José: Editorial Universidad Estatal a Distancia, 1980. 359p. bibliog. (Serie Estudios Sociopolíticos, no. 6).
Given the importance of the González Flores presidency (1914-17) it is not surprising that there are many studies on the president and his times. The Oconitrillo biography, although somewhat thin on the personal side of the man, does cover adequately the principal issues of the González Flores presidency and his subsequent activities as a private citizen. The financial crisis precipitated by World War I and the closing of European ports to Costa Rica's principal export, coffee, led González Flores to propose various financial reforms, most of them involving state intervention. The strength of Oconitrillo's study, in comparison with other works on González Flores, is the excellent coverage of the interaction between the president and the legislature. The study is based on newspapers, published documents, and secondary sources.

222 **Un siglo de política costarricense: crónica de 24 campañas presidenciales.** (A century of Costa Rican politics: a chronicle of 24 presidential campaigns.)
Eduardo Oconitrillo García. San José: Editorial Universidad Estatal a Distancia (EUNED), 1982. 2nd ed. 295p. bibliog.
Although lacking in documentation and analysis this book adequately reviews all Costa Rican presidential campaigns from 1889 to 1978. It is sharply focused on the candidates and their campaigns and does not deal with the implementation of public policy. The first edition, covering twenty-three presidential campaigns, was published by EUNED in 1981.

223 **Los Tinoco, 1917-1919.** (The Tinocos, 1917-19.)
Eduardo Oconitrillo García. San José: Editorial Costa Rica, 1980.
240p. bibliog.
A popular account of the rule of President Federico Tinoco and his brother Joaquín,
Minister of War, from January 1917 until August 1919. The author contends that the
Tinoco administration was harmful to the country's economy, that it hindered the
development of republican institutions, and that it limited individual liberties.

224 **Agustín de Iturbide y Costa Rica.** (Agustín de Iturbide and Costa Rica.)
Hernán G. Peralta. San José: Editorial Costa Rica, 1968. 2nd ed.
526p. bibliog.
Following Agustín de Iturbide's achievement of independence for Mexico in 1821
Costa Ricans began an intense debate over their possible relationship with the Mexican
empire. This debate is the focus of Peralta's work, which details the discussion in each
of Costa Rica's four principal cities: San José, Cartago, Heredia, and Alajuela. The
detailed coverage is justified when one considers that this is the formative period of
Costa Rican nationhood.

225 **La epopeya del civismo costarricense.** (The epic of Costa Rican civic
life.)
José María Pinaud. San José: Ministerio de Cultura, Juventud y
Deportes, 1979. 162p. (Serie del Rescate, no. 5).
The presidential election of 1889 in Costa Rica is sometimes considered the first
genuinely free election in Central American history. This essay covers the campaign
and the election which the opposition party won. The victor, President José Joaquín
Rodríguez, took office as scheduled. Although lacking in documentation the book does
include photographs of the leading participants. Interviews with Ricardo Jiménez
Oreamuno and Ricardo Fernández Guardia add interest to the essay. The first edition
was published in San José by Imprenta La Tribuna in 1942.

226 **Revista de Costa Rica en el siglo XIX.** (Journal of Costa Rica in the 19th
century.)
San José: Tipografía Nacional, 1902. 404p. bibliog.
Contains a number of the writings of important observers of the 19th-century Costa
Rican scene. Among them are Bishop B. A. Thiel's monograph on the population of
Costa Rica; Máximo Soto-Hall's comments on the National War; R. J. Valenciano's
review of the Church hierarchy, 1851-1900; and Paul Biolley's excellent, comprehen-
sive bibliography of foreign works about Costa Rica in the 19th century.

227 **De Calderón a Figueres.** (From Calderón to Figueres.)
Eugenio Rodríguez Vega. San José: Editorial Universidad Estatal a
Distancia, 1981. 2nd ed. 269p. bibliog.
The appeal of this book is the fresh, wide-eyed view of a teenage participant in the
significant political and military events of the 1940s. Rodríguez states that as a young
man he had a passion for note-taking. Some of these notes he reproduces here, along
with a general framework and commentary on the events leading up to the revolution
of 1948 and immediately afterwards. An excellent collection of photographs helps
recapture the mood of the period.

228 **Lucha social y guerra civil en Costa Rica, 1940-1948.** (The social conflict and civil war in Costa Rica, 1940-48.)
Manuel Rojas Bolaños.   San José: Editorial Porvenir, 1982. 3rd ed. 172p. bibliog. (Colección Debate).

Essentially an economic interpretation of the revolution of 1948 the present work begins with a lengthy introduction focusing on economic history, and especially on the economic crisis of 1929-38. One background chapter treats the history of the Communist Party of Costa Rica, 1931-42. In the section on the revolution itself the author, a sociologist, pays particular attention to class conflict and to the evolution of the social democratic ideology. The first edition was published by Editorial Porvenir in 1979.

229 **Costa Rica en la segunda guerra mundial, 7 de diciembre de 1941, 7 de diciembre de 1943.** (Costa Rica in World War II, 7 December 1941 to 7 December 1943.)
Edited by Juan Francisco Rojas Suárez.   San José: Imprenta Nacional, 1943. 342p.

The government of Rafael Calderón Guardia authorized this publication, which is a collection of laws, decrees, and statements concerning Costa Rica's participation in World War II. Costa Rica declared war on Japan, Germany, and Italy in December 1941. Actions taken against citizens of these countries are recorded here, including the names of over 200 individuals who were expelled from Costa Rica.

230 **The anti-imperialist career of Alejandro Alvarado Quirós.**
Richard V. Salisbury.   *Hispanic American Historical Review*, vol. 57, no. 4 (Nov. 1977), p. 587-612.

Alvarado Quirós (1876-1945) was a distinguished Costa Rican diplomat and public servant who played a leading role in Costa Rican foreign relations and in the Pan American Union movement in the 1920s and 1930s. Unlike radical critics of United States foreign policy in Central America, who were often ignored for ideological reasons, his aristocratic lineage, even demeanour, and his overall conservatism gained him a hemispheric audience for his anti-imperialist views.

231 **Los productores directos en el siglo del café.** (Direct producers in the century of coffee.)
Mario Samper Kutschbach.   *Revista de Historia*, vol. 4, no. 7 (July-Dec. 1978), p. 123-217. bibliog.

This article, taken from the author's PhD dissertation at the University of California, Berkeley, attempts to account for numbers and percentages of labourers, artisans, and *campesinos* [rural population] in the Costa Rican workforce at different periods of time up to 1935. It is a detailed study of proletarianization and class conflict which is based solidly on census records and archival sources and which takes previous studies fully into account. Samper relates his data to the expansion of foreign commerce and industrialization, to the changing ideologies and class structures of the times, and to labour–capital conflicts.

232 **La fase oculta de la guerra civil en Costa Rica.** (The covert aspects of the civil war in Costa Rica.)
Jacobo Schifter. San José: Editorial Universitaria Centroamericana, 1981. 2nd ed. 158p. bibliog. (Colección Seis).

Schifter's point of view is that the true populist movement in Costa Rica was that of the Calderón Guardia and Picado administrations in 1940-48, as compared to the so-called revolution of 1948 led by José Figueres. The latter, Schifter argues, lacked mass support and was reformist. Ultimately, the Figueres movement tended to become authoritarian and confrontational. Its purpose was to diversify the economy and modernize the country from the top down. Numerous statistical charts on elections and commerce since 1948 support his interpretation.

233 **Costa Rican trade and navigation ties with United States, Germany and Europe: 1840 to 1885.**
Thomas Schoonover. *Jahrbuch für Geschichte von Staat, Wirtschaft und Gesellschaft Lateinamerikas*, vol. 14 (1977), p. 269-309.

Schoonover challenges the prevalent view that Great Britain dominated Costa Rican trade in the 19th century. He argues instead that the British exercised 'competitive leadership' with other countries, particularly Germany and the United States, and documents the rise in United States interest in Central American trade, investment, and transit routes, and the gradual British withdrawal after 1850. Detailed tables on Costa Rican exports, imports, and shipping are presented. Of special interest, since less has been written on this topic, is the author's description of the strong German, especially Prussian, involvement in mid-19th-century Central America and Costa Rica. This was reflected in German colonization efforts as well as in commercial and maritime activities. The author also points out how the rise of coffee and banana export sectors led to dependence on foreign markets and capital, and eventually to the importation of foodstuffs.

1948-

234 **El 48.** (The 48.)
Miguel Acuña V. San José: Lehmann, 1975. 386p. maps.

Without an index or bibliography and with few footnotes this book is difficult to judge and to use for the reconstruction of political and military events centring on the revolution of 1948. Nevertheless, the author, who conducted some fifty interviews of participants in the revolution, conveys a sense of immediacy and familiarity with the events of that time. The section on the military conflict during 1948 appears to be the most authoritative.

235 **Historia económica de Costa Rica, 1950-1970.** (The economic history of Costa Rica, 1950-70.)
Carlos Araya Pochet. San José: Editorial Fernández-Arce, 1975. 2nd ed. 159p. bibliog.
Professor Araya, a historian educated in Costa Rica and Spain, describes the economic growth of Costa Rica in the two decades between 1950 and 1970. Per capita income, one of the standard measures of economic growth, increased from $195 to $570, one of the highest increases in the world for that period. Nevertheless, as Araya points out, this economic growth did not signify that Costa Rica was in a process of social and economic development. He concludes that, despite relative advances in political development and in education, Costa Rica was still in the standard Latin American pattern of dependency on agricultural exports at the end of two decades of remarkable economic growth. He also concludes that the Central American Common Market had few favourable effects on the Costa Rican economy.

236 **Costa Rica and the 1948 revolution: rethinking the social democratic paradigm.**
Lowell Gudmundson. *Latin American Research Review*, vol. 19, no. 1 (1984), p. 235-42.
In this review essay Gudmundson reports on books and articles by Costa Rican writers Oscar Aguilar, Daniel Camacho, Rodolfo Cerdas, Jacobo Schifter, Jorge Enrique Romero, Jorge Mario Salazar, and Manuel Rojas, who challenge the conventional interpretation of the revolution of 1948 as the creating force for social democracy in Costa Rica. Gudmundson holds that their criticism of the idea that the revolution was led by electoral purists and populists is sound; he argues that they are more accurately labelled neoliberals and transformists. In short, the revolution was not as radical, according to these revisionists, as was previously thought.

237 **Costa Rica contemporánea.** (Contemporary Costa Rica.)
Edited by Chester Zelaya. San José: Editorial Costa Rica, 1982- . 2nd ed. 2 vols. maps. bibliog.
The information explosion of recent years made possible the publication of this remarkable collection of sixteen articles on different topics by the country's leading experts. The topics are geography (Carlos Meléndez); political parties (Jacobo Schifter); elections (Wilburg Jiménez Castro); foreign policy (Gonzalo Facio); social and economic development (Oscar Arias); agrarian policy (José Manuel Salazar Navarrete); industry (Claudio Soto Badillo); commerce (Alvaro Arguedas); Central American economic integration (Eduardo Lizano); population (Marcos Bogan Miller); health (Bogan Miller and Jessie Orlich Montejo); employment (Esteban Lederman, Ponciano Torales, and Juan Diego Trejos); education (Carlos Monge Alfaro); letters (Virginia Sandoval de Fonseca); art (Ricardo Ulloa); and music (Bernal Flores).

The Costa Rica reader.
See item no. 9.

Costa Rica: a geographical interpretation in historical perspective.
See item no. 22.

Temblores, terremotos, inundaciones y erupciones volcánicas en Costa Rica

1608-1910. (Tremors, earthquakes, floods and volcanic eruptions in Costa Rica 1608-1910.)
See item no. 44.

Costa Rica en el siglo XIX. (Costa Rica in the 19th century.)
See item no. 64.

Talamanca, el espacio y los hombres. (Talamanca, space and man.)
See item no. 65.

Genealogías de Cartago hasta 1850. (Genealogies of Cartago from 1850.)
See item no. 248.

Monografía de la población de la Republica de Costa Rica en el siglo XIX. (A monograph of the population of the Republic of Costa Rica in the 19th century.)
See item no. 252.

Jamaican blacks and their descendants in Costa Rica.
See item no. 265.

Etnografía histórica de Costa Rica (1561-1615). (An historical ethnography of Costa Rica, 1561-1615.)
See item no. 277.

Historia eclesiástica de Costa Rica: del descubrimiento a la erección de la diócesis, 1502-1850. (The ecclesiastical history of Costa Rica: from the discovery to the establishment of the diocese, 1502-1850.)
See item no. 290.

1884, el estado, la iglesia y las reformas liberales. (1884, the state, the Church and the liberal reforms.)
See item no. 291.

A history of protestantism in Costa Rica.
See item no. 294.

Reseña histórica de la iglesia en Costa Rica desde 1502 hasta 1850. (Historical overview of the Church in Costa Rica from 1502 until 1850.)
See item no. 297.

La iglesia costarricense y la cuestión social. (The Costa Rican Church and the social question.)
See item no. 298.

Peasants of Costa Rica and the development of agrarian capitalism.
See item no. 312.

Aspects of power distribution in Costa Rica.
See item no. 320.

La dinastía de los conquistadores: la crisis del poder en la Costa Rica contemporánea. (The dynasty of the conquerors: the crisis of power in contemporary Costa Rica.)
See item no. 321.

Social reform in Costa Rica: social security and the presidency of Rafael Angel Calderón.
See item no. 348.

Democracy in Costa Rica.
See item no. 354.

Costa Rica: a meaningful democracy.
See item no. 362.

The presidents of Costa Rica.
See item no. 365.

La elección de un presidente: Costa Rica, 1978-1982. (The election of a President: Costa Rica, 1978-82.)
See item no. 368.

Análisis electoral de una democracia: estudio del comportamiento político costarricense durante el período 1953-1974. (The electoral analysis of a democracy: a study of Costa Rican political behaviour during 1953-74.)
See item no. 376.

The Costa Rican election of 1953: a case study.
See item no. 377.

Costa Rican electoral trends, 1953-1966.
See item no. 378.

Costa Rica.
See item no. 397.

Democracia y partidos políticos en Costa Rica, 1950-1962. (Democracy and political parties in Costa Rica, 1950-62.)
See item no. 404.

Liberación Nacional en la historia política de Costa Rica, 1940-1980. (National Liberation in the political history of Costa Rica, 1940-80.)
See item no. 405.

Crisis de 1929 y la fundación del Partido Comunista en Costa Rica. (The crisis of 1929 and the founding of the Communist Party in Costa Rica.)
See item no. 406.

Análisis de la trayectoria electoral de Costa Rica: 1953-1970. (Analysis of the electoral trajectory of Costa Rica: 1953-70.)
See item no. 407.

Liberación Nacional in Costa Rica: the development of a political party in a transitional society.
See item no. 408.

Las ideas políticas en Costa Rica. (Political ideas in Costa Rica.)
See item no. 415.

The social democratic ideology in Latin America: the case of Costa Rica's Partido Liberación Nacional.
See item no. 416.

Ricardo Jiménez Oreamuno, "su pensamiento." (Ricardo Jiménez Oreamuno, 'his thinking'.)
See item no. 417.

Siete ensayos políticos: fuentes de la democracia social en Costa Rica. (Seven political essays: sources of social democracy in Costa Rica.)
See item no. 418.

The disturbing influence in Central America of the Nicaraguan Canal Treaty with the United States of America and its conflict with the treaty rights of Costa Rica.
See item no. 421.

Costa Rica, relaciones exteriores de una república en formación 1847-1849. (Costa Rica, foreign relations of a republic in formation 1847-49.)
See item no. 427.

Costa Rican relations with Central America, 1900-1934.
See item no. 428.

Los contratos Webster–Mora y las implicaciones sobre Costa Rica y Nicaragua. (The Webster–Mora contracts and their implications for Costa Rica and Nicaragua.)
See item no. 430.

Arms and politics in Costa Rica and Nicaragua, 1948-1981.
See item no. 432.

Costa Rica and the 1920-1921 Union Movement: a reassessment.
See item no. 438.

The deterioration of relations between Costa Rica and the Sandinistas.
See item no. 441.

The United States and Central America, 1944-1949.
See item no. 444.

Domestic politics and foreign policy: Costa Rica's stand on recognition, 1923-1934.
See item no. 446.

Las alianzas conflictivas: las relaciones de Estados Unidos y Costa Rica desde la Segunda Guerra Mundial a la guerra fría. (Conflicting alliances: the relations of the United States and Costa Rica from the Second World War to the Cold War.)
See item no. 448.

De nuestra historia patria: hechos militares y políticos. (Our country's history: military and political events.)
See item no. 450.

La Constitución de 1949: antecedentes y proyecciones. (The constitution of 1949: antecedents and projections.)
See item no. 452.

Las constituciones de Costa Rica. (The constitutions of Costa Rica.)
See item no. 455.

Génesis del gobierno de Costa Rica: a través de 160 años de vida independiente. (The genesis of government in Costa Rica in 160 years of independent life.)
See item no. 461.

The economic cycle in Latin American agricultural export economies, 1880-1930: a hypothesis for investigation.
See item no. 479.

Costa Rica hoy: la crisis y sus perspectivas. (Costa Rica today: the crisis and its perspectives.)
See item no. 482.

Historia económica y hacendaria de Costa Rica. (An economic and financial history of Costa Rica.)
See item no. 484.

British investments in Costa Rica.
See item no. 498.

Ciento cinco años de vida bancaria en Costa Rica. (150 years of banking in Costa Rica.)
See item no. 501.

The case of Costa Rica.
See item no. 513.

The formation of the coffee estate in nineteenth-century Costa Rica.
See item no. 520.

Agrarian policies in dependent societies: Costa Rica.
See item no. 553.

El ferrocarril al Atlántico en Costa Rica: 1871-1874. (The railway to the Atlantic in Costa Rica: 1871-74.)
See item no. 570.

Historia de la aviación en Costa Rica. (The history of aviation in Costa Rica.)
See item no. 572.

Costa Rica Railway Company Ltd. and Northern Railway Company.
See item no. 573.

La Iglesia y el sindicalismo en Costa Rica. (The Church and syndicalism in Costa Rica.)
See item no. 578.

Formación de la fuerza laboral costarricense: una contribución a la historia económica social y administrativa de Costa Rica. (Formation of the Costa Rican labour force: a contribution to the economic, social and administrative history of Costa Rica.)
See item no. 582.

El movimiento obrero en Costa Rica, 1830-1902. (The workers' movement in Costa Rica, 1830-1902.)
See item no. 584.

Artesanos y obreros costarricenses, 1880-1914. (Costa Rican workers and artisans, 1880-1914.)
See item no. 592.

Consenso y represión: una interpretación socio-política de educación costarricense. (Consensus and repression: a sociopolitical interpretation of Costa Rican education.)
See item no. 611.

La ingeniería en Costa Rica, 1502-1903: ensayo histórico. (Engineering in Costa Rica, 1502-1903: an historical essay.)
See item no. 621.

Baratijas de antaño. (Musings from the past.)
See item no. 625.

Historia y antología de la literatura costarricense. (History and anthology of Costa Rican literature.)
See item no. 631.

Historical sources in Costa Rica.
See item no. 686.

National Museum of Costa Rica: one hundred years of history.
See item no. 687.

Historians and history writing in Costa Rica.
See item no. 691.

José Santos Lombardo.
See item no. 696.

Los presidentes. (The presidents.)
See item no. 707.

Rafael Yglesias Castro.
See item no. 708.

Laude, evocación de Mora: el hombre, el estadista, el héroe, el mártir. (Praise, evocation of Mora: the man, the statesman, the hero, the martyr.)
See item no. 709.

Alfredo González Flores.
See item no. 715.

Juan Manuel de Cañas.
See item no. 717.

Juan Mora Fernández.
See item no. 720.

Dr. José María Montealegre: contribución al estudio de un hombre y una época poco conocida de nuestra historia. (Dr José María Montealegre: a contribution to the study of a man and an era little known in our history.)
See item no. 726.

Juan Vázquez de Coronado: conquistador y fundador de Costa Rica. (Juan Vázquez de Coronado: conqueror and founder of Costa Rica.)
See item no. 727.

Otilio Ulate and the traditional response to contemporary political change in Costa Rica.
See item no. 728.

Rogelio Fernández Güell: escritor, poeta y caballero andante. (Rogelio Fernández Güell: writer, poet and knight-errant.)
See item no. 729.

Calderón Guardia.
See item no. 731.

Máximo Fernández.
See item no. 732.

Keith and Costa Rica: a biographical study of Minor Cooper Keith.
See item no. 734.

Juan Vázquez de Coronado y su ética en la conquista de Costa Rica. (Juan Vázquez de Coronado and his ethics in the conquest of Costa Rica.)
See item no. 735.

Jorge Volio y el Partido Reformista. (Jorge Volio and the Reform Party.)
See item no. 736.

Apuntes de don Rafael Yglesias Castro sobre su vida privada y actuaciones públicas. (Notes of Rafael Yglesias Castro on his public activities and private life.)
See item no. 737.

Rafael Francisco Osejo.
See item no. 738.

Historical dictionary of Costa Rica.
See item no. 739.

Population

General

238 **Población, fecundidad y desarrollo en Costa Rica, 1950-1970.**
(Population, fecundity and development in Costa Rica, 1950-70.)
Olda María Acuña B., Carlos F. Denton L.   Heredia, Costa Rica:
Instituto de Estudios Sociales en Población, Universidad Nacional,
1984. 150p. bibliog. (Informe de Trabajo, no. 39).

Costa Rica's rate of natural population increase, which was high up to 1950, even
higher in the period 1950-60 (approximately four per cent per year), and dropping to a
relatively stable two-and-a-half per cent since 1975, is the subject of this study. Aided
by forty-nine statistical tables the authors undertake to explain the relationship of
Costa Rica's natural population increase with the strategy of economic development in
place at the time and the National Family Planning Programme, which was established
in 1965.

239 **The Costa Rican family planning program.**
Manuel J. Carvajal, David T. Geithman, Lydia B. Neuhauser.   In:
*The organization of family planning programs: India, China, Costa
Rica, Venezuela, Lebanon*, edited by Rushikesh M. Maru (et al.).
Washington, DC: Smithsonian Institution, Interdisciplinary
Communications Program, 1976, p. 225-34. bibliog. (Occasional
Monographs Series, no. 8).

The authors describe both private and public institutional efforts on behalf of family
planning, with the purpose of explaining the sharp decline in fertility in Costa Rica in
the 1963-73 period. There were 1,139.7 children under five years of age per 1,000
women of reproductive age in 1963, but only 818.4 in 1973. Judging from the
percentage of women participating in one or more family planning programmes the
authors conclude that these programmes have been effective.

240 **An economic analysis of migration in Costa Rica.**
Manuel J. Carvajal, David T. Geithman. *Economic Development and Cultural Change*, vol. 23, no. 1 (Oct. 1974), p. 105-22.
Simply put, the purpose of the authors is to prove that when Costa Ricans migrate from one place to another within Costa Rica they do it for economic reasons, that is, to improve their standard of living. Utilizing data from the 1963 census the authors show that settled migrants (in their new residence for three years or more) earn substantially higher incomes than recent migrants and non-migrants. Other variables such as gender, age, and education are considered in the analysis. The authors suggest possible public policy changes based on their conclusions.

241 **La población de Costa Rica.** (The population of Costa Rica.)
Mario E. Fernández Arias, Anabelle Schmidt de Rojas, Víctor Basauri. San José: Universidad de Costa Rica, Instituto de Investigaciones Sociales, 1976. 199p. maps. bibliog.
Extracting data from censuses as late as 1973, the authors present an array of characteristics of the Costa Rican population. The narrative is supplemented by 114 easy-to-read charts and graphs and eleven maps. The focus is on the 20th century, although data on earlier periods is included. Supplementary chapters discuss the relation of rapid population growth to economic development, and project Costa Rican population to the year 2000. This study was published again in 1977 as part of the volume entitled *Población de Costa Rica y orígenes de los costarricenses* (San José: Editorial Costa Rica, Biblioteca Patria series, no. 5).

242 **Population and urban trends in Central America and Panama.**
Robert W. Fox, Jerrold W. Huguet. Washington, DC: Inter-American Development Bank, 1977. 224p. bibliog.
Chapter Two (p. 58-83) of this important work is entirely on Costa Rica. Fox, a sociologist, and Huguet, a demographer, answer most questions about Costa Rican population trends in these pages. Although the last census available to be used by the authors was the 1973 census, the comprehensiveness of the data makes the work still useful. Crude birth rates, death rates, age-specific fertility rates, urban–rural ratios and much more are shown in tabular form and analysed in the narrative. Twenty tables are included. Projections of population to the year 2000 are shown by sex, province, and urbanized areas. The availability of comparable data on the other Central American countries in the other chapters adds to the usefulness of the work to students of Costa Rica.

243 **Demography and development: the lessons of Costa Rica.**
Charles F. Gallagher. *American Universities Field Staff Reports, South America*, no. 16 (1980), 14p.
More on demography than development, this essay attempts to answer some of the questions raised by the sharp drop in Costa Rica's crude birthrate (from 48.3 per 1000 in 1959 to 29.9 per 1000 in 1973), infant mortality, and death rate. The author discusses employment, educational problems, and family planning policies in relation to demography and development.

244 **Migraciones internas en Costa Rica.** (Internal migrations in Costa Rica.)
Wilburg Jiménez Castro. Washington, DC: Pan American Union, Department of Social and Economic Affairs, 1956. 163p. maps. bibliog.

The author, director of the Department of Census and Statistics in Costa Rica, attempts a reconstruction of all internal migratory movements in Costa Rica from the precolumbian era to 1950. Maps and tables make it easy for the reader to follow these movements.

245 **Origins of population, Turrialba, Costa Rica, 1948.**
Paul C. Morrison, Carroll Schwartz. *Journal of Geography*, vol. 62, no. 8 (Nov. 1963), p. 352-61.

Morrison and Schwartz provide data on the population growth of the town of Turrialba from less than a thousand in 1864 to over 6,000 in 1964. Characteristics of the population such as age and origin are also provided. Turrialba expanded in the banana boom years of 1912-18 and the coffee boom years of 1928-32.

246 **The distribution of population in Costa Rica.**
Robert Edward Nunley. Washington, DC: National Academy of Sciences–National Research Council, 1960. 71p. maps. bibliog.
(National Research Council (United States) Publication no. 743).

Professor Nunley uses a historical-geographical analysis to trace the growth and distribution of the population of Costa Rica from the colonial period until 1950. A series of maps (early colonial, 1824, 1844, 1864, 1892, 1927, and 1950) demonstrates the progressive formation of towns, transport developments, and the expansion of commercial agriculture. Appendix A gives a useful list of population statistics of Costa Rica by cities and provinces from 1569 to 1950.

247 **Dinámica demográfica, planificación familiar y política de población en Costa Rica.** (Demographic dynamics, family planning and population policy in Costa Rica.)
Luis Rosero Bixby. *Demografía y Economía*, vol. 15, no. 1 [no. 45] (1981), p. 59-84. bibliog.

This is an excellent introduction to Costa Rican population issues. The article summarizes recent changes in birth, death, and fertility rates, emphasizing the very rapid drop in fertility rates that occurred between 1960 and 1976, and it describes Costa Rica's National Plan for Family Planning and Sex Education, inaugurated in 1968. According to the author the Costa Rican government should adopt a permanent population policy as a necessary element in its development plans.

248 **Genealogías de Cartago hasta 1850.** (Genealogies of Cartago from 1850.)
Víctor Sanabria Martínez. San José: Servicios Secretariales, 1957. 6 vols.

These six volumes contain genealogies of hundreds of families from Cartago before 1850. Because of the importance of Cartago as capital and 'cradle of the Costa Rican population', according to the author, this compilation is especially valuable for Costa

Rican genealogy as a whole. The information comes from birth, baptismal, death, and other Church records. Archbishop Sanabria finished this work in 1949 and the massive project was carried to its conclusion by the Costa Rican Academy of History. He discusses some general racial and migration data in the preface.

249 **Population perception and policy in Costa Rica.**
Thomas G. Sanders. *American University Field Staff Reports, Mexico and Caribbean Area* Series, vol. 8, no. 1 (Jan. 1973), p. 1-16.
Sanders discusses the phenomenal growth of Costa Rica's population in the 1950s and the early 1960s and the recognition of this growth as a problem on the part of the people and government of Costa Rica. Several possible explanations for the decline in fecundity after 1963 are offered.

250 **Estimaciones demográficas de la región central de Costa Rica, 1950-1973.** (Demographic estimates of the central region of Costa Rica, 1950-73.)
Annabelle Schmidt de Rojas. San José: Universidad de Costa Rica, Facultad de Ciencias Sociales, Instituto de Investigaciones Sociales, 1977. 154p. (Avances de Investigación, no. 26).
A statistical study of fertility, mortality, and migration in the central region of Costa Rica (where approximately 60 per cent of the population lives) based on the censuses of 1950, 1963, and 1973. The analysis deals with important differences in fertility and mortality in the different years and presents data on the characteristics of migrants.

251 **The decline of fertility in Costa Rica: literacy, modernization and family planning.**
J. Mayone Stycos. *Population Studies*, vol. 36, no. 3 (March 1982), p. 15-30.
As indicated in the title, Professor Stycos links Costa Rica's sharp fertility decline in the 1960s and 1970s to literacy, modernization, and the introduction of the National Family Planning Programme in 1968. Stycos, a sociologist, bases his analysis on excellent demographic data from the censuses of 1950, 1963, and 1973.

252 **Monografía de la población de la República de Costa Rica en el siglo XIX.** (A monograph of the population of the Republic of Costa Rica in the 19th century.)
Bernardo Augusto Thiel. San José: Ministerio de Economía y Hacienda, Dirección General de Estadística y Censos, 1951. 43p.
First published in 1902, Thiel's work is now considered a classic study that carefully analyses colonial documents, local Church records, and the censuses of 1864, 1883, and 1892 to arrive at the size and ethnic make-up of the Costa Rican population during all historical periods.

253 **The population of Costa Rica and its natural resources.**
William Vogt. Washington, DC: Pan American Union, 1946. 2:).

The author maintains that the people of Costa Rica are putting their future at grave risk by destroying the country's natural resources. There are sections on the land, the flora and fauna, and water. The work is also available in Spanish, published by the same publisher.

254 **A survey of attitudes related to Costa Rican population dynamics.**
F. B. Waisanen (et al.). San José: Programa Interamericano de Información Popular of the American International Association for Economic and Social Development, 1966. 189p. bibliog.

Contracted by the United States Agency for International Development the authors conducted surveys to provide information on social, cultural, and other factors affecting people's attitudes toward family planning in Costa Rica. Such information could then be used by the media to promote family planning.

Minorities

255 **América Indígena.** (Indigenous America.)
Mexico City: Interamerican Indigenist Institute. vol. 34 (April-June 1974), p. 291-486.

This issue of the periodical *América Indígena* is dedicated almost entirely to the Indians of Costa Rica. A total of fifteen articles, all in Spanish, by archaeologists, historians, anthropologists, and linguists treat various aspects of Indian life in Costa Rica. An article on the condition of contemporary Costa Rican Indians by Gonzalo Rubio Orbe, director of the Interamerican Indigenous Institute, and Carlos Aguilar's general article on Indian settlements provide an appropriate introduction to the special issue, as half the remaining articles are ethnographic and deal with specific tribes or settlements. The final article reviews the status of legislation concerning Indians in Costa Rica. When one considers that the Indian population in 1974 was only approximately 8,000 the publication is a remarkable one.

256 **Localidades indígenas costarricenses.** (Indigenous Costa Rican localities.)
María Eugenia Bózzoli de Wille. San José: Editorial Universitaria Centroamericana, 1975. 2nd ed. 231p. bibliog. (Colección Aula).

The object of this book is to identify the places where Indians live and to provide sufficient baseline data about their living conditions to serve future investigators interested in social change among the Indians. Approximately 8,000 Indians lived in Costa Rica in 1968.

257 **El nacimiento y la muerte entre los bribris.** (Birth and death among the Bribris.)
María Eugenia Bózzoli de Wille. San José: Editorial Universidad de Costa Rica, 1979. 264p. bibliog.

An outstanding study done as a PhD dissertation in anthropology at the University of Georgia in 1975 (available from University Microfilms, Ann Arbor, Michigan, order no. 76-6378). The author's work with the Bribri, however, dates from 1965, when she began to collect information about them. Extensive work with informants, plus a thorough analysis of the observations of others, results in a complete picture of the Bribris' beliefs about birth and death. It is the most thorough study on the subject yet published.

258 **Symbolic aspects of Bribri roles on the occasions of birth and death.**
María Eugenia Bózzoli de Wille. In: *Sex roles and social change in native lower Central American societies*, edited by Christine A. Loveland, Franklin O. Loveland. Urbana, Illinois: University of Illinois Press, 1982, p. 142-65. bibliog.

An ethnographic study of the Bribri Indians of the Talamanca region. It focuses on pregnant women and on those responsible for burials, two groups who complement each other as they oversee the transition stages from non-being to being, and from being to spirit-being. Sex roles are clearly revealed in Bribri mythology and symbolism.

259 **Social relations and cultural persistence (or change) among Jamaicans in a rural area of Costa Rica.**
Roy S. Bryce-Laporte. PhD dissertation, University of Puerto Rico, 1962. 247p. maps. bibliog.

Bryce-Laporte focuses on a town he calls 'New Sligoville', reportedly the most Jamaican community in the Province of Limón, and undertakes a descriptive study of the social relations and cultural persistence among Jamaicans and their offspring in this town. The author divides the town into three generations in order to study changing values with regard to the Church, diet, relationship to the land, language, etc. Bryce-Laporte returned to the town ten years later and his observations of the subsequent visit are published in Carlos Meléndez and Quince Duncan, *El negro en Costa Rica* (San José: Editorial Costa Rica, 1972).

260 **El negro en Costa Rica: antología.** (The negro in Costa Rica: anthology.)
Quince Duncan, Carlos Meléndez Chaverri. San José: Editorial Costa Rica, 1981. 8th ed. 258p. bibliog.

In this book, a Costa Rican historian (Meléndez) and a black Costa Rican novelist (Duncan) combine to present an anthology of their own writings and those of others on blacks in Costa Rica. Meléndez covers such topics as blacks in the colonial period, the Jamaican immigration, and Marcus Garvey in Costa Rica; Duncan writes on black culture in the Limón area, Limonese speech, and contemporary racial relations. Also included are an Afro-Costa Rican bibliography and biographical sketches of prominent blacks. The first edition was published by the Editorial Costa Rica in 1972.

261 **Los aborígenes de Costa Rica.** (The aborigines of Costa Rica.)
Carlos Gagini. San José: Imprenta Trejos Hermanos, 1917. 206p.
bibliog.

A general survey of the Indian tribes of Costa Rica, based primarily on a reading of
chronicles and other secondary accounts. Heavy emphasis falls on a criticism of these
sources and on Indian dialects and vocabulary. An appendix of indigenous names is a
major part of the work (p. 85-206).

262 **Costa Rican Jewry: an economic and political outline.**
Lowell Gudmundson. In: *The Jewish presence in Latin America*,
edited by Judith Laikin Elkin, Gilbert W. Merkx. Boston: Allen and
Unwin, 1987, p. 219-31.

A succinct history of the small Polish Jewish colony of Costa Rica. Most Jewish
immigrants arrived in Costa Rica in the 1930s and most of the male immigrants became
pedlars of cloth and clothing for the Mil Colores store. By 1978, although they
constituted less than one per cent of the total population, descendants of the
immigrants had become over-represented in the professions, especially medicine, and
many had become successful merchants and industrialists. The story of their economic
success, the occasional outburst of anti-Semitism during political campaigns, and the
evolution of quite favourable economic and diplomatic relations between Israel and
Costa Rica is well told in this article.

263 **Estudio de comunidades indígenas: zonas Boruca-Térraba y China
Kichá.** (A study of indigenous communities: the Boruca-Térraba and
China Kichá.)
San José: Instituto de Tierras y Colonización, 1964. 203p. maps.

An ethnographic reconnaissance of two Indian communities, the present work provides
details on economic matters, household composition, the Indian world-view, and the
local political system.

264 **An ethnic geography of Costa Rica's Atlantic zone.**
Charles W. Koch. In: *Graduate Studies in Latin America at the
University of Kansas*, edited by Charles L. Stansifer. Lawrence,
Kansas: Center of Latin American Studies, University of Kansas, 1980,
vol. 4, p. 7-18.

A handy summary of Koch's dissertation (University of Kansas, 1975) on the Jamaican
blacks who worked for the Northern Railway Company. Using the railway company's
records as evidence of class differentiation, Koch sheds new light on their adjustment
to Costa Rica. He attributes the life and work patterns of these blacks to their social
and economic situation and not to race or culture.

265 **Jamaican blacks and their descendants in Costa Rica.**
Charles W. Koch. *Social and Economic Studies*, vol. 26, no. 3
(Sept. 1977), p. 339-61. bibliog.

This is a social history of blacks in the Caribbean coastal Atlantic zone of Costa Rica
beginning with their introduction from Jamaica as banana and railroad workers in the
1870s. The author discusses immigration patterns, national policies which have affected

the workers of the region, and the influence of racism on these policies and on the general relations between races in the region and country. The work has a solid documentary base.

266 **Cultural change, social conflict, and changing distributions of authority in the Caribbean lowlands of Costa Rica.**
Everett E. Logue. Winston-Salem, North Carolina: Overseas Research Center, Wake Forest University, 1977. 119p. bibliog. (Developing Nations Monograph Series One, no. 7).

Although highly theoretical, this study provides descriptive data unavailable elsewhere about the Bribri Indians of Talamanca and their changing cultural patterns as a result of state intervention, missionary activity, and banana-industry operations. The focus of the study is on the cultural change occurring among the Bribri as they became peasants or as they became subject to the demands and pressures of the society around them. Fieldwork was done in the village of Amubri in 1973 and 1974.

267 **Legislación indigenista de Costa Rica.** (Indian legislation of Costa Rica.) Edited by Carlos Meléndez Chaverri. Mexico City: Instituto Indigenista Interamericano, 1957. 50p. (Ediciones Especiales del Instituto Indigenista Interamericano, no. 30).

Following a short summary of the situation of the small Indian population in Costa Rica, Meléndez compiles a list of laws and decrees pertaining to the Indians. Of special interest is the last section, which includes laws passed in Costa Rica as a result of recommendations from the Instituto Indigenista Interamericano.

268 **The adaptation of West Indian Blacks to North American and Hispanic culture in Costa Rica.**
Michael D. Olien. In: *Old roots in new lands: historical and anthropological perspectives on black experiences in the Americas*, edited by Ann M. Pescatello. Westport, Connecticut: Greenwood Press, 1977, p. 132-56. bibliog. (Contributions in Afro-American and African Studies, no. 31).

The focus of this authoritative article is the adaptation of West Indian (mainly Jamaican) banana workers to life on the Caribbean coast of Costa Rica. According to Olien, two events, the abandonment of banana production in this area by the United Fruit Company in 1942 and the revolution of 1948, contributed greatly to their integration into the Costa Rican polity.

269 **Black and part-black populations in colonial Costa Rica: ethnohistorical resources and problems.**
Michael D. Olien. *Ethnohistory*, vol. 27, no. 1 (1980), p. 13-29.

Olien calls attention to the need for research on the origins and development of the black population of Costa Rica's Caribbean coast and makes specific suggestions as to where research material on this subject may be found. At the same time he provides an historical overview of the black population, reviews the secondary literature, and poses specific questions that remain unanswered.

270 **Levels of urban relationships in a complex society: a Costa Rican case.**
Michael D. Olien. In: *Urban anthropology: research perspectives and strategies*, edited by Elizabeth M. Eddy. Athens, Georgia: University of Georgia Press, 1968, p. 83-92. (Southern Anthropological Society Proceedings, no. 2).

While in Limón doing research on the black population of the surrounding area Professor Olien undertook an informal anthropological study of Limón and its unique urban situation. He describes Limón's problems as the nation's principal port, its relation to the Caribbean coastal hinterland, the interrelationships between resident blacks, whites, and Chinese, and the city's international relations. An introductory section places Limón in the context of Costa Rican urbanization.

271 **The negro in Costa Rica: the role of an ethnic minority in a developing society.**
Michael D. Olien. Winston-Salem, North Carolina: Overseas Research Center, Wake Forest University, 1970. 61p. bibliog. (Developing Nations Monograph Series One, no. 3).

Fieldwork on the Caribbean coast of Costa Rica for this study was carried out in 1963-65. The study reviews the historical record of slave migrations in the colonial period, resulting in a small black population on the Caribbean coast, and the importation of West Indian blacks in the late 19th century to work on the Northern Railway and United Fruit Company banana plantations in the same area. Characteristics of contemporary blacks are summarized.

272 **Los caminos del indigenismo.** (The roads of Indianism.)
Mayobanex Ornes. San José: Editorial Costa Rica, 1980. 221p. bibliog.

The author, a lawyer, summarizes the condition of Indians in Costa Rica from the colonial period and brings up to date legislation covering them. He also discusses Indian policy variations at different times in Costa Rica's history, and institutions affecting the Indians. He gives special attention to the National Commission of Indian Affairs and the Land and Colonization Institute. He closes with his own long list of policy recommendations.

273 **El judío en Costa Rica.** (The Jew in Costa Rica.)
Jacobo Schifter, Lowell Gudmundson, Mario Solera Castro. San José: Editorial Universidad Estatal a Distancia, 1979. 385p. bibliog. (Serie Estudios Sociopolíticos, no. 4).

Following a lengthy introduction on Polish Jewry, justified because most Jewish immigrants to Costa Rica came from Poland, two key chapters in this book focus on the immigration movement itself and on political reactions to the Jewish presence in Costa Rica. The numbers are small: most immigrants came during the decade of the 1930s and no more than eighty-five came in any one year. The typical immigrant, according to the authors, was young, poor, not orthodox, and earned his living through commerce. Documents on Jews in Costa Rica proved to be scarce, but the authors supplemented research in written materials by lengthy and repeated interviews with members of the Jewish community in San José. Personal stories collected in this manner offer insight into the assimilation process.

274 **The Boruca of Costa Rica.**
Doris Z. Stone. Cambridge, Massachusetts: Peabody Museum of
American Archaeology and Ethnology, Harvard University, 1949. 50p.
map. bibliog. (Papers of the Peabody Museum, vol. 26).
An excellent account of the few surviving Boruca Indians of the South Pacific zone of
Costa Rica. No more than 700 were counted in the 1945 census. Although the author
apologizes for the introductory nature of the volume, which was the result of four visits
to the region in 1946, it comprehensively covers the Borucas' religion, customs, dress,
and daily activities. Kraus Reprint Company of Millwood, New York published a
reprint of this work in 1975.

275 **Notes on present-day pottery making and its economy in the ancient
Chorotegan area.**
Doris Z. Stone. *Middle American Research Records*, vol. 1, no. 16
(30 Dec. 1950), p. 269-79.
An illustrated ethnographic study, this article describes the pottery process from clay-
gathering to marketing. Clay-gatherers were men and boys but all twenty-seven potters
studied were women. The study was carried out in three towns in Guanacaste, Costa
Rica.

276 **The Talamanca tribes of Costa Rica.**
Doris Z. Stone. Cambridge, Massachusetts: Peabody Museum of
Archaeology and Ethnology, Harvard University, 1962. 108p. bibliog.
(Papers of the Peabody Museum, vol. 43:2).
Stone's purpose in this work is 'to give a picture of the manner of living and the way of
thinking of the Talamancan in 1956-59'. The focus is on about 900 Bribri Indians and
1,600 Cabécar Indians. By providing comprehensive coverage of language, customs,
subsistence activities, religion, folklore, recreation, and art the author accomplishes
her purpose. The narrative is well organized and is strengthened by excellent
supporting material including photographs and an appendix which contains an article
by Carlos Meléndez Chaverri on the last king of Talamanca. A Spanish edition (San
José, 1961) is available.

277 **Etnografía histórica de Costa Rica (1561-1615).** (An historical
ethnography of Costa Rica, 1561-1615.)
Elías Zamora Acosta. Sevilla, Spain: Universidad de Sevilla, 1980.
163p. bibliog. (Publicaciones del Seminario de Antropología
Americana, vol. 16).
This is the first book of its kind about Costa Rica. Zamora Acosta utilizes sources in
the Archives of the Indies in Sevilla to reconstruct political, economic, and social life in
Costa Rica during the first three generations after the conquest, 1561-1615. The study
combines anthropological and historical methodology. One cannot say that he is totally
successful in reconstructing the life of the Indians during that period, but, given the
relative scarcity of previous studies and the paucity of documentary evidence (the
result of the Spanish crown's neglect of Costa Rica and the lack of interest by the
conquerors), the result is an impressive work of scholarship. The work is one part of a
series sponsored by the Department of Anthropology and Ethnology of America at the
Universidad de Sevilla to reconstruct the ethnohistory of colonial Guatemala.

Migration

278 **Les migrations intérieures à Costa Rica: une approche régionales [*sic*] au problème.** (Costa Rican internal migration: a regional approach to the problem.)
Guillermo A. Carvajal. *Revista Geográfica*, no. 98 (July-Dec. 1983), p. 91-114. maps.

Besides providing statistical and cartographical explanations of internal migrations in Costa Rica, the author offers a regional and economic interpretation of each major migratory movement. An account of the major migration literature is also offered. Official Ministry of Planning subdivisions (Atlantic, South Pacific, North, and Metropolitan) are the units analysed and not the provinces. The focus is on the 1968-73 period. There are eight maps.

279 **Emigrantes a la conquista de la selva: estudio de un caso de colonización en Costa Rica, San Vito de Java.** (Emigrants conquering the jungle: case-study of a colonization in Costa Rica, San Vito de Java.)
Herzel Gera Weizmann. Geneva, Switzerland: Intergovernmental Committee for Migrations, 1982. 63p. maps.

There is controversy over the experimental colonizaticn project launched by the Costa Rican government in 1952 when 117 Italian peasant families began a new life in San Vito de Java, a small agricultural community near the Panamanian border. This book, by an Israeli agricultural technician who has visited the colony representing the Intergovernmental Committee on Migration, takes the positive view: that the expansion of settlement and coffee production and the permanence of the colony in a border area has been of great benefit. He admits, however, that the colonists and the government of Italy, which co-sponsored the project, derived less benefit than Costa Rica.

Costa Rica: a geographical interpretation in historical perspective.
See item no. 22.

Densities of population in Holdridge life zones in Costa Rica: an empirical approach.
See item no. 32.

Population pressure upon resources in Costa Rica.
See item no. 36.

Costa Rica: evolución territorial y principales censos de población. (Costa Rica: territorial evolution and principal population censuses.)
See item no. 50.

Talamanca, el espacio y los hombres. (Talamanca, space and man.)
See item no. 65.

Los nicarao y los chorotega según las fuentes históricas. (The Nicarao and the Chorotega acccrding to historical sources.)
See item no. 113.

Costa Rica: la frontera sur de Mesoamérica. (Costa Rica: the southern border of Mesoamerica.)
See item no. 122.

Mesoamerican influences among Talamanca and Western Guaymi Indians.
See item no. 142.

Costa Rica: tierra y poblamiento en la colonia. (Costa Rica: land and population in the colonial period.)
See item no. 168.

La población de la ciudad de Cartago en los siglos XVII y XVIII. (The population of the city of Cartago in the 17th and 18th centuries.)
See item no. 188.

Black into white in nineteenth century Spanish America: Afro-American assimilation in Argentina and Costa Rica.
See item no. 209.

Leyendas y tradiciones borucas. (Boruca legends and traditions.)
See item no. 281.

"What happen": a folk-history of Costa Rica's Talamanca coast.
See item no. 286.

Religión y magia entre los indios de Costa Rica de origen sureño. (Religion and magic of the Indians of Costa Rica of southern origin.)
See item no. 289.

La esposa del bribri es la hermana de Dios. (The wife of the Bribri is the sister of God.)
See item no. 292.

Socioeconomic fertility determinants in Costa Rica, 1963-1973.
See item no. 304.

Ethnicity and livelihoods: a social geography of Costa Rica's Atlantic zone.
See item no. 305.

Family, household and intergenerational relations in a "Jamaican" village in Limón, Costa Rica.
See item no. 314.

Report on income distribution and poverty in Costa Rica.
See item no. 324.

Urban poverty and economic development: a case study of Costa Rica.
See item no. 326.

Land tenure and the rural exodus in Chile, Colombia, Costa Rica, and Peru.
See item no. 330.

Peripheral capitalism and rural–urban migration: a study of population movements in Costa Rica.
See item no. 331.

Population

Ethnic diversity on a corporate plantation: Guaymí labor on a United Brands subsidiary in Costa Rica and Panama.
See item no. 580.

El movimiento obrero en Costa Rica, 1830-1902. (The workers' movement in Costa Rica, 1830-1902.)
See item no. 584.

El negro en la literatura costarricense. (Blacks in Costa Rican literature.)
See item no. 635.

Lenguas indígenas costarricenses. (Indigenous Costa Rican languages.)
See item no. 654.

Estudios de lingüística chibcha. (Studies of Chibcha linguistics.)
See item no. 656.

Diccionario bribri–español, español–bribri. (A Bribri–Spanish, Spanish–Bribri dictionary.)
See item no. 664.

Las lenguas indígenas de Centro América: con especial referencia a los idiomas aborígenes de Costa Rica. (The indigenous languages of Central America: with special reference to the indigenous languages of Costa Rica.)
See item no. 665.

Bibliografía costarricense de ciencias sociales, no. 2. (A Costa Rican social science bibliography, no. 2.)
See item no. 743.

Folklore

280 **El gran incógnito: visión interna del campesino costarricense.** (The great
unknown: an internal view of the Costa Rican peasant.)
Luis Barahona Jiménez. San José: Editorial Costa Rica, 1975. 223p.

Here is an example of the highbrow (the author, a philosopher) attempting to
understand and explain the character of the lowbrow (the Costa Rican peasant). He
does it both by means of interpreting the literature dealing with the peasant and by his
own personal observations. The work can be criticized because it is impressionistic but
at the same time the comments on the Costa Rican peasant's religious beliefs, his
amusements, his artisanry, his vices, and his family relationships are careful,
sympathetic, and reflective. An appendix of peasant vocabulary and sayings is
included. The present work is a revision of articles originally published in the *Revista
de los Archivos Nacionales* in 1946 and 1947.

281 **Leyendas y tradiciones borucas.** (Boruca legends and traditions.)
Adolfo Constenla Umaña. San José: Editorial Universidad de Costa
Rica, 1979. 165p. maps. bibliog.

At the time when Constenla conducted his reasearch on the Boruca language and
legends there were only 800 Boruca Indians left. Thus, Constenla's successful effort to
save some of the Boruca legends by interviewing Espíritu Santo Maroto is a valuable
contribution to cultural preservation. The text of most of the legends is reproduced in
Boruca and Spanish. Constenla, a linguist, also supplies in this book a discussion of the
Boruca language and a Boruca–Spanish lexicon.

282 **La carreta costarricense.** (The Costa Rican oxcart.)
Constantino Láscaris Comneno, Guillermo Malavassi. San José:
Ministerio de Cultura, Juventud y Deportes, 1975. 210p. bibliog. (Serie
del Folclor, no. 1).

The work consists of two parts: the first explains the origin of the Costa Rican oxcart,
which in the 19th century was vital for the transportation of coffee to the ports and
which has now become an item in the handcraft industry, and the development of its
specific characteristics; the second is an anthology of writings about the oxcart.

283 **El costarricense.** (The Costa Rican.)
Constantino Láscaris Comneno. San José: Editorial Universitaria
Centroamericana, 1983. 4th ed. 477p. bibliog. (Colección Séptimo
Día).

Constantino Láscaris was a Spanish philosopher who taught for many years at the
Universidad de Costa Rica. Following the Salvador de Madariaga tradition of
analysing national character Láscaris takes the mundane – speech, cuisine, religious
beliefs, and folk practices – and builds an understanding of Costa Rican national
character. It is not what one would call a formal book; it is based on interviews, visits
to all parts of Costa Rica, and reflections on the Costa Rican way of doing things.

284 **Costa Rica y su folclore.** (Costa Rica and its folklore.)
Evangelina de Núñez. San José: Imprenta Nacional, 1956, 395p.

Núñez has tried to collect in this one volume 'all that gave life and splendor to this
blessed land', and that was handed down by word of mouth or in written form. In this
book, therefore, you will find prayers, songs, superstitions, sayings, refrains,
descriptions of games and dances, accounts of national symbols and shields, poems,
customs, legends, stories, biographical sketches, and miscellaneous commentaries. It is
not very well organized and it is not clear where all the information comes from, but it
is a good place to start to get the flavour of Costa Rican folklore.

285 **Plantas medicinales de Costa Rica y su folclore.** (Medicinal plants of
Costa Rica and their folklore.)
Esteban Núñez Meléndez. San José: Editorial Universidad de Costa
Rica, 1982. 3rd ed. 318p. bibliog.

After some introductory remarks on the Indian background, plant geography, and the
history of medicine in Costa Rica, Núñez, a Puerto Rican professor of pharmacy, gets
to the heart of the book: a list of medicinal plants found in Costa Rica (p. 101-267).
The arrangement is alphabetical, classified by families of plants. Scientific terms are
kept to a minimum in the entries, but, in case of need, a glossary of scientific terms is
appended. The first edition was published in 1975 by the Editorial Universidad de
Costa Rica.

286 **"What happen": a folk-history of Costa Rica's Talamanca coast.**
Paula Palmer. San José: Ecodesarrollos, 1977. 351p. maps.

Paula Palmer, a Peace Corps volunteer English teacher, collected these stories while
teaching at Cahuita (on the Caribbean coast of Costa Rica, south of Puerto Limón)
during 1974-77. Arranged chronologically by generations, the stories describe fishing,

crafts, coastal trade, the activities of the banana companies, schools, religious activities, and amusements. Palmer succeeds in combining her own words with oral history, the traditional Afro-Caribbean method of preserving a record of events and customs, to present an authentic picture of life on the Caribbean coast.

287 **Popular medicine in Puntarenas, Costa Rica: urban and societal features.**
Miles Richardson, Barbara Bode. New Orleans, Louisiana: Middle American Research Institute, Tulane University, 1972. 26p. bibliog.

Cultural anthropologists Richardson and Bode attempt to explain how residents of Puntarenas view orthodox, heretic, and non-empirical healers. Much of the explanation is highlighted by an extensive interview with a Puntarenas restaurant owner who describes her approaches to modern physicians, midwives, *curanderos* [healers], and naturists. Fieldwork for the study was carried out during the summer of 1967. This article is a reprint from Publication no. 24, Middle American Research Institute, Tulane University, 1971.

288 **Curanderismo tradicional del costarricense.** (Traditional healing of Costa Rica.)
Alia Sarkís, Víctor M. Campos. San José: Editorial Costa Rica, 1981. 2nd ed. 176p.

This work is not a study of *curanderismo* [healing] but rather a compilation of folk remedies classified by illness. Scientific names are included for all plants suggested as remedies. The book is based on the work of two pharmacy students at the University of Costa Rica and on the authors' interviews in the Central Valley and the Atlantic zone. The first edition was published by the Editorial Costa Rica in 1978.

El uso de algunas plantas medicinales en Costa Rica. (The use of some medicinal plants in Costa Rica.)
See item no. 82.

The Talamanca tribes of Costa Rica.
See item no. 276.

La esposa del bribri es la hermana de Dios. (The wife of the Bribri is the sister of God.)
See item no. 292.

The study of San José, Costa Rica, street culture: codes and communication in lower-class society.
See item no. 328.

Culture, politics and medicine in Costa Rica: an anthropological study.
See item no. 337.

Family context and illness behavior in Costa Rica.
See item no. 339.

Folklore

The urban patient: health-seeking behavior in the health care system of San José, Costa Rica.
See item no. 342.

Refranes y dichos populares usuales en Costa Rica. (Proverbs and customary popular expressions in Costa Rica.)
See item no. 658.

Dr. Moreno Cañas: a symbolic bridge to the demedicalization of healing.
See item no. 724.

A report on folklore research in Costa Rica.
See item no. 760.

Religion

289 **Religión y magia entre los indios de Costa Rica de origen sureño.**
(Religion and magic of the Indians of Costa Rica of southern origin.)
Carlos H. Aguilar Piedra. San José: Universidad de Costa Rica, 1965.
83p. bibliog. (Publicaciones de la Universidad de Costa Rica, Serie
Historia y Geografía, no. 6).

Ideas on the Supreme Being, fate, the soul, and shamanism among the Bribri and
Cabécar of Talamanca and among the Huetar, Coto, Térraba, and Boruca Indians of
the South Pacific region are the subject of this study. Professor Aguilar bases his
interpretations on earlier ethnological works (especially those of Henri Pittier, Doris
Stone, and William Gabb) and on inferences from archaeological objects.

290 **Historia eclesiástica de Costa Rica: del descubrimiento a la erección de la
diócesis, 1502-1850.** (The ecclesiastical history of Costa Rica: from the
discovery to the establishment of the diocese, 1502-1850.)
Ricardo Blanco Segura. San José: Editorial Costa Rica, 1967. 401p.
bibliog.

Building on the work of previous Church historians Bernardo Augusto Thiel and
Víctor Manuel Sanabria, Blanco Segura presents in exhaustive detail an account of
Catholic Church activities in Costa Rica *before* the naming of the first bishop in 1850.
The two most persistent themes of the book are, in the colonial period, missionary
relations with the Indians, and, in the independence period, the much-resented
ecclesiastical dependence on Nicaragua and Guatemala and the desire to have a
separate bishopric. The study rests on a solid foundation of primary and secondary
sources and will not soon be superseded. It was originally published in 1960 in the
Revista de los Archivos Nacionales.

291 **1884, el estado, la iglesia y las reformas liberales.** (1884, the state, the Church and the liberal reforms.)
Ricardo Blanco Segura. San José: Editorial Costa Rica, 1984. 374p. bibliog.

The year 1884 was important in the history of Costa Rica because the Church–state conflict then reached a climax, resulting in the expulsion of the Jesuit order and Bishop Bernardo Augusto Thiel. Blanco Segura builds up to this point with lengthy expositions (covering the first 140 pages) on liberalism, freemasonry, and the background of the Church and the Jesuits. He then discusses the expulsion, the anticlerical laws of the Próspero Fernández presidency (1882-85), and the personalities involved. Not unexpectedly, Blanco Segura, Costa Rica's leading Church historian, defends the Bishop and the Jesuit order against the Liberal accusations.

292 **La esposa del bribri es la hermana de Dios.** (The wife of the Bribri is the sister of God.)
María Eugenia Bózzoli de Wille. *América Indígena*, vol. 36, no. 1 (Jan.-March 1976), p. 15-37. bibliog.

This article discusses five tales of mythical beings which illustrate the role of women in Bribri society. The Bribri Indians, whose language is related to Chibcha, live in southern Costa Rica.

293 **Protestant–Catholic relations in Costa Rica.**
Richard L. Millett. *Journal of Church and State*, vol. 12, no. 1 (Winter 1970), p. 41-57.

What stands out in this succinct survey of Catholic–Protestant relations is the bitterness of the relationship until the 1960s. Thereafter, according to Millett, the Episcopal Mission succeeded in mediating the extreme views of both sides. The study is based on secondary sources, although valuable insights into the Protestant perspective are provided by the Strachan papers from the Latin American Mission Archive in San José.

294 **A history of Protestantism in Costa Rica.**
Wilton Nelson. Lucknow, India: Lucknow Publishing House, 1963. 258p.

A condensation of the author's ThD 1958 dissertation at Princeton Theological Seminary (available on microfilm from University Microfilms, Ann Arbor, Michigan, order no. 73-20304). A Spanish version was published in San José by Publicaciones IINDEF in 1983 (362 pages). It is a solid and well-documented study of the development of Protestantism in Costa Rica from the middle of the 19th century. The emphasis falls on the 1891-1961 period. A statistical appendix furnishes estimates of the Protestant population in Costa Rica by denomination in 1956 and 1960.

295 **Presbítero doctor Francisco Calvo (Ganganelli): organizador de la masonería en Costa Rica.** (The priest Francisco Calvo (Ganganelli): organizer of the freemasons in Costa Rica.)
Rafael Obregón Loría.   San José: Imprenta Borrasé, 1963. 114p. bibliog.

Calvo was an unusual man. A priest, he was the son of a priest and the grandson of a priest. His liberalism, his interest in politics, and especially his fight against the Church hierarchy on behalf of freemasonry in Costa Rica in the 1860s and 1870s are the themes Obregón dwells on in this slim volume.

296 **Costa Rica: la Iglesia Católica y el orden social.** (Costa Rica: the Catholic Church and the social order.)
Andrés Opazo Bernales.   San José: Departamento Ecuménico de Investigaciones, 1987. 217p.

In the first chapter of this sociological study the author sets the stage by discussing the Costa Rican political economic model in the period following the revolution of 1948, worker and peasant movements of that era, and the Catholic Church's general position on social issues during the archbishopric of Carlos Humberto Rodríguez Quirós (1960-78) and afterwards. Thereafter the author focuses on specific cases of pastoral action and local religious movements during the 1970s and 1980s, as in Golfito, San Gabriel de Aserrí, and Chacarita. Opazo admires the social leadership of Archbishop Víctor Sanabria in the 1940s and considers such leadership from the hierarchy to be lacking subsequently.

297 **Reseña histórica de la iglesia en Costa Rica desde 1502 hasta 1850.** (Historical overview of the Church in Costa Rica from 1502 until 1850.)
Víctor Sanabria Martínez.   San José: Departamento Ecuménico de Investigaciones, 1984. 290p.

Archbishop Sanabria left this incomplete manuscript (dated 1946) when he died in 1952. Church officials prepared it for publication in 1984 without further editing or additions. It is a succinct account of the Church's activities in the colonial period. Its contributions include outlining the details of the dependence of Costa Rica's ecclesiastical authorities on Nicaragua and Guatemala, narrating the fortunes of the Franciscan missions in Talamanca and elsewhere, and explaining the origins of Cartago's shrine, Nuestra Señora de los Angeles. Despite the title the book does not extend to the 19th century. It is well documented but is based not on archival sources but on published documents and secondary materials.

298 **La iglesia costarricense y la cuestión social.** (The Costa Rican Church and the social question.)
Gustavo Adolfo Soto Valverde.   San José: Editorial Universidad Estatal a Distancia, 1985. 571p. bibliog.

The strength of this book – massive detail on the chosen topic – is also its weakness. The author deserves credit for amassing from a variety of ecclesiastical sources details on the Costa Rican Catholic Church's position on social issues, particularly in the critical period of 1940-43. However, the lengthy citations and diversions on ecclesiastical history detract from the author's purpose, which is to demonstrate that the social reforms of President Rafael Calderón Guardia (1940-44) were a direct result of deeply rooted Christian concepts as expressed by Archbishop Víctor Sanabria and other Church spokesmen.

299 And in Samaria.
Mildred Spain.   Dallas: Central American Mission, 1954. 2nd ed. 328p.

The author narrates the story of the origin and development of the missionary work of the Dallas-based Central American Mission (Protestant), whose work began in Costa Rica.

300 The Catholic Church and politics in Nicaragua and Costa Rica.
Philip J. Williams.   Pittsburgh, Pennsylvania: University of Pittsburgh Press, 1989. 228p. bibliog.

The best overall English-language treatment of the Catholic Church's recent activities in Costa Rica is, without dispute, this monograph by Williams. The section on Costa Rica (p. 97-181) is extensive, balanced, and based on archival as well as secondary sources. While many Costa Rican religious historians have given little attention to the failure of the Church to speak out on social issues in the 1952-78 period, Williams has no such inhibitions. He points out, for example, that of some 325 documents issued by Church leaders between 1953 and 1970 'only 61 treated social and political questions, and many in a most cursory manner'. Efforts to activate the Church in the 1980s are covered in the third and final chapter on Costa Rica.

Anatomía patriótica. (A patriotic anatomy.)
See item no. 1.

La patria esencial. (The essence of the country.)
See item no. 2.

Costa Rican life.
See item no. 4.

Los costarricenses. (The Costa Ricans.)
See item no. 5.

The Costa Ricans.
See item no. 6.

El nacimiento y la muerte entre los bribris. (Birth and death among the Bribris.)
See item no. 257.

El judío en Costa Rica. (The Jew in Costa Rica.)
See item no. 273.

La Iglesia y el sindicalismo en Costa Rica. (The Church and syndicalism in Costa Rica.)
See item no. 578.

El pensamiento político-social de monseñor Sanabria. (The socio-political thought of Monsignor Sanabria.)
See item no. 699.

Monseñor Sanabria: apuntes biográficos. (Monsignor Sanabria: biographical notes.)
See item no. 704.

Obispos, arzobispos y representantes de la santa sede en Costa Rica. (Bishops, archbishops and representatives of the Papacy in Costa Rica.)
See item no. 705.

Who shall ascend; the life of R. Kenneth Strachan: of Costa Rica.
See item no. 714.

Bernardo Augusto Thiel, segundo obispo de Costa Rica: apuntamientos históricos. (Bernardo Augusto Thiel, second Bishop of Costa Rica: historical notes.)
See item no. 733.

Social Conditions

General

301 **La familia en Costa Rica.** (The family in Costa Rica.)
Olda María Acuña B., Carlos F. Denton L. San José: Ministerio de
Cultura, Juventud y Deportes, Instituto de Estudios Sociales en
Población, 1979. 98p. bibliog.
The authors analyse the structure and function of families within the Costa Rican
economic and social system. The work is based on a comparison of marriage, divorce,
fertility, family planning, and female employment statistics found in the 1963 and 1973
censuses.

302 **Cultural change in a Costa Rican village.**
Manuel Alers-Montalvo. PhD dissertation, Michigan State
University. 1953. 185p. bibliog. (Available from University Microfilms,
Ann Arbor, Michigan, order no. 7154).
A study of seventy families in the village of San Juan Norte, near Turrialba. It deals
with cultural changes as a result of the introduction of potable water, vegetable
gardens, and a new variety of sugar-cane.

303 **Rural development in Costa Rica.**
Jeffrey Ashe. New York: Acción International, 1978. 110p. map.
bibliog.
Using the regional divisions adopted by the Ministry of Planning (North Pacific,
Northern Plains, etc.), and not the provinces, this study provides data on employment,
local associations, housing, transport and migration in each of Costa Rica's regions
except the urbanized Central Valley. Recommendations centre on job creation and
improvement of agricultural production. This study was originally undertaken by the
Institute of Municipal Development and Assistance (IFAM) and published by IFAM in
Spanish in 1976.

304 **Socioeconomic fertility determinants in Costa Rica, 1963-1973.**
Manuel J. Carvajal, David T. Geithman. In: *New perspective on the demographic transition.* Washington, DC: Smithsonian Institution Interdisciplinary Communications Program, 1976, p. 95-162. bibliog. (Occasional Monograph Series, no. 4).
This study focuses on changes in fertility rates during 1963-73. The authors suggest that fertility declined in this period because of improvement of family income in Costa Rica and a general increase of economic opportunities.

305 **Ethnicity and livelihoods: a social geography of Costa Rica's Atlantic zone.**
Charles W. Koch. PhD dissertation, University of Kansas, 1975. 508p. bibliog. (Available from University Microfilms, Ann Arbor, Michigan, order no. 75-30058).
Koch's thesis is that the different settlement and agricultural patterns of the Jamaican and Hispanic settlers of the Atlantic region of Costa Rica are determined by material rather than cultural factors. In the process of proving this, he provides a wealth of well-documented information on the Northern Railway Company, the banana industry (particularly the United Fruit Company), agricultural patterns, physical factors affecting agriculture, and the history of the area.

306 **Turrialba: social systems and the introduction of change.**
Edited by Charles Price Loomis (et al.). Glencoe, Illinois: Free Press, 1953. 288p. maps. bibliog.
Loomis, a sociologist, directed this study by an interdisciplinary team that included representatives of agriculture, anthropology, economics, demography, political science, nutrition, and education. The team's purpose was to illuminate the nature of the social systems of Turrialba, a small town which happened to be the headquarters of the Interamerican Institute of Agricultural Sciences, and to examine the introduction of change from different disciplinary angles. It is a classic effort, typical of the 1950s, by social scientists who were hoping to unlock the mysteries of slow economic development and discover how to accelerate it.

307 **Some aspects of life on a large Costa Rican coffee finca.**
Paul C. Morrison, Thomas L. Norris. *Papers of the Michigan Academy of Science, Arts and Letters*, vol. 38 (1953), p. 331-46.
Based on a study of Aquiares, a large coffee *finca* [estate] near Turrialba, the article pays attention to the attitudes of different *finca* residents toward recreation, religion, education, social contact, housing, and production. Photographs are included.

308 **Costa Rica: a country at the crossroads.**
N. Nikiforova. *International Affairs* (Moscow), vol. 10 (Oct. 1981), p. 113-19.
Nikiforova presents the Soviet view of the current economic, political, and social status of Costa Rica. Although primarily descriptive, the article attacks United States influence and multinational corporations and emphasizes Costa Rica's dependence on

foreign capital. The position of the People's Vanguard Party (Communist) is explained.

309 **Poverty and labour market in Costa Rica.**
Mary Pollack. Santiago, Chile: International Labour Organization, 1987. 37p. bibliog. (Documento de Trabajo no. 288).
Based on data from household surveys on employment and unemployment carried out in 1971 and 1982, this study analyses the effects of the economic crisis on different groups, particularly low-income groups. The results show that poverty increased from 1971 to 1982, that more household members than before are employed in the informal sector, and, not surprisingly, that householders headed by women, older persons, and handicapped persons are more likely to be indigent than others.

310 **Rural electrification and development: social and economic impact in Costa Rica and Colombia.**
John Saunders (et al.) Boulder, Colorado: Westview Press, 1978. 180p. bibliog. (A Westview Replica Edition).
The comparison of rural electrification in the two countries hinges on the emphasis on cooperatives in Costa Rica and state enterprise in Colombia. Although the study provides little guidance on which method is superior it does provide a variety of data on household electricity consumption and energy costs, assesses the social impact of electrification, and makes suggestions on alternative energy sources and the role of energy in development.

311 **Agrarian capitalism and the transformation of peasant society: coffee in Costa Rica.**
Mitchell A. Seligson. Buffalo, New York: Council on International Studies, State University of New York at Buffalo, 1975. 66p. bibliog. (Special Studies Series, no. 69).
In this short essay, backed by statistical charts on land distribution and coffee production, Seligson relates the rise and decline of the coffee oligarchy, the rise of the bureaucracy and middle classes, and the problems of peasants. He maintains that far from having an equitable land distribution system, Costa Rica has more rural landless and subsistence farmers than is generally believed.

312 **Peasants of Costa Rica and the development of agrarian capitalism.**
Mitchell A. Seligson. Madison, Wisconsin: University of Wisconsin Press, 1980. 220p. bibliog.
The sharp focus of this book is on peasants. In the first part the approach is historical, in an effort to explain the impact of coffee and banana cultivation on peasant conditions. In the second part the author, a political scientist, uses anthropological, sociological, and political science methodology to analyse such issues as social stratification among peasants, peasant organizations, and land reform. Seligson shows that peasant response to agrarian capitalism has been basically non-violent. In the final chapter, entitled 'Demise of the Peasantry', Seligson points out that international market conditions and technology since the 1960s have drastically reduced the operating room for peasants and consequently their numbers have declined.

313 **Poder político y democracia en Costa Rica.** (Political power and democracy in Costa Rica.)
José Luis Vega Carballo.   San José: Editorial Porvenir, 1982. 168p. bibliog. (Colección Debate).

The author, a sociologist, attempts to explain the relationship among key ingredients of Costa Rican political and social life: monoculture, class structure, emergence of new social classes, capitalism, and dependency – all in relation to Costa Rica's unique democratic system.

Social structure

314 **Family, household and intergenerational relations in a "Jamaican" village in Limón, Costa Rica.**
Roy Simon Bryce-Laporte.   In: *The family in the Caribbean: proceedings of the Second Conference on the Family in the Caribbean, Aruba, Netherlands Antilles, December 1-5, 1969*, edited by Stanford N. Gerber. Rio Piedras, Puerto Rico: Institute of Caribbean Studies, University of Puerto Rico, 1973, p. 65-93. bibliog.

This paper was extracted from the author's thesis (q.v.). Here he seeks to explain the intergenerational relationships in Limón. Contrary to what one would expect according to the theories of Radcliffe-Brown, the relations in the village tended to be tense or less comfortable between 'alternate generations' and more relaxed in 'proximate generations'. The author demonstrates these relationships with case-studies and attempts to explain the generational aspect.

315 **Sociocultural contrasts in rural and urban settlement types in Costa Rica.**
Victor Goldkind.   *Rural Sociology*, vol. 26, no. 4 (Dec. 1961), p. 365-80.

Among the topics discussed in this article are contrasting rural and urban attitudes toward manual labour, employment of women, and leisure time. The smaller the urban centre, the author finds, the less distance there is between social classes.

316 **The structure of leadership and its characteristics in a Costa Rica community.**
David E. W. Holden.   *América Indígena*, vol. 27, no. 1 (Jan. 1967), p. 55-68.

An explanation of the 'sociometric' method of determining leadership structures, and an outline of the results of the application of this method in the small, rural community of Pejivalle. The author, a sociologist, did his investigation at the request of the Costa Rican Land and Colonization Institute.

317 **Class status in rural Costa Rica: a peasant community compared with an hacienda community.**
Charles Price Loomis, Reed M. Powell.   In: *Materiales para el estudio de la clase media en la América Latina*, edited by Theo R. Crevenna. Washington, DC: Panamerican Union, 1950-51, vol. 5, p. 1-23. (Publicaciones de la Oficina de Ciencias Sociales).
Loomis and Powell argue that Costa Rican democracy is partly due to the relatively strong position of the 'peasant proprietor', or small farmer. However, on the basis of a comparative analysis of San Juan Sur, a peasant-proprietor type of community, and Atirro, an *hacienda* (both are near Turrialba), they conclude that peasant proprietors are being reduced to peonage by large landholders and corporate farms. The authors reached their findings by identifying community leadership networks and interviewing individuals in the two communities.

318 **Social class and social mobility in a Costa Rican town.**
Sakari Sariola.   Turrialba, Costa Rica: Inter-American Institute of Agricultural Sciences, 1954. 136p. bibliog. (Inter-American Institute of Agricultural Sciences, Miscellaneous Publication, no. 5).
The town under study is Turrialba. The author is a well-known Latin American sociologist. The result is a thorough examination of the characteristics of the lower, middle, and upper classes of Turrialba. One hundred and forty-two heads of households responded to the author's questions concerning place of birth, occupation, nationality, household possessions, participation in activities, and personal relations.

319 **The 'dual society' thesis in Latin America: a reexamination of the Costa Rican case.**
Mitchell A. Seligson.   *Social Forces*, vol. 51, no. 1 (Sept. 1972), p. 91-8.
On the basis of data collected from Costa Rica in the 1960s on birth control, church attendance, chaperonage and other matters, Seligson challenges the view that Latin American society can be assumed to divide into traditional and modern sectors. According to Seligson, a more accurate description of Costa Rican society is value homogeneity since he has discovered few attitudinal differences between lower classes and middle classes.

320 **Aspects of power distribution in Costa Rica.**
Samuel Z. Stone.   In: *Contemporary cultures and societies of Latin America*, edited by Dwight B. Heath. New York: Random House, 1974. 2nd ed. p. 404-21.
A summary of the author's controversial doctoral dissertation in sociology at the University of Paris which was published as *La dinastía de los conquistadores* (Dynasty of the conquerors) in 1975. Through an imaginative use of genealogy and class analysis Stone shows that the coffee planter élite which rose to prominence in the mid-19th century was directly descended from the political and economic élite of the colonial period. Stone maintains that although the descendants of the conquerors split into factions and have had to share a degree of political power with the middle and lower classes in the 20th century they still dominate politics and commerce. Since it is a summary Stone relies on a few examples to demonstrate his point.

321 **La dinastía de los conquistadores: la crisis del poder en la Costa Rica contemporánea.** (The dynasty of the conquerors: the crisis of power in contemporary Costa Rica.)
Samuel Z. Stone. San José: Editorial Universitaria Centroamericana, 1975. 3rd ed. 623p. map. bibliog. (Colección Seis).

For a commentary on the English-language summary of this book see the previous item. The book-length study in Spanish treats the reader to many insights into the development of classes and the sources of power at different times in Costa Rica's history. It traces in great detail the connections between the contemporary political and economic élite and the first Spanish arrivals in the 16th century. Genealogical charts demonstrate the close connections among the original settlers and the so-called coffee élite which rose to prominence in the middle of the 19th century. The small size of the population of Costa Rica at an early period in its history is an important factor which Stone believes allowed the power continuity to develop, but he discusses other factors as well. Although some commentators have perhaps overemphasized the contrast between the élitism revealed by this study and Costa Rica's reputation for democracy Stone himself is careful to point out that the Costa Rican élite had many divisions and that especially in the 20th century non-élite groups and individuals have gained access to political positions and to wealth.

322 **Some variables of lower and middle class in two Central American cities.**
Robert C. Williamson. *Social Forces*, vol. 41, no. 2 (Dec. 1962), p. 195-207.

The article is based on information gathered from 474 families in San Salvador, El Salvador, and from 245 families in San José, Costa Rica during 1958 and 1960. Class characteristics investigated were: communication, mobility, nationalism, kinship, conformity, optimism, and marital adjustment. Results indicated fewer differences among the classes in the two cities and less conformity consciousness than expected.

Social problems

323 **Cannabis in Costa Rica: a study of chronic marihuana use.**
Edited by William E. Carter. Philadelphia, Pennsylvania: Institute for the Study of Human Issues, 1980. 331p. bibliog.

This book is the result of a two-year multidisciplinary study of chronic marijuana use in Costa Rica. The study was funded by the National Institute of Drug Abuse. Forty drug users were compared to carefully selected controls (non-users) for the purpose of examining possible environmental factors leading to drug use and the subsequent effects of chronic intake. The results demonstrated almost no significant difference in personality, intelligence, REM [rapid eye movement] sleep, etc. between the drug users and the controls. In addition to providing comparative data on the drug users, the book is full of valuable information on working-class culture and life in San José.

324 **Report on income distribution and poverty in Costa Rica.**
Manuel J. Carvajal. Washington, DC: Rural Development Division,
Bureau for Latin America and the Caribbean, United States Agency
for International Development, 1979. 74p. bibliog. (Working
Document Series Costa Rica, General Working Document, no. 2).

This report presents a statistical analysis of income distribution in Costa Rica and
relates poverty to fertility rates, child mortality, internal migration, illiteracy, and
housing. It also makes recommendations on tax and credit policy so as to benefit the
poor.

325 **Poverty in Costa Rica: methodological problems in the determination of
some of its characteristics.**
Víctor Hugo Céspedes S., Alberto di Mare, Claudio González Vega,
Eduardo Lizano Fait. San José: United States Agency for
International Development, 1977. 288p.

Although the authors claim no theoretical breakthrough in their discussion of poverty
they do present a methodology for investigation of poverty and, at the same time, they
present massive data extracted from the 1973 census on the characteristics of the poor
in Costa Rica. They also make specific recommendations on how to improve the study
of poverty. They find, not surprisingly, that the poor in Costa Rica are mostly rural,
lacking in education, have more children than the non-poor, and are likely to be
unemployed. The study, a translation of the original Spanish version, was funded by
the Agency for International Development (USAID) and is an attempt to delineate
some of the demographic, social, and economic characteristics which accompany the
condition of poverty.

326 **Urban poverty and economic development: a case study of Costa Rica.**
Bruce H. Herrick, Barclay Hudson. New York: St. Martin's Press,
1981. 188p. maps. bibliog.

This study of poverty in Costa Rica, for which data were collected in San José in 1977,
is designed to throw light on the issue of poverty in general and on government policy.
The authors show that in San José poverty is not limited to slum areas (*tugurios*), and
that 'contrary to conventional wisdom, rural to urban migration was not a direct major
cause of urban poverty'. The discussion touches upon shifts in employment
opportunities, unemployment, and the anti-poverty strategy and institutional framework in Costa Rica. Final recommendations include a revision of the current 'spatial'
perception of poverty which guides government policy.

327 **Situation, principal problems and prospects for the economic and social
development of Costa Rica.**
Washington, DC: Organization of American States, 1974. 145p.

Produced by the Permanent Executive Committee of the Inter-American Economic
and Social Council of the Organization of American States, this survey reviews social
statistics, social legislation, and the overall economic situation of Costa Rica in the
1973-74 period. There follows discussion of national socio-economic objectives,
strategies, and prospects. The final section covers international cooperation for the
economic development of Costa Rica, past and future.

328 **The study of San José, Costa Rica, street culture: codes and communication in lower-class society.**
J. Bryan Page.   In: *Drugs, rituals and altered states of consciousness*, edited by Brian M. Du Toit. Rotterdam: A. A. Balkema, 1977, p. 207-14. bibliog.

The author was part of a team of anthropologists who studied marijuana use in San José. In this article he provides a scholarly glimpse into the *pachuco* [street talk] of the marijuana user.

329 **Imagen de la mujer que proyectan los medios de comunicación de masas en Costa Rica.** (The image of women projected by the mass media in Costa Rica.)
Teresita Quiroz M., Barbara Larraín E.   San José: Universidad de Costa Rica, Facultad de Ciencias Sociales, Instituto de Investigaciones Sociales, 1978, 344p. bibliog. (Avances de Investigación, no. 34).

Basing their comments on statistical data from the census of 1973 and comparisons with data from other countries, the authors clearly show the subordinate position of women in Costa Rican society. The heart of their study is an analysis of the images of women projected by television, radio, and popular magazines through soap operas and advertisements. Although the analysis is of the images and not on their possible impact, the authors conclude that the mass media are instruments of male domination.

330 **Land tenure and the rural exodus in Chile, Colombia, Costa Rica, and Peru.**
R. Paul Shaw.   Gainesville, Florida: University Presses of Florida, 1976. 180p. bibliog. (Latin American Monographs, 2nd series, no. 19).

The principal question posed by this book is what effect might agrarian reform and land redistribution have on rural–urban migration and employment patterns. The Costa Rican experience from 1950 to 1963, plus similar experiences in Chile, Colombia, and Peru, lead the author to conclude that land reform does have beneficial side-effects, namely slowing rural–urban migration and reducing open unemployment in cities.

331 **Peripheral capitalism and rural–urban migration: a study of population movements in Costa Rica.**
J. Edward Taylor.   *Latin American Perspectives*, Issues 25/26, vol. 7, no. 2, 3 (Spring-Summer 1980), p. 75-90. map. bibliog.

According to the author, previous studies of rural–urban migration give too much attention to pull factors and too little to push factors. His explanation of why rural workers have migrated to the Central Valley of Costa Rica is that conditions in rural areas forced workers out. In the early 20th century falling coffee prices forced consolidation and out-migration of peasants and in the mid-20th century expansion of cattle production for export forced peasants off the land.

Family

332 **Family and kinship among the San José working class.**
William E. Carter, William R. True. In: *Family and kinship in Middle America and the Caribbean: proceedings of the 14th seminar of the Committee on Family Research of the International Sociological Association, Curaçao, September 1975*, edited by Arnaud F. Marks, René A. Römer. Willemstad, The Netherlands: Institute of Higher Studies in Curaçao, Department of Caribbean Studies of the Royal Institute of Linguistics and Anthropology, 1987, p. 227-50. bibliog.

This study of Costa Rican family life is based on eighty-two life-histories collected by the authors between 1973 and 1975, as part of a larger interdisciplinary investigation of cannabis use (q.v.). They note among the San José working class the predominance of a traditional pattern of strong, stable, and cohesive family systems, brought to the capital by migrants from the countryside.

333 **The Costa Rican family.**
Manuel J. Carvajal. In: *The family in Latin America*, edited by Man Singh Das, Clinton J. Jesser. Sahibabad, India: Vikas, 1980, p. 335-87. bibliog.

Census data from 1950 to 1973 are used extensively by Carvajal in this lengthy article to delineate social and economic aspects of the Costa Rican family. Characteristics such as size, household composition, income, and patterns of consumption are discussed, and material on birth rates, migration, education, literacy, health, social security coverage and housing complements the specific coverage of the family. Thirty-four statistical tables support the narrative. A short section on the history of family planning in Costa Rica is included.

334 **Costa Rican family structure.**
Setha M. Low. In: *First child and family formation*, edited by Warren B. Miller, Lucile Newman. Chapel Hill, North Carolina: Carolina Population Center, University of North Carolina, 1977, p. 128-44.

In setting the stage for her study, Low summarizes what is known about the Costa Rican family and women's role in society, along with Costa Rican attitudes toward contraception, abortion, and illegitimacy. She argues for the mother–child dyad as a family unit. The study itself focuses on the strategies developed by single mothers with a single child to provide the necessities for their children. The research sample included 453 individuals contacted through several health clinics. Seven specific cases of single women are examined in detail. The study was conducted in the mid-1970s.

Costa Rican life.
See item no. 4.

Los costarricenses. (The Costa Ricans.)
See item no. 5.

The Costa Ricans.
See item no. 6.

Costa Rica: transition to land hunger and potential instability.
See item no. 17.

Costa Rica's frontier legacy.
See item no. 18.

La base funcional de ciudades pequeñas: ejemplo costarricense. (The functional base of small cities: a Costa Rican example.)
See item no. 29.

Revista Geográfica. (Geographical Review.)
See item no. 31.

Population pressure upon resources in Costa Rica.
See item no. 36.

Nicoya, a cultural geography.
See item no. 38.

Vacaciones en Costa Rica. (Vacation in Costa Rica.)
See item no. 66.

Arqueología criminal americana. (American criminal archaeology.)
See item no. 154.

Costa Rica: tierra y poblamiento en la colonia. (Costa Rica: land and population in the colonial period.)
See item no. 168.

Población, fecundidad y desarrollo en Costa Rica, 1950-1970. (Population, fecundity and development in Costa Rica, 1950-70.)
See item no. 238.

The Costa Rican family planning program.
See item no. 239.

Demography and development: the lessons of Costa Rica.
See item no. 243.

Dinámica demográfica, planificación familiar y política de población en Costa Rica. (Demographic dynamics, family planning and population policy in Costa Rica.)
See item no. 247.

Population perception and policy in Costa Rica.
See item no. 249.

A survey of attitudes related to Costa Rican population dynamics.
See item no. 254.

Social relations and cultural persistence (or change) among Jamaicans in a rural area of Costa Rica.
See item no. 259.

Jamaican blacks and their descendants in Costa Rica.
See item no. 265.

Social Conditions

Cultural change, social conflict, and changing distributions of authority in the Caribbean lowlands of Costa Rica.
See item no. 266.

El gran incógnito: visión interna del campesino costarricense. (The great unknown: an internal view of the Costa Rican peasant.)
See item no. 280.

Costa Rica: la Iglesia Católica y el orden social. (Costa Rica: the Catholic Church and the social order.)
See item no. 296.

Culture, politics and medicine in Costa Rica: an anthropological study.
See item no. 337.

Family context and illness behavior in Costa Rica.
See item no. 339.

The meaning of nervios: a sociocultural analysis of symptom presentation in San José, Costa Rica.
See item no. 340.

Patterns of Costa Rican politics.
See item no. 369.

Power structure and its communication behavior in San José, Costa Rica.
See item no. 370.

Sons of the establishment: elite youth in Panama and Costa Rica.
See item no. 372.

Development and participation in Costa Rica: the impact of context.
See item no. 388.

Costa Rica's political turmoil: can production support the welfare state?
See item no. 396.

A multidimensional view of power in San José, Costa Rica.
See item no. 464.

An analysis of rural food distribution in Costa Rica.
See item no. 468.

Costa Rica hoy: la crisis y sus perspectivas. (Costa Rica today: the crisis and its perspectives.)
See item no. 482.

Income distribution and economic development: some intra-country evidence.
See item no. 488.

Equitable growth: the case of Costa Rica.
See item no. 493.

Hacia una interpretación del desarrollo costarricense: ensayo sociológico. (Towards an interpretation of Costa Rican development: a sociological essay.)
See item no. 495.

Social aspects of the banana industry.
See item no. 525.

The structure of decision-making in Paso.
See item no. 539.

Un área rural en desarrollo: sus problemas económicos y sociales en Costa Rica. (A rural area in development: its economic and social problems in Costa Rica.)
See item no. 545.

The impact of communication on rural development: an investigation in Costa Rica and India.
See item no. 575.

Las luchas sociales en Costa Rica, 1870-1930. (Social struggles in Costa Rica, 1870-1930.)
See item no. 583.

El movimiento obrero en Costa Rica, 1830-1902. (The workers' movement in Costa Rica, 1830-1902.)
See item no. 584.

The phonological correlates of social stratification in the Spanish of Costa Rica.
See item no. 655.

La mujer costarricense a través de cuatro siglos. (The Costa Rican woman over four centuries.)
See item no. 695.

Autobiografías campesinas. (Rural autobiographies.)
See item no. 700.

Bibliografía costarricense de ciencias sociales, no. 2. (A Costa Rican social science bibliography, no. 2).
See item no. 743.

Bibliography of poverty and related topics in Costa Rica.
See item no. 750.

Social Services, Health and Welfare

335 Nervios in rural Costa Rica.
Peggy F. Barlett, Setha M. Low. *Medical Anthropology*, vol. 4, no. 4 (Fall 1980), p. 523-64.

The data for this article were obtained in 1977 by means of interviews of all households in the two small towns of Paso and Toco in Puriscal canton in Costa Rica. Approximately twenty-five per cent of the adults in these towns indicated that they had attacks of *nervios* [nerves], a general complaint covering physical as well as mental symptoms. The complaint was not found to correlate with socio-economic status or power inequalities.

336 Los problemas de la salud en Costa Rica: políticas y estrategias. (Health problems in Costa Rica: politics and strategies.)
Juan Jaramillo Antillón. San José: Ministerio de Salud, 1983, 143p. maps. bibliog.

Minister of Health Jaramillo provides in this book over one hundred pages of statistical data on medicine and public health in Costa Rica. In the narrative portion (p. 1-138) he comments on specific health problems. Taking a comprehensive view of public health he addresses issues such as social security, hospital administration, alcoholism, and air pollution as well as government policy toward specific diseases, malnutrition, and mortality. The 1984 publication is a corrected version of the first edition, published in 1983.

337 Culture, politics and medicine in Costa Rica: an anthropological study.
Setha M. Low. South Salem, New York: Redgrave, 1985.

Almost everything anyone could want to know about health services in Costa Rica is contained in this thorough and methodologically sophisticated book. The perspective is that of the patient, how he or she sees medical institutions, the variety of health services, and the response of physicians and other informal curers. The author analyses the three types of the health care system: professional medicine, popular medicine (including pharmacists), and folk medicine. All of this is done against a background of information about Costa Rican demographic characteristics and especially the role of the family in Costa Rican society. Case-histories of patients enhance the appeal of the book.

338 **The effect of medical institutions on doctor–patient interaction in Costa Rica.**
Setha M. Low. *Health and Society*, vol. 60, no. 1 (1982), p. 17-50. bibliog.

Professor Low observed doctor–patient interaction at two hospitals and two clinics in San José for the purpose of determining the level of patient satisfaction. She finds that the setting and the personnel did make a difference. For example, patients at the Hospital San Juan de Dios had fewer complaints than those at the Social Security Hospital. The study is carefully done, supported by interviews and an ample bibliography of secondary sources, and concludes with policy recommendations. In the introduction there is an excellent review of the public health system.

339 **Family context and illness behavior in Costa Rica.**
Setha M. Low. *Medical Anthropology*, vol. 6, no. 4 (Fall 1982), p. 253-68.

Professor Low finds that family influences on health care in Costa Rica are very strong, that families of satisfied patients utilize all three health sectors – professional, popular, and folk – for medical consultation, and that families of dissatisfied patients use only the professional sector. The article is based on intensive interviews of nine families.

340 **The meaning of nervios: a sociocultural analysis of symptom presentation in San José, Costa Rica.**
Setha M. Low. *Culture, Medicine, and Psychiatry*, vol. 5, no. 1 (March 1981), p. 25-47.

Nervios is often used by Costa Ricans as an explanation of bodily ailments. By means of interviews of 457 patients over a twenty-month period Professor Low arrives at various conclusions about the attitudes of Costa Ricans toward health symptoms, health care, family life, and cultural patterns.

341 **Patient satisfaction: a comparative study of different levels of health care in Costa Rica.**
Setha M. Low. In: *Old roots in new lands: historical and anthropological perspectives*, edited by J. H. Morgan. New York: University Press of America, 1983, p. 125-39.

In this analysis of doctor–patient interaction Professor Low examines the expectations of patients and their satisfaction and places such interaction in its cultural and historical context. Interviews were conducted at the Hospital San Juan de Dios and Social Security Hospital in San José.

342 **The urban patient: health-seeking behavior in the health care system of San José, Costa Rica.**
Setha M. Low. *Urban Anthropology*, vol. 10, no. 1 (1981), p. 27-52.
Professor Low, a medical anthropologist, describes the professional, popular, and folk medicine sectors in San José and how patients perceive and use them.

343 **Health care in Costa Rica: boom and crisis.**
Carmelo Mesa-Lago. *Social Science and Medicine*, vol. 21, no. 1 (1985), p. 13-21. bibliog.
In the 1960-80 period Costa Rica's advances in health care placed the country in the second position in Latin America in overall health care. But the fivefold increase in costs and the economic crisis of the 1980s endangered the progress made. In this article Mesa-Lago provides data and analysis to explain the boom and crisis. The article is divided into five sections: the first outlines the historical development of health care; the second provides statistical data on the extent of population coverage; the third analyses the financial aspects of health care; the fourth describes regional differences; and the last deals with Costa Rica's response to rising health costs. In the conclusion, Meso-Lago offers suggestions of his own on further adjustments that should be made to maintain Costa Rica's leadership position.

344 **Salud: puente para la paz.** (Health: bridge for peace.)
Edgar Mohs. San José: Libro Libre, 1986. 208p.
As paediatrician, director of the Children's Hospital in San José, Vice-minister of Health, and finally as Minister of Health, Mohs has regularly commented on Costa Rica's public health system and its role in the promotion of peace and prosperity. This book collects his observations on science, public health, and social security which he made in a newspaper column from 1978 to 1985.

345 **Health without wealth? Costa Rica's health system under economic crisis.**
Lynn M. Morgan. *Journal of Public Health Policy*, vol. 8, no. 1 (Spring 1987), p. 86-105. bibliog.
After carefully surveying the advances made by Costa Rica in satisfying the health care needs of its population, Morgan addresses the cutbacks forced on Costa Rica's health administrators by the economic crisis of the 1980s. Her contention that the economic crisis severely affected health care is supported by statistics on disease, nutrition, health expenditures, infant mortality, outpatient consultations, and on other related matters. In addition to the statistical material Morgan provides a discussion of Costa Rica's dependence on outside financial support for health care and an excellent summary of the political debate over health policy.

346 **International politics and primary health care in Costa Rica.**
Lynn M. Morgan. *Social Science and Medicine*, vol. 30, no. 2 (1990), p. 211-19. bibliog.
Costa Rica's excellent reputation for providing primary health care in the last two decades is deserved, writes Morgan, but there is one area of failure. Despite beginning a highly publicized programme in 1978 to enhance community participation in health, Costa Rica abandoned the effort four years later after the election of Luis Alberto

Monge. The primary explanation for the programme's failure is, according to Morgan, that pressures for community participation came from outside Costa Rica, principally from the international agencies, and not from within. She also discusses other causes: partisan politics, a threat to political stability, economic recession, and policy shifts by international agencies. In effect, community participation was abandoned because it offered hope for more rapid change than the political élite was prepared to accept.

347 **Las luchas por el seguro social en Costa Rica.** (The fight for social security in Costa Rica.)
Mark B. Rosenberg. San José: Editorial Costa Rica, 1980. 211p.

Professor Rosenberg, a political scientist, offers a political analysis of the origin and expansion of the Costa Rican social security system, one of the most comprehensive in Latin America. The book focuses on the efforts of the Calderón Guardia administration (1940-44) to establish the system and the efforts of later administrations to expand it. Support for social security came from élite political groups, although workers were supposed to be the principal beneficiaries. For an English-language version one could consult his PhD dissertation, completed in 1976 at the University of Pittsburgh (available from University Microfilms, Ann Arbor, Michigan, order no. BGK77-13033).

348 **Social reform in Costa Rica: social security and the presidency of Rafael Angel Calderón.**
Mark B. Rosenberg. *Hispanic American Historical Review*, vol. 61, no. 2 (May 1981), p. 278-96.

In contrast to the generally held view that social security in Costa Rica was a result of popular demand, Rosenberg maintains that President Calderón Guardia inaugurated the programme largely on his own. Rosenberg points out that social security was instituted in 1942 with little planning and little popular support. Once he realized the need for support Calderón relied on the Catholic Church, labour unions, and the Communist Party to popularize the programme. Interviews, private correspondence, and government documents are the principal sources for Rosenberg's interpretation.

349 **Social security policymaking in Costa Rica: a research report.**
Mark B. Rosenberg. *Latin American Research Review*, vol. 14, no. 1 (1979), p. 116-33. bibliog.

This is a solid, succinct account of the development of the social security concept in Costa Rica, its legislative mandate in the 1960s, and the expansion of its coverage in the 1970s.

350 **Health aspects of the community development project, rural area, Turrialba, Costa Rica, 1948-51.**
Nevin S. Scrimshaw (et al.). *American Journal of Tropical Medicine and Hygiene*, vol. 2, no. 4 (July 1953), p. 583-92.

This article covers the health aspects of a rural development project in the Turrialba area carried out in 1948-51. Data on social structure, leadership, diet, health conditions, and use of public health facilities by 140 families are included.

351 **Organization of medical sciences in Costa Rica: problems of an underdeveloped area.**
Frederick T. Wolf. Nashville, Tennessee: Graduate Center of Latin American Studies, Vanderbilt University, 1965. 6p.

The author, a biologist at Vanderbilt University, visited Costa Rica in 1961 and 1963 to gather information on the principal diseases, hospitals, mobile health clinics, laboratories, the Ministry of Health, associations of nurses and physicians, and the School of Medicine at the Universidad de Costa Rica. His report is accurate, readable, and succinct.

Plantas medicinales de Costa Rica y su folclore. (Medicinal plants of Costa Rica and their folklore.)
See item no. 285.

Popular medicine in Puntarenas, Costa Rica: urban and societal features.
See item no. 287.

Curanderismo tradicional del costarricense. (Traditional healing of Costa Rica.)
See item no. 288.

Los problemas económicos del desarrollo en Costa Rica. (Economic problems of development in Costa Rica.)
See item no. 487.

Dr. Moreno Cañas: a symbolic bridge to the demedicalization of healing.
See item no. 724.

Bibliografía costarricense de ciencias sociales, no. 2. (A Costa Rican social science bibliography, no. 2).
See item no. 743.

Human Rights

352 **La Declaración Universal de Derechos Humanos: comentarios y texto.**
(The Universal Declaration of Human Rights: comments and text.)
Asociación Costarricense Pro-Naciones Unidas. San José: Editorial
Juricentro, 1979. 216p. bibliog. (Colección Derechos del Hombre).
In celebration of the thirtieth anniversary of the Universal Declaration of Human
Rights, the Costa Rican association in favour of the United Nations asked prominent
Costa Rican citizens for their opinions. This book, which brings together their
comments, amply demonstrates Costa Rica's commitment to human rights.

353 **Libertades públicas en Costa Rica.** (Public liberties in Costa Rica.)
Rubén Hernández Valle. San José: Editorial Juricentro, 1980. 250p.
Beginning with a commentary on the theoretical basis for individual human rights,
Professor Hernández proceeds to analyse the constitutional and legal foundation for
these rights in Costa Rica.

Politics

General

354 **Democracy in Costa Rica.**
Charles D. Ameringer. New York: Praeger, 1982. 138p. bibliog.
An essay touching on Costa Rican national character, political dynamics, and foreign relations, this is probably the best general explanation of the origins and character of Costa Rican democracy available in English. Although Ameringer treats the basic traditionally understood ingredients of Costa Rican democracy – education, isolation, and equal land distribution – the emphasis falls on the period since the revolution of 1948 and on the ability of Costa Rica's political system to modernize.

355 **Grupos de presión en Costa Rica.** (Pressure groups in Costa Rica.)
Oscar Arias Sánchez. San José: Editorial Costa Rica, 1980. 5th ed. 124p. bibliog.
The author, who became president of Costa Rica in 1986, submitted this work as his thesis for a licentiate degree in law. It was first published by the Editorial Costa Rica in 1971. The book is an impressionistic comparison of pressure groups in Costa Rica, the United States, England, and France, and contains little information about specific pressure groups.

356 **Quién gobierna en Costa Rica?: un estudio del liderazgo formal en Costa Rica.** (Who governs in Costa Rica?: a study of the formal leadership of Costa Rica.)
Oscar Arias Sánchez. San José: Editorial Universitaria Centroamericana, 1976. 378p. bibliog. (Colección Seis, Serie Mayor).
Formal leadership in this study means specifically all 461 cabinet ministers, legislators, and Supreme Court judges who served in Costa Rica from 1948 to 1974. The objective is to single out socio-economic characteristics of these leaders for the purpose of determining if any changes took place with respect to access to leadership. The author

concludes that, contrary to popular opinion, the middle and lower classes have had little success in breaking into the political élite. He also studies the career paths of the formal leadership. This study by Arias, who was elected president in 1986 on a campaign to strengthen democracy, was his doctoral dissertation in political science.

357 **Liberalismo: veinticinco años de ANFE.** (Liberalism: twenty-five years of ANFE.)
San José: Asociación Nacional de Fomento Económico (ANFE), 1984. 173p.

In commemoration of its 25th anniversary, ANFE collected for this volume the presidential addresses of its presidents (including Fernando Trejos Escalante, Fernando Guier, and Alberto di Mare) since its founding and a few additional speeches delivered on special occasions. The speeches of course reflect ANFE's ideal of political liberalism and a free society for Costa Ricans.

358 **Are Latin Americans politically rational?: citizen participation and democracy in Costa Rica.**
John A. Booth.   In: *Political participation in Latin America*, edited by John A. Booth, Mitchell A. Seligson. New York: Holmes & Meier, 1978, vol. 1, p. 88-113.

The traditional view is that the Third World masses are unlikely to follow rational patterns of political action. However, this study (in two volumes) of political activity in Costa Rica (including voting, consulting government officials, and involvement in community improvement associations), concludes that Costa Ricans of all classes, take action that they believe useful in pursuing their particular goals. In other words, they act rationally in the political arena.

359 **Democracy and citizen action in Costa Rica: the modes and correlates of popular participation in politics.**
John A. Booth.   PhD dissertation, University of Texas, Austin, 1975. 467p. (Available from University Microfilms, Ann Arbor, Michigan, order no. 75-25,011).

Democracy and citizen participation in politics are the two central themes of this dissertation. After a thorough discussion of the theory of democracy and of the historical background of the Costa Rican political system the author presents the results of his investigation of the political activities of 1,446 randomly selected heads of families in Costa Rica. The data were collected in 1973 by means of interviews. Seventeen types of political activity, such as voting and serving as a member of a civic organization, were identified. The usefulness of the study is enhanced by frequent comparisons with political participation data from other countries. Booth's conclusions concerning the breadth and depth of democracy in Costa Rica are positive.

360 **Structure and levels of political participation in Costa Rica: comparing peasants with city dwellers.**
John A. Booth, Mitchell A. Seligson. In: *Political participation in Latin America,* vol. 2, *Politics and the poor,* edited by John A. Booth, Mitchell A. Seligson. New York: Holmes and Meier, 1979, p. 62-75.

Defining political participation as actions that influence or attempt to influence the distribution of public goods, the authors explore the difference in the styles and levels of participations between urban dwellers and peasants in Costa Rica. In contrast to the generally held belief that peasants are less participatory, the authors find that in Costa Rica peasants are more active than urban dwellers in community project development and in education organizations. Urban dwellers, however, do vote more often and contact political officials more often. Data for this study were collected by questionnaires in 1972 and 1973.

361 **Costa Rica: free, honest elections with costly campaigns.**
George A. Bowdler, Patrick Cotter. In: *Voter participation in Central America, 1954-1981,* George A. Bowdler, Patrick Cotter. Washington, DC: University Press of America, 1982, p. 204-35.

Despite some organizational problems and some debatable historical interpretations this is a good overall view of Costa Rican political parties, political culture, the electoral system, presidential campaigns, voter turn-out, and recent elections. The introduction covers the religious, military, and economic background of Costa Rica and its relations with other countries. In the concluding section the authors make suggestions on the limiting of campaign expenditures.

362 **Costa Rica: a meaningful democracy.**
James L. Busey. In: *Political systems of Latin America,* edited by Martin C. Needler. New York: Van Nostrand Reinhold Company, 1967, 2nd ed., p. 113-28. maps. bibliog. (Van Nostrand Political Science Series).

An impressionistic account of the country's political history and system by a political scientist who specializes in Latin American government and politics. His impressions are overwhelmingly favourable. The article contains excellent brief descriptions of the constitution of 1949, political parties, the executive, the legislature, the judicial power, and the electoral system, but is weak on autonomous agencies.

363 **Foundations of political contrast: Costa Rica and Nicaragua.**
James L. Busey. *Western Political Quarterly,* vol. 11, no. 3 (Sept. 1958), p. 627-59.

Hampered by the paucity of research on the political systems of Costa Rica and Nicaragua in the 1950s, Busey nevertheless contributes a pioneering study of factors favouring democracy in Costa Rica and discouraging it in Nicaragua. He discusses fundamental causal factors such as history, ethnic homogeneity, natural resources, topography, and climate as well as immediate factors such as education, literacy, and land distribution.

364 Notes on Costa Rican democracy.
James L. Busey. Boulder, Colorado: University of Colorado Press, 1962. 84p. map. bibliog. (University of Colorado Studies, Series in Political Science, no. 2).

In seeking to explain Costa Rica's unusually successful democratic system of government Professor Busey, a political scientist, takes a conventional approach. He describes the political landscape in the first part of the book: constitution, executive power, political parties, elections, and the legislative assembly. In the second part, called 'Causal Elements', he relates social and economic history and land distribution to the political system.

365 The presidents of Costa Rica.
James L. Busey. *The Americas*, vol. 18, no. 1 (July 1961), p. 55-70.

Although stressing the absence of military presidents and the strength of the democratic transition, the author, in this synthesis of Costa Rican presidents, doubts whether Costa Rica is 'the idyllic utopia . . . that some have imagined'.

366 Actitudes políticas del costarricense: análisis de opinión de dirigentes y partidarios. (The political attitudes of Costa Ricans: an analysis of the opinions of leaders and partisans.)
Mario Carvajal Herrera. San José: Editorial Costa Rica, 1978. 330p. bibliog.

To the surprise of the author and many others who admire the flexibility of the Costa Rican political system this study shows that the Costa Rican electorate is rather apathetic toward political change. By means of questionnaires submitted in 1972 to leaders of political parties, pressure groups, and the Catholic Church, and to political party followers, Carvajal uncovers the hostility to change. He believes that the tendency for the Costa Rican electorate to favour the exchange of one party for another every four years, paradoxically also inhibits change because the incumbent government has too little time to effect structural change. The background of Costa Rica's elections, 1953 to 1974, is adequately explained. The present study is a translation and expansion of the author's doctoral dissertation in political science at the University of Kansas. It is available in English from University Microfilms, Ann Arbor, Michigan, order no. 73-11,862.

367 Políticas de crecimiento urbano: la experiencia de Costa Rica. (The politics of urban growth: the experience of Costa Rica.)
Edited by Manuel J. Carvajal. San José: Dirección General de Estadísticas y Censos, 1977. 288p. maps. bibliogs.

As a result of a grant from the Tinker Foundation a team of Costa Rican and North American scholars undertook this impressive study of urban growth in Costa Rica. The interdisciplinary approach produces large quantities of statistical data and analysis of topics that affect urbanization: infrastructure (particularly transportation and power), industrial and agricultural production, land and housing markets, and public policies. Furthermore, the roles of specific interest groups such as chambers of commerce receive treatment. Surprisingly little information, however, is offered on specific cities.

368 **La elección de un presidente: Costa Rica, 1978-1982.** (The election of a President: Costa Rica, 1978-82.)
Charles F. Denton, Olda María Acuña B. San José: Ministerio de Cultura, Juventud y Deportes, Instituto del Libro, 1984. 142p. bibliog.

The period covered in this book is primarily 1978-82, with some material on the period following the election of Luis Alberto Monge to the presidency of Costa Rica in 1982. Rather than an analysis of Monge's candidacy *per se*, the book traces the changing public opinion of Costa Ricans leading to Monge's election. The authors are president and executive director of a public polling firm; they administered over sixty opinion polls between 1978 and 1982. Concluding statements centre on the political culture of Costa Rican citizens.

369 **Patterns of Costa Rican politics.**
Charles F. Denton. Boston, Massachusetts: Allyn and Bacon, 1971. 113p. bibliog. (Allyn and Bacon Series in Latin American Politics).

Research during 1967-68 while on a Fulbright-Hays Fellowship led to the preparation of this book. Consciously following what the author calls a 'pan-disciplinarian' approach, Professor Denton describes the economic environment, class structure, and social mobilization, and follows with a description of political institutions, the political party system, and voting behaviour. Public interest groups and other institutions such as the Catholic Church are discussed.

370 **Power structure and its communication behavior in San José, Costa Rica.**
Harold T. Edwards. *Journal of Inter-American Studies*, vol. 9, no. 2 (April 1967), p. 236-47.

The intent of this article is to test the 'reputational' method of determining community power in a cross-cultural context. The results show two separate power groups in San José with some intercommunication. These cliques corresponded to political affiliation and to some extent professional and economic interests. The methodology and analysis is similar to that of David E. W. Holden's study of a rural community (q.v.).

371 **Elections and the election process in Costa Rica in 1986.**
William L. Furlong. *Universities Field Staff International Reports, Latin America*, no. 12 (1986), p. 1-9.

Written just after the victory of Oscar Arias over Rafael Calderón Guardia, Jr in the election of 2 February 1986, this article is a straightforward description of the electoral system and the election itself. It covers minor parties, campaign styles, issues, and results, and focuses heavily on the presidential campaign rather than on the legislative or municipal campaigns. It successfully captures the special flavour of the Costa Rican elections as a 'civic fiesta', and it fully supports Costa Rica's reputation as Latin America's most developed democracy.

372 **Sons of the establishment: elite youth in Panama and Costa Rica.**
Daniel Goldrich. Chicago, Illinois: Rand McNally, 1966. 139p. map.
bibliog. (Studies in Political Change).

A study of the political attitudes of young people in élite high schools of Panama and
Costa Rica, based on questionnaires distributed in 1961 and 1963. Although the results
are not surprising it is useful to have solid documentation of the general faith of Costa
Ricans in their political system as compared to the lack of such faith in Panama.
Attitudes toward reform, violence, international business, and other countries are
among other subjects examined.

373 **Costa Rica.**
Lowell Gudmundson. In: *Latin America and Caribbean:*
contemporary record, edited by Jack W. Hopkins. New York: Holmes
and Meier, 1985. Vol. III, 1983-84, p. 496-515. map.

This article is one of a series of articles on Costa Rica focusing on the economic crisis,
the 'tug of war with the International Monetary Fund', and the efforts of Costa Rica to
maintain neutrality in 1984 as pressure from the Ronald Reagan administration
increased. The author also discusses developments in the presidential campaign of 1986
and an upheaval in the Costa Rican Communist party. A 'statistical profile' of the
country focusing on the 1980-82 years is included.

374 **Costa Rican interpretations of Costa Rican politics.**
Edward J. Heubel. *Latin American Research Review,* vol. 35, no. 2
(1990), p. 217-25.

In a bibliography of predominantly English-language titles this article, an extensive
commentary on five recent books in Spanish on Costa Rican politics, should be helpful.
Two of the books reviewed are by former President Oscar Arias and one is by
someone else on Arias' successful campaign for the presidency in 1986. The
commentary provides a good summary of Costa Rican political issues, foreign and
domestic, in the 1980s.

375 **Legislative–executive policy-making: the cases of Chile and Costa Rica.**
Steven W. Hughes, Kenneth J. Mijeski. Beverly Hills, California:
Sage Publications, [*c.*1973]. 59p. bibliog. (Comparative Legislative
Studies Series).

In this attempt to assess the roles of the executive and legislative branches of
government in Chile and Costa Rica between 1958 and 1970 the authors examine how
legislation is initiated. Using several tests for dominance they conclude that in Costa
Rica the legislature rather than the executive is dominant in policy-making. Executive
dominance is the norm in most Latin American and Western European countries.

376 **Análisis electoral de una democracia: estudio del comportamiento político costarricense durante el período 1953-1974.** (The electoral analysis of a democracy: a study of Costa Rican political behaviour during 1953-74.)
Wilburg Jiménez Castro.   San José: Editorial Costa Rica, 1977. 43, [94]p. maps. bibliog.

A multiplicity of colourful maps, statistical charts, and graphic illustrations make this the most complete and most readily understood book on Costa Rican elections. The book, which is of folio size, is a political atlas containing forty-three pages of narrative and fifty-one pages of maps and charts. It is not a study of the issues or the political positions of the candidates. It is, rather, a compilation of data on registered voters, ballots cast, abstention and the like from the six elections – for the presidency, the National Assembly, and municipal offices – held between 1953 and 1974, as well as an account of Costa Rica's electoral tribunal system.

377 **The Costa Rican election of 1953: a case study.**
Harry Kantor.   Gainesville, Florida: University of Florida Press, 1958. 68p. bibliog. (Latin American Monograph Series, no. 5).

Professor Kantor's study is a straightforward political analysis of the election of 1953 with chapters on political development before 1953, the structure of government, the electoral system, and the election itself. The focus is on the candidates José Figueres and Fernando Castro and their campaigns rather than on regional or class origins of voters.

378 **Costa Rican electoral trends, 1953-1966.**
John D. Martz.   *Western Political Quarterly*, vol. 20, no. 4 (Dec. 1967), p. 888-909.

This article is one of the first analyses, in English, of Costa Rican election trends. It contains a discussion of constitutionally established election procedures, a survey of Costa Rican politics, a description of the country's political parties, and an analysis of the elections of 1953, 1958, 1962, and 1966. National Assembly, municipal, and presidential elections are covered. Analysis of the strengths and weaknesses of the National Liberation Party is particularly well done.

379 **Presidential power in Latin American politics.**
Kenneth J. Mijeski.   In: *Costa Rica: the shrinking of the presidency*, edited by Thomas V. DiBacco. New York: Praeger, 1977, p. 56-71. bibliog. (Praeger Special Studies in International Politics and Government).

Mijeski's essay on the Costa Rican presidency provides a summary of the historical and constitutional background of the Costa Rican tendency to limit executive powers. There are short sections on the autonomous agencies, described as Costa Rica's fourth branch of government, and on the National Assembly. Subsequent sections treat the presidencies of Mario Echandi, José Figueres, and Daniel Oduber. Ironically, as Mijeski points out, Figueres, who was largely responsible for the constitution of 1949, carried sufficient prestige and flamboyant style to overcome some of the limitations on the presidency.

380 **De Sandino a Stalin: recuerdos de Eduardo Mora Valverde.** (From
Sandino to Stalin: memoirs of Eduardo Mora Valverde.)
Eduardo Mora Valverde. San José: Editorial Revolución, 1988. 149p.
For an understanding of the peculiarities of the Communist Party of Costa Rica and for
a glimpse at the personal side of its leaders this book serves very well. As the younger
brother of Manuel Mora Valverde, who founded the Communist Party in 1931, and as
a lifelong member of the party himself, Eduardo Mora has been in a position to see at
first hand and from the beginning the party's successes and failures. What the book
lacks in organization is compensated for by the candid and offhand appraisal of Costa
Rican politics from the 1930s to the 1950s. A word of caution: to follow Mora's
personal story one needs a grasp of the basic facts of Costa Rican history.

381 **Discursos: 1934-1979.** (Speeches: 1934-79.)
Manuel Mora Valverde. San José: Editorial Presbere, 1980. 741p.
For an understanding of the role played by the Communist Party of Costa Rica in the
history of Costa Rica this collection of speeches by Manuel Mora Valverde is
indispensable. Mora founded the party in 1931 and served as secretary-general for fifty
years; he also frequently served as a deputy in the National Assembly. The speeches
collected here cover foreign relations, Church–state relations, and a host of topics
relative to political conflicts, social conditions, and labour in Costa Rica. Gilberto
Calvo and Francisco Zúniga Díaz deserve credit for selecting, editing, and introducing
the political context of the speeches.

382 **Voices from Costa Rica.**
Andrew Reding. *World Policy Journal*, vol. 3, no. 2 (Spring 1986),
p. 317-45.
In interviews with three former Costa Rican presidents (José Figueres, Daniel Oduber,
and Rodrigo Carazo) and with Javier Solís, the last a member of a leftist political
coalition known as the People United, Reding probes Costa Rican opinion on several
issues: reasons for the country's democratic development; Costa Rican resistance to
pressures from the Ronald Reagan administration to strengthen the military and to
support the Contras; and the Costa Rican response to the economic crisis. Comments
on the founding of the University for Peace, which is headed by Carazo, and on
pressures from the International Monetary Fund (IMF) and the United States Agency
for International Development (USAID) to adopt unpopular economic measures
round out the interviews.

383 **Thinking about Costa Rica's political future: a comment.**
Mark B. Rosenberg. *Inter-American Economic Affairs*, vol. 31, no. 1
(Summer 1977), p. 89-94.
In November 1976 an open symposium on Costa Rica's political future was held and
the principal paper was delivered by Oscar Arias Sánchez who was then Minister of
National Planning and who took office as President in May 1986. Rosenberg, a political
scientist, questions in this brief analysis the possibility of realizing Arias' two main
goals, namely, increasing citizen participation in politics and decentralization of the
state.

384 **Costa Rica.**
Mitchell A. Seligson. In: *Latin America and Caribbean Contemporary Record*, edited by Jack W. Hopkins. New York: Holmes and Meier, 1983- . Vol. I, 1981-82, p. 399-408. map. bibliog.

This article takes a rather alarming look at Costa Rica's economic and political crisis. The author focuses on terrorism and the economic crisis, predicting either a profound reshaping of the social welfare system in Costa Rica or, in the worst instance, 'the end of democratic rule'. Seligson's perspective is, in a sense, a photograph of the attitude of many observers during the peak of the economic crisis in 1982. Coverage of the important political and economic events of the year is very useful in orienting analysts, students, and tourists to the mood of 1982. Nevertheless, hindsight tells us that the excitement of a crisis sometimes leads to exaggeration. Readers should look at succeeding volumes of the Latin American and Caribbean series (three more appear in the bibliography: q.v.) for later views.

385 **Costa Rica.**
Mitchell A. Seligson. In: *Latin America and Caribbean Contemporary Record*, edited by Jack W. Hopkins. New York: Holmes and Meier, 1983- . Vol. II, 1982-83, p. 460-74.

Seligson covers the economic crisis, neutrality in the face of United States conflict with Nicaragua, terrorism, and the then newly elected President Luis Alberto Monge's strategy to combat these problems. Statistics on price indexes, unemployment, and other economic indicators are included. While not as alarmist as his article in Vol. I of the present series (q.v.), the article presents a very bleak economic and social picture of 1983.

386 **Costa Rica and Jamaica.**
Mitchell A. Seligson. In: *Competitive elections in developing countries*, edited by Myron Weiner, Ergun Özbudun. Durham, North Carolina: Duke University Press, 1987, p. 147-98.

Costa Rica and Jamaica are generally considered, according to scholarly standards, to be exceptionally democratic. Yet both are small, highly dependent on foreign trade, and not highly developed economically, all characteristics which, according to political theories of democracy, presuppose them toward authoritarianism rather than democracy. Seligson attempts to explain why Costa Rica and Jamaica are exceptions. In his explanation of Costa Rica's case he focuses on the absence of large estates and labour exploitation in the colonial period, the early establishment of an electoral system, and post-1948 origins of a modern political party system.

387 **Democratic stability and economic crisis: Costa Rica, 1978-1983.**
Mitchell A. Seligson, Edward N. Muller. *International Studies Quarterly*, vol. 31, no. 3 (Sept. 1987), p. 301-26. bibliog.

This very important article partially explains how Costa Rica's democratic political system survived the economic crisis of the early 1980s. The principal purpose of the article is to test the hypothesis of Seymour M. Lipset that effectiveness and legitimacy are better indicators of a political system's survivability than economic crises. Using the results of surveys conducted in 1978-79 in Costa Rica and other countries the authors establish that Costa Ricans have a high level of faith in their government. Follow-up surveys conducted in 1980 and 1983, during the economic crisis, indicated that although Costa Ricans turned against political leadership, they maintained their support for the political system. High-quality analysis is shown in the discussion of the economic situation, in the surveys and in the tabular display of survey results, and in the discussion of the study's place in the academic literature.

388 **Development and participation in Costa Rica: the impact of context.**
Mitchell A. Seligson. In: *Political participation in Latin America*, edited by John A. Booth, Mitchell A. Seligson. New York: Holmes and Meier, 1978-79, vol. 1, p. 145-53. bibliog.

In this two-volume work and using data he gathered in 1972-73 in addition to the national census figures of 1973, the author analyses political participation among male peasants in different communities at four levels of development. He concludes, to his surprise, that in Costa Rica the level of political participation is actually higher in less-developed communities than it is in areas with a higher standard of living. Contributions to volume 2 are also listed in this bibliography (q.v.).

389 **Ordinary elections in extraordinary times: the political economy of voting in Costa Rica.**
Mitchell A. Seligson, Miguel Gómez B. In: *Elections and democracy in Central America*, edited by John A. Booth, Mitchell A. Seligson. Chapel Hill, North Carolina: University of North Carolina Press, 1989, p. 158-84. bibliog.

After discussing the theoretical political science literature on the political effects of economic crisis, Seligson and Gómez focus on Costa Rica. Specifically, their purpose is to explore the impact of the economic crisis of the early 1930s on the voting behaviour of Costa Ricans. Ordinarily, voters choose extremist parties in times of economic crises; the authors show that this did not happen in Costa Rica. Other expected voting behaviour, according to conventional theory, would be for sharp shifts in political party alignment to occur or for abstention to rise. Neither of these occurred. On the basis of interviews of voters in 1978 and 1985 Seligson and Gómez speculate on the reason for Costa Rica's deviation from the norm.

390 **Trust, efficacy, and modes of political participation: a study of Costa Rican peasants.**
Mitchell A. Seligson. *British Journal of Political Science*, vol. 10, no. 1 (Jan. 1980), p. 75-98.

Seligson criticizes political participation studies because they tend mistakenly to conclude that citizens who place their trust in government do not also engage in protest actions. The results of his survey of 531 adult male peasants in 1972-73 lead Seligson to conclude that Costa Rican peasants frequently vote, participate in community projects, demand government services, and they also occasionally strike or engage in land invasions. The study is an aid to understanding the importance of attitudes in predicting the full range of political participation.

391 **Unconventional political participation: cynicism, powerlessness, and the Latin American peasant.**
Mitchell A. Seligson. In: *Political participation in Latin America*, edited by John A. Booth, Mitchell A. Seligson. New York: Holmes and Meier, 1978, vol. 2, p. 134-46.

A survey of three types of Costa Rican peasants (squatters, small-holders, and landless) reveals that small-holders generally trust government agencies and are efficacious in attaining government services, while landless peasants generally feel powerless and cynical about government. Squatters, however, tend to have higher levels of cynicism and efficacy than the other two peasant types. The survey was carried out in late 1972 and early 1973.

392 **Community power brokers and national political parties in rural Costa Rica.**
James Sewastynowicz. *Anthropological Quarterly*, vol. 56, no. 3 (July 1983), p. 107-15.

In this political-anthropological study the author emphasizes the positive aspects of the activities of power brokers in small towns in Costa Rica. Power brokers, typically merchants, serve as mediators between the national government in San José and local community interests. Through their influence they deliver votes for national candidates and economic benefits to their community. Fieldwork for this study was done in Pejivalle in 1976 and 1977.

393 **Estado empresario y lucha política en Costa Rica.** (The state as entrepreneur and the political struggle in Costa Rica.)
Ana Sojo. San José: Editorial Universitaria Centroamericana, 1984. 287p. bibliog.

After a chapter on Karl Marx's theory of the state, this book reviews the historical relationship between the state and private enterprise and then focuses sharply on the policies of the presidential administrations of José Figueres and Daniel Oduber (1970-78). The thesis is that, through the ideology of the ruling National Liberation Party and certain provisions of the Constitution of 1949, autonomous agencies have become so powerful as to create a state bourgeoisie under a system of state capitalism. Several autonomous agencies, including the Costa Rican Development Corporation and the Costa Rican Petroleum Refinery, are examined in detail.

394 **Costa Rican election factbook, February 6, 1966.**
Paul G. Stephenson. Washington, DC: Institute for the Comparative Study of Political Systems, 1965. 44p.

Prepared specifically for the Costa Rican elections of 6 February 1966, this booklet is a model guide for election observers. It contains a brief historical introduction, an explanation of the electoral system, biographical sketches of all important political figures, sketches of the political parties, a guide to the principal issues, and electoral statistics for the three previous elections. A supplement was published by the same publisher in 1969 (*Costa Rica: election factbook*, no. 2) for the elections of 1 February 1970 but unfortunately none has been published since.

395 **Social characteristics of Costa Rican decision makers.**
Dorothy M. Stetson. *Journal of Politics*, vol. 31, no. 3 (Aug. 1969),
p. 799-803.
The author interviewed twenty-eight deputies of the National Assembly, thirty-two
civil servants, and twenty directors of autonomous agencies with a view to determining
common social characteristics. Among other interesting facts concerning their age and
backgrounds she found that as a group the decision-makers were well educated and
well travelled.

396 **Costa Rica's political turmoil: can production support the welfare state?**
Samuel Z. Stone. *Caribbean Review*, vol. 10, no. 1 (Winter 1981),
p. 42-6.
The main purpose of this article is to explain the difficulties that Costa Rican political
leaders have had in maintaining a growing bureaucracy and a welfare state and at the
same time satisfying the demands of increasingly strident interest groups, labour
unions, the old coffee élite, and the new industrialists. The author, a sociologist, uses
economic and political data to account for social class divisions, and offers an
interpretation of the historical differences between Costa Rica and the other Central
American countries. He also provides an analysis of the effects of the Sandinista
revolution of 1979 on Costa Rican internal politics and international relations.

397 **Costa Rica.**
Robert D. Tomasek. In: *Political forces in Latin America: dimensions
of the quest for stability*, edited by Ben G. Burnett, Kenneth F.
Johnson. Belmont, California: Wadsworth, 1970, 2nd ed., p. 91-114.
maps. bibliog.
The present article provides a sharp focus on Costa Rica's political parties, the political
party system, the electoral process, the presidency, and political personalities of the
decades of the 1950s and 1960s. It is an excellent discussion of the uniqueness of Costa
Rica's political system.

398 **Costa Rica: crisis y desafíos.** (Costa Rica: crisis and challenges.)
Edelberto Torres Rivas (et al.). San José: Departamento Ecuménico
de Investigaciones, 1987. 219p.
Crisis – that much used word in Costa Rica in the 1980s – in this case means primarily a
political and moral crisis. Such is the principal unifying perception of the nineteen
social scientists, labour union leaders, political analysts, and others who attended a
three-day conference in San José in February 1987. The perceived failure of the Costa
Rican political system to halt the widening gap between the rich and the poor and the
failure of the Central American republics to resolve their international differences
appeared to concern the delegates the most, although attention was given also to the
problem of international indebtedness.

Politics. General

399 The 1970 election in Costa Rica.
Henry Wells. *World Affairs*, vol. 133, no. 1 (June 1970), p. 13-28.

A straightforward political analysis of the election of 1970 in Costa Rica. The National Liberation Party won the election at all three levels: presidential, assembly, and municipal, thus continuing a trend of alternation of political power. Results at all levels are discussed. The victory of José Figueres and his party is explained from the perspective of personality, campaign strategy and tactics, and party organization.

400 Costa Rica: problems of social democracy.
Robert G. Wesson. In: *Politics, policies and economic development in Latin America*, edited by Robert Wesson. Stanford, California: Hoover Institution Press, 1985, p. 213-35.

This article has a twofold appeal. First, it is an exceptionally clear statement of the political-economic model which has evolved in Costa Rica since the 1940s. Wesson interprets it as a social democracy, a creation of the National Liberation Party and José Figueres which brought many benefits to Costa Rica. Second, the article clearly describes the economic crisis which befell Costa Rica in the late 1970s and early 1980s. Wesson's interpretation is summed up by his statement: 'the political strategy of jobs for many and benefits for all ran out when the public sector became too big and too inefficient and corrupt for the private sector to support it'.

401 One road to democracy with development: José Figueres and the social democratic project after 1948.
Anthony Winson. In: *Central America: democracy, development and change*, edited by John M. Kirk, George W. Schuyler. New York: Praeger, 1984. p. 89-100.

In this succinct, reflective article which attempts to account for Costa Rica's successful transition from a liberal oligarchy to liberal democratic politics similar to that of the advanced capitalist countries, Winson gives much of the credit to President José Figueres. His explanation covers the founding of the National Liberation Party, the decision to outlaw the Communist Party, and the growth of state power, particularly the nationalization of banking and the power industry.

402 What price political stability? The 1966 presidential campaign in Costa Rica.
John Yochelson. *Public and International Affairs*, vol. 5, no. 1 (Spring 1967), p. 278-307.

A thorough examination of the 1966 presidential election. The article considers in depth the strengths and weaknesses of the competing political parties (National Unification and National Liberation) and their respective candidates (José Joaquín Trejos and Daniel Oduber) and suggests that Trejos' narrow victory damaged both political parties and weakened Costa Rica's political system. Interviews with leading politicians were the principal source of information.

403 **Democracia en Costa Rica?: cinco opiniones polémicas.** (Democracy in Costa Rica?: five polemical opinions.)
Edited by Chester Zelaya. San José: Editorial Universidad Estatal a Distancia, 1983. 2nd revd. ed. 260p. bibliogs. (Serie Estudios Sociopolíticos, no. 1).

In 1977 the hour had apparently arrived when Costa Rican scholars grew tired of foreign analyses of their political system and decided to do it themselves. The result is a stimulating interdisciplinary debate among five of Costa Rica's best-known scholars on the origins and nature of Costa Rican democracy. Chester Zelaya (historian) cites evidence that local and foreign observers alike considered Costa Rica democratic as early as the 1830s. Oscar Aguilar Bulgarelli (historian) traces the evolution of the practice of democracy from the colonial period to contemporary times. Daniel Camacho (sociologist) doubts the strength of democracy in Costa Rica, pointing out that Costa Rica has had its autocrats as well as its democrats. Rodolfo Cerdas Cruz (sociologist) also takes a semi-negative view, claiming that democracy in Costa Rica is really liberal democracy, which, he says, has its limitations. Jacobo Schifter (political scientist) argues that Costa Rica became democratic after 1948 by chance, not because of the strength of democratic ideas but because other opposing forces neutralized each other. Each chapter has a separate bibliography. The first edition was published in 1977 by the same publisher; the second edition contains revisions in two of the five presentations.

Political parties

404 **Democracia y partidos políticos en Costa Rica, 1950-1962.** (Democracy and political parties in Costa Rica, 1950-62.)
Oscar R. Aguilar Bulgarelli. San José: Litografía e Imprenta LIL, 1977. 175p. bibliog.

In this purely political analysis the author tends to minimize the ideological foundation of Costa Rican political parties. Instead, he emphasizes that in the years 1950-62 politics centred on the National Liberation Party headed by José Figueres and on opposition to that party with a corresponding minimum of ideological controversy. The second half of the book contains material on the National Liberation Party from the personal archive of Jorge Rossi, one of the Party's leaders in the 1950s. A second edition was published in San José by Universidad Estatal a Distancia in 1981.

405 **Liberación Nacional en las historia política de Costa Rica, 1940-1980.** (National Liberation in the political history of Costa Rica, 1940-80.)
Carlos Araya Pochet. San José: Editorial Nacional de Textos, 1982. 219p. bibliog.

A synthesis of the history of the National Liberation Party, with a chapter on its origins, a chapter on its activities in the 1970s, and four chapters detailing diverse aspects of the party in the 1950s and 1960s. The focus is on the institutionalization of the party rather than on personalities. The book is a revision of the author's 1968 thesis in history at the University of Costa Rica, first published in 1969 by the Editorial Costa Rica.

406 **Crisis de 1929 y la fundación del Partido Comunista en Costa Rica.** (The crisis of 1929 and the founding of the Communist Party in Costa Rica.) Ana María Botey, Rodolfo Cisneros. San José: Editorial Costa Rica, 1984. 146p. bibliog.

A documented, Marxist approach to the origins of the Communist Party in Costa Rica. More than half the book is introductory, covering the capitalist structure of the economy before 1930 and pioneering workers' movements. The third chapter describes the effects of the economic crisis of 1929 on Costa Rica, and the fourth and last chapter explains the origins of the Communist Party.

407 **Análisis de la trayectoria electoral de Costa Rica: 1953-1970.** (Analysis of the electoral trajectory of Costa Rica: 1953-70.) Mario Carvajal Herrera. *Revista de la Universidad de Costa Rica*, no. 32 (Dec. 1971), p. 31-43.

A handy guide to the five Costa Rican elections between 1953 and 1970. The author, a political scientist and prominent member of the National Liberation Party, comments on the electoral process, political parties, the democratic tradition, and the increasing percentage of voters.

408 **Liberación Nacional in Costa Rica: the development of a political party in a transitional society.** Burt H. English. Gainesville, Florida: University of Florida Press, 1971. 185p. bibliog. (Latin American Monographs, 2nd series, no. 8).

This scholarly monograph contains a succinct account of the rise of the National Liberation Party, which the author considers 'the oldest, best organized, [and] most viable modern party' in Central America. It also provides a description of the party's ideology and an analysis of its electoral strength in the presidential and congressional elections of 1953, 1958, 1962, and 1966.

409 **Experience of the Communists in Costa Rica.** Francisco Espinosa. *World Marxist Review*, vol. 6, no. 7 (July 1963), p. 40-2.

In this article Francisco Espinosa, a member of Costa Rica's People's Vanguard (Communist) Party, provides a short history of the position of Costa Rican communists on events and issues in the 1931-63 period. The article is especially helpful in explaining positions taken by the People's Vanguard Party toward the Rafael Calderón Guardia and José Figueres administrations.

410 **Costa Rica: conditions for revolution.** Eduardo Mora Valverde. *World Marxist Review*, vol. 23, no. 10 (Oct. 1980), p. 23-5.

Mora, Deputy General Secretary of the People's Vanguard (Communist) Party of Costa Rica, reports in this article on the thirteenth congress of his party, held in June 1980. The party reaffirmed its allegiance to the Soviet Union, its hostility to the

People's Republic of China, and its adherence to the policy of a successful Communist revolution in Costa Rica without recourse to violence.

411 **Costa Rica, Honduras, and Panama.**
Neale J. Pearson. In: *Communism in Central America and the Caribbean*, edited by Robert G. Wesson. Stanford, California: Hoover Institution Press, 1982, p. 94-116.

This article briefly reviews the origins of the Communist Party in Costa Rica, its participation (as the People's Vanguard Party) in government in the 1940s, and its role in political opposition after the revolution of 1948. Communist-affiliated trade unions are discussed. Pearson also offers a summary of Costa Rica's diplomatic relations with the Soviet Union, Cuba, and other Marxist countries.

412 **Acción Democrática, orígenes del Partido Liberación Nacional: de León Cortés a José Figueres.** (Democratic Action, origins of the National Liberation Party: from León Cortés to José Figueres.)
Jorge Enrique Romero Pérez. San José: Editorial Nueva Década, 1983. 244p. bibliog.

Although lacking a disciplinary perspective and a clear organization, this book provides information about individuals and groups which were involved in the formation of Acción Democrática during the Cortés presidency (1936-40). One can trace the evolution of this progressive political grouping to the creation of the National Liberation Party through the speeches and writings of its leaders and position papers of various sections of the party. Such internal evidence is the raw material for this book.

413 **La enfermedad de la izquierda costarricense.** (The sickness of the Costa Rican left.)
Patricia Vega. *Aportes*, vol. 4, no. 18 (March-April 1984), p. 4-13.

By means of interviews with the principal leftist political figures Patricia Vega focuses attention on various schisms and conflicts which weakened the political left in 1983-84.

414 **La crisis de los partidos políticos tradicionales de Costa Rica.** (The crisis of the traditional political parties of Costa Rica.)
José Luis Vega Carballo. [San José]: Ediciones Academia Costarricense de Bibliografía, 1978. 25p.

The author argues that several studies of Costa Rican political parties are unsatisfactory because they fail to take into account the social class origins of these parties.

Ideology

415 **Las ideas políticas en Costa Rica.** (Political ideas in Costa Rica.)
Luis Barahona Jiménez. San José: Departamento de Publicaciones,
Ministerio de Educación Pública, 1977. 453p.

This is a greatly enlarged and revised edition of the author's *El pensamiento político en Costa Rica* which was published in 1972. After early chapters on the colonial and independence periods, the author organizes the main part of the book according to specific political figures and their political ideas. These figures are grouped under such headings as Catholic anti-liberalism, positivism, anarchism, liberalism, reformism, social democracy, and socialism. In the second half of the book excerpts from the major political thinkers have been selected for an anthology of Costa Rican political thought. The author is considered to be the founder of the Christian Democratic Party in Costa Rica.

416 **The social democratic ideology in Latin America: the case of Costa
Rica's Partido Liberación Nacional.**
Susanne Bodenheimer. *Caribbean Studies*, vol. 10, no. 3 (Oct. 1970),
p. 49-96. bibliog.

Because of its thoroughness and its closely reasoned class analysis this article is a very important contribution to an understanding of the National Liberation Party. Although focused primarily on ideology it covers the party's origins, personal rivalries, and its actions on specific issues once in office. True to the title, it also covers the Party's relation to comparable social democratic parties in Latin America. This article was translated into Spanish and published as a booklet by Editorial EDUCA (San José) in 1984.

417 **Ricardo Jiménez Oreamuno, "su pensamiento."** (Ricardo Jiménez
Oreamuno, 'his thought'.)
Ricardo Jiménez Oreamuno, selected and edited by Eugenio Rodríguez
Vega. San José: Editorial Costa Rica, 1980. 459p. bibliog. (Biblioteca
Patria, no. 17).

Having been president of Costa Rica three times (1906-10, 1924-28, 1932-36) during the liberal era of Costa Rican politics, Ricardo Jiménez Oreamuno is deservedly named 'a typical Costa Rican liberal' by Eugenio Rodríguez, who edited this volume and prepared the bibliography. Rodríguez organizes Jiménez' writings under six categories: major writings, other works, presidential messages, declarations to the press, letters, and literary writings. Altogether the volume collects commentary, mainly political, on practically every issue raised on the Costa Rican scene in the first half of the 20th century.

418 **Siete ensayos políticos: fuentes de la democracia social en Costa Rica.**
(Seven political essays: sources of social democracy in Costa Rica.)
Eugenio Rodríguez Vega. San José: Fundación Friedrich Ebert:
Centro de Estudios Democráticos de América Latina, 1982. 319p.
bibliog.

Most historians and political commentators think of Costa Rican social democracy as starting in the 1940s with the ideas of Rodrigo Facio or the revolution of 1948. Rodríguez, who defines social democracy as embracing the concepts of liberty, freedom, tolerance, civilism [that is, anti-militarism], and love of education, contributes to the history of ideas in Costa Rica by tracing the origins and evolution of these concepts in Costa Rica to 19th-century figures like Tomás Guardia. He follows up these ideas in essays on Alfredo González Flores, Jorge Volio, and Rodrigo Facio.

419 **La social democracia en Costa Rica.** (Social democracy in Costa Rica.)
Jorge Enrique Romero Pérez. San José: Editorial Universidad Estatal
a Distancia, 1982. 2nd ed. 326p. bibliog.

The focal point of this book is the thought of Rodrigo Facio, considered to be the intellectual creator of the Centre for the Study of National Problems in the 1940s and of the National Liberation Party. Facio died in 1961 at the age of 44. The Centre and the Party have been the organizations most clearly identified with social democracy in Costa Rica. Romero Pérez is a lawyer and sociologist. This work was first published in 1977.

420 **Ideas políticas elementales.** (Elementary political ideas.)
José Joaquín Trejos Fernández. San José: Libro Libre,
1985. 233p.

In this volume are gathered selected speeches by former President Trejos (1966-70). The first few touch on broad issues of democracy and development but the principal focus of the speeches given since 1970 is on issues of economic development in Costa Rica.

The Costa Ricans.
See item no. 6.

El desarrollo nacional en 150 años de vida independiente. (National development during 150 years of independence.)
See item no. 153.

Costa Rica: a democratic revolution.
See item no. 161.

Desarrollo de las ideas filosóficas en Costa Rica. (The development of philosophical ideas in Costa Rica.)
See item no. 167.

Costa Rica: moderate democratization of a civil oligarchy.
See item no. 171.

Política y reforma en Costa Rica, 1914-1958. (Politics and reform in Costa Rica, 1914-58.)
See item no. 173.

Orden y progreso, la formación del estado nacional en Costa Rica. (Order and progress, the formation of the national state in Costa Rica.)
See item no. 174.

Costa Rica y sus hechos políticos de 1948: problemática de una década. (Costa Rica and its political acts of 1948: problem of a decade.)
See item no. 198.

León Cortés y su época. (León Cortés and his era.)
See item no. 204.

Alfredo González Flores, estadista incomprendido. (Alfredo González Flores, a misunderstood statesman.)
See item no. 221.

Un siglo de política costarricense: crónica de 24 campañas presidenciales. (A century of Costa Rican politics: a chronicle of 24 presidential campaigns.)
See item no. 222.

Los Tinoco, 1917-1919. (The Tinocos, 1917-19.)
See item no. 223.

De Calderón a Figueres. (From Calderón to Figueres.)
See item no. 227.

La fase oculta de la guerra civil en Costa Rica. (The covert aspects of the civil war in Costa Rica.)
See item no. 232.

Presbítero doctor Francisco Calvo (Ganganelli): organizador de la masonería en Costa Rica. (The priest Francisco Calvo (Ganganelli): organizer of the freemasons in Costa Rica.)
See item no. 295.

The Catholic Church and politics in Nicaragua and Costa Rica.
See item no. 300.

Poder político y democracia en Costa Rica. (Political power and democracy in Costa Rica.)
See item no. 313.

Costa Rica: caught between two worlds.
See item no. 424.

Costa Rica: Gesellschaft und Kultur eines Staates mit ständiger aktiver und unbewaffneter Neutralität. (Costa Rica: the society and culture of a state practising active and unarmed neutrality.)
See item no. 434.

De nuestra historia patria: hechos militares y políticos. (Our country's history: military and political events.)
See item no. 450.

La Constitución de 1949: antecedentes y proyecciones. (The constitution of 1949: antecedents and projections.)
See item no. 452.

Estudio sobre las instituciones autónomas de Costa Rica. (A study of the autonomous institutions of Costa Rica.)
See item no. 460.

El poder ejecutivo en Costa Rica. (The executive power in Costa Rica.)
See item no. 465.

Bureaucratic politics and social policy: the emergence of Costa Rica's welfare state.
See item no. 466.

La clase política y el poder judicial en Costa Rica. (Politics and judicial power in Costa Rica.)
See item no. 467.

Obras de Rodrigo Facio. (The works of Rodrigo Facio.)
See item no. 474.

Fear of adjusting: the social costs of economic policies in the 1970s.
See item no. 476.

Costa Rica.
See item no. 477.

Nuevos rumbos para el desarrollo costarricense. (New directions for Costa Rican development.)
See item no. 486.

The limits of reform development in contemporary Costa Rica.
See item no. 489.

Costa Rica: two great assets and many problems.
See item no. 494.

Reforma agraria y poder político. (Agrarian reform and political power.)
See item no. 536.

Population growth, economic progress, and opportunities on the land: the case of Costa Rica.
See item no. 550.

Don Pepe: a political biography of José Figueres of Costa Rica.
See item no. 698.

La lucha sin fin: Costa Rica, una democracia que habla español. (The/battle without end: Costa Rica, a Spanish-speaking democracy.)
See item no. 702.

Figueres and Costa Rica: an unauthorized political biography.
See item no. 706.

Los presidentes. (The presidents.)
See item no. 707.

Rafael Yglesias Castro.
See item no. 708.

Alfredo Gonzalez Flores, "su pensamiento." (Alfredo González Flores, 'his thought'.)
See item no. 721.

Otilio Ulate and the traditional response to contemporary political change in Costa Rica.
See item no. 728.

Calderón Guardia.
See item no. 731.

Máximo Fernández.
See item no. 732.

Jorge Volio y el Partido Reformista. (Jorge Volio and the Reform Party.)
See item no. 736.

Foreign Relations

General

421 **The disturbing influence in Central America of the Nicaraguan Canal Treaty with the United States of America and its conflict with the treaty rights of Costa Rica.**
Chandler P. Anderson. Washington, DC: Gibson, 1917. 50p.
The canal treaty referred to in the title is the Bryan–Chamorro Treaty, signed by Nicaragua and the United States in 1914. It gave the United States the right to build an inter-oceanic canal along the San Juan river, which serves as the border between Nicaragua and Costa Rica. Anderson's treatise is a legal defence of the position of Costa Rica that the Bryan–Chamorro Treaty violates Costa Rica's rights to the San Juan as spelled out in a previous treaty between Costa Rica and Nicaragua.

422 **Costa Rica.**
Morris J. Blachman, Ronald G. Hellman. In: *Confronting revolution: security through diplomacy in Central America*, edited by Morris J. Blachman, William M. LeoGrande, Kenneth E. Sharpe. New York: Pantheon Books, 1986. p. 156-82.
Although the authors respect the political and economic progress Costa Rica has made, they insist that 'democratic resiliency in Costa Rica rests on a weak social and economic foundation endangered by intense economic and political international pressures'. They see four structural problems: excessive dependency on the export of bananas and coffee; high demand for imports by the new urban middle class; growth of autonomous agencies; and an inadequate tax system. What is more, they see strong pressures from the United States, mainly stemming from Washington's commitment to eliminate the Sandinistas from Nicaragua, which threaten to militarize Costa Rica. The second half of the article describes clearly the pressures from the United States for Costa Rica to become involved in the war against the Sandinistas, and it also describes Costa Rica's reaction to that pressure.

131

423 **Costa Rica: the end of the fiesta.**
Richard E. Feinberg. In: *From gunboats to diplomacy: new U.S.*
policies for Latin America, edited by Richard Newfarmer. Baltimore,
Maryland: Johns Hopkins University Press, 1984, p. 102-15.

From gunboats to diplomacy was written on the eve of the 1984 presidential election in
order to delineate a new foreign policy for the Democratic Party of the United States.
The article on Costa Rica by noted economist Richard E. Feinberg focuses on the
economic and political crisis of Costa Rica, including a discussion of the relations
between the Ronald Reagan administration and Costa Rican President Luis A. Monge
(1982-86). The author concludes that the United States policy of provoking conflict
between Costa Rica and Nicaragua prevents economic recovery for the country.

424 **Costa Rica: caught between two worlds.**
William L. Furlong. *Journal of Interamerican Studies and World*
Affairs, vol. 29, no. 2 (Summer 1987), p. 119-54.

This article emphasizes problems, both domestic and international, faced by Costa
Rica in the mid-1980s. Internal political and economic problems are sketched as a
background to a full discussion of the dilemma Costa Rica faced in its effort to
maintain a healthy relationship with the United States without becoming a vehicle of
President Ronald Reagan's opposition to the Sandinista government of Nicaragua.
Relations with Nicaragua are covered in detail, following up differences highlighted by
Robert Tomasek in his 1984 article, 'The Deterioration of Relations between Costa
Rica and the Sandinistas' (q.v.). Other topics covered are United States military
relationships with Costa Rica, President Luis Alberto Monge's declaration of neutrality
in December 1983, and the Oscar Arias Peace Plan.

425 **Costa Rica–Mexico, 1978-1986: de la concertación a la confrontación.**
(Costa Rica–Mexico, 1978-86: from agreement to confrontation.)
H. Rodrigo Jauberth Rojas. Mexico City: Centro de Investigación y
Docencia Económicas, 1987. 459p.

Rather than a traditional analysis of the diplomatic relations between the two
countries, as the title suggests, this book is both a source book and a polemic. Over
half is devoted to annexes, which include lengthy citations from other publications,
copies of newspaper articles, and interviews with dignitaries about Mexican–Costa
Rican relations. The focus is on the Central American policy of the United States and
the target of the polemic seems to be Costa Rican leaders who, according to the
authors, have identified themselves too closely with the United States. Nevertheless,
the theme of Costa Rican relations with Mexico is so important and has been so
neglected by scholars that any book on the subject, however flawed, is welcome.

426 **Neutrality Costa Rican style.**
Jennie Lincoln. *Current History*, vol. 84, no. 500 (March 1985),
p. 118-21, 136.

The Costa Rican version of neutrality became important when President Luis Alberto
Monge declared his nation's neutrality on 17 November 1983. He meant military
neutrality and not necessarily political neutrality. Lincoln analyses the declaration in
the light of domestic politics, relations with Nicaragua and the United States, the
Contadora peace effort, and Costa Rica's economic crisis.

427 **Costa Rica, relaciones exteriores de una república en formación 1847-**
1849. (Costa Rica, foreign relations of a republic in formation 1847-49.)
Clotilde Maria Obregón.   San José: Editorial Costa Rica, 1984. 305p.
maps. bibliog.

It is important to note that this monograph, which originally was a two-volume history
thesis at the University of Costa Rica on the Castro Madriz presidency (1847-49), has
an excellent introductory section (p. 15-83) covering the general, political, economic,
and social situation of Costa Rica in the mid-1840s. Concerning foreign relations, the
author covers the establishment of Costa Rica's relations with the rest of the world,
with emphasis on specific Central American countries and the issue of Central
American union and on Felipe Molina's important mission to Europe in 1848. The
study makes good use of Costa Rican archival sources, but unfortunately does not
utilize archival materials from other countries.

428 **Costa Rican relations with Central America, 1900-1934.**
Richard V. Salisbury.   Buffalo, New York: Council on International
Studies, State University of New York at Buffalo, 1975. 88p. bibliog.
(Special Studies, no. 71).

The title clearly delineates the scope of this work, a pioneering one in the sense that it
is one of the first accounts of Costa Rican foreign relations based on a thorough
examination of archival materials. In contrast to the popular assumption that the small
Central American nations remain passive in the face of foreign pressures Professor
Salisbury finds that the Costa Rican Foreign Ministry 'pursued remarkably innovative,
independent, and activist policies' in this period. Of particular interest are Costa Rica's
recognition policy, its reaction to the Nicaraguan civil strife of the 1920s, and its
attitude toward intervention in general.

429 **The attitude of the United States toward the Colombia–Costa Rica**
arbitral proceedings.
Leon F. Sensabaugh.   *Hispanic American Historical Review*, vol. 19,
no. 1 (Feb. 1939), p. 16-30.

Based primarily on United States diplomatic materials, the article contains a brief
history of the border dispute between Colombia and Costa Rica. The dispute was
successfully arbitrated in 1900, three years before Panama threw off Colombian
sovereignty and became Costa Rica's neighbour to the south. Because of the possibility
that arbitration might affect its interests in inter-oceanic transportation the United
States opposed arbitration.

430 **Los contratos Webster–Mora y las implicaciones sobre Costa Rica y**
Nicaragua. (The Webster–Mora contracts and their implications for
Costa Rica and Nicaragua.)
Paul Woodbridge A[lvarado].   San José: Editorial Costa Rica, 1967.
94p. map. bibliog. (Serie La Propia).

This compressed book sheds light on three contracts signed by William Webster in
1857 and 1858 with the Costa Rican government. Webster was an Englishman who was
hired by Cornelius Vanderbilt, president of the Accessory Transit Company, to reopen
the San Juan river transit route, and the contracts were designed to put the transit

route under Costa Rican instead of Nicaraguan control. Woodbridge's account is based on archival sources.

With Central American countries

431 **Costa Rica–Panama arbitration: argument of Costa Rica before the arbitrator Hon. Edward Douglas White.**
Washington, DC: Gibson Brothers, 1913-14. 6 vols.

President Loubet of France made a boundary award in 1900 in an arbitration between Costa Rica and Colombia. The dispute over the boundary continued, however, after Panama separated from Colombia in 1903. In 1910 Costa Rica and Panama signed an agreement to hold a second arbitration, and it is to this arbitration that the six volumes are addressed. Although couched inevitably in formal legal prose they contain a wealth of geographical and historical information, including the comments of travellers to the area and the scientific results of surveys, as well as information on the treaties and foreign relations of Costa Rica. The second volume contains Costa Rica's answer to Panama's argument and the last four volumes (published by the Commonwealth Company, Rosslyn, Virginia in 1913) contain relevant documents. Entries under Luis Matamoros (q.v.) and John Bassett Moore (q.v.) also pertain to the Costa Rica–Panama arbitration.

432 **Arms and politics in Costa Rica and Nicaragua, 1948-1981.**
Stephen Earley. Albuquerque, New Mexico: Latin American Institute, University of New Mexico, 1982. 54p. bibliog. (Research Paper Series, Latin American Institute, no. 9).

This research paper, after brief coverage of Nicaraguan–Costa Rican relations in the pre-1979 period, focuses sharply on the flow of arms from Costa Rica during the Sandinista revolution in Nicaragua in 1978-79. Newspaper reports of official Costa Rican government complicity in the arms traffic, uncovered in an investigation in 1961, are the principal sources of information.

433 **Neutralidad y democracia combativa.** (Neutrality and combative democracy.)
Carlos José Gutiérrez Gutiérrez. Heredia, Costa Rica: Fundación Friedrich Ebert, Centro de Estudios Democráticos de América Latina, 1987. 215p.

As one of Costa Rica's best-known students of international relations, as one of the authors of President Luis Alberto Monge's Declaration of Neutrality (1983), and as Minister of Foreign Relations when the declaration was made, Gutiérrez has special credibility on the subject of Costa Rica's policy toward conflict in Central America. This book presents a number of his speeches on his own personal participation and Costa Rica's involvement in the crisis of Central American international relations in the mid-1980s.

434 **Costa Rica: Gesellschaft und Kultur eines Staates mit ständiger aktiver und unbewaffneter Neutralität.** (Costa Rica: the society and culture of a state practising active and unarmed neutrality.)
Edited by Andreas Maislinger. Innsbruck, Austria: Inn-Verlag Innsbruck, 1986. 431p.

Thirty-two articles on Costa Rica primarily during the Luis Alberto Monge administration (1982-86). The emphasis falls on foreign relations, particularly Costa Rica's efforts to maintain its neutrality in relation to the Nicaraguan conflict, and the economic crisis of the time. Four articles are in English and the rest are in German. English summaries are included.

435 **Costa Rica–Panama arbitration: report submitted to the representative of Costa Rica by Luis Matamoros, consulting engineer of the government of Costa Rica.**
Luis Matamoros. Washington, DC: Gibson Brothers, 1913. 159p.

Matamoros criticizes the Panama–Costa Rica Boundary Commission which provided details leading to the Loubet Award. Matamoros claims that the geologists and engineers who surveyed the Sixaola river valley did a superficial job and that a more thorough survey would lead to the conclusion that the whole valley properly belongs to Costa Rica. A report on the region by geologist Benjamin L. Miller is appended.

436 **Costa Rica–Panama arbitration: memorandum on *uti possidetis.***
John Bassett Moore. Rosslyn, Virginia: Commonwealth Company, 1913. 51p.

John Bassett Moore, the eminent international lawyer from the United States, explains the legal principle of *uti possidetis*, how it has been used in the adjustment of boundary disputes in Latin America, and how it applies to the Costa Rica–Panama boundary dispute. He concludes that earlier treaties between Colombia and the Central American countries and territorial references in Costa Rica's constitutions do little to clarify the dispute.

437 **Los derechos de Costa Rica y Nicaragua en el Rio San Juan.** (The rights of Costa Rica and Nicaragua on the San Juan river.)
Felipe Rodríguez Serrano. San José: Lehmann, 1983. 63p. map.

Rodríguez Serrano, a lawyer and public official in Nicaragua until 1977, takes a legal approach to the problem of the Costa Rica–Nicaragua boundary. He summarizes diplomatic discussions, provides the texts of the various treaties on the subject, and focuses on the Grover Cleveland Award of 1888 and subsequent delineation of the boundary.

438 **Costa Rica and the 1920-1921 Union Movement: a reassessment.**
Richard V. Salisbury. *Journal of Interamerican Studies and World Affairs*, vol. 19, no. 3 (Aug. 1977), p. 393-418. bibliog.

Many historians have commented on Costa Rica's antipathy to the idea of Central American union, but this article is the first serious study of Costa Rica's attitude toward a particular union movement. Salisbury explains the nationalist–unionist debate, which ended with Costa Rica's rejection of federation, at a time when the issue was intensely examined by Costa Rican leaders.

439 **The Costa Rican role in the Sandinista victory.**
Mitchell A. Seligson, William J. Carroll, III. In: *Nicaragua in revolution*, edited by Thomas W. Walker. New York: Praeger, 1982. p. 331-43.

Readers should pass over the historical introduction, which contains errors and misinterpretations, and turn to the heart of the article which deals with Costa Rican public opinion about the Sandinista revolution in neighbouring Nicaragua. The article reports the results of a 1978 survey of opinion on the Sandinistas, on the interest of Costa Ricans in helping the Sandinistas, and on the prospects for a victory for communism in Nicaragua. Costa Ricans, not surprisingly, were ambivalent about the Sandinistas several months before the Sandinista victory in 1979.

440 **Nuestro límite con Nicaragua: estudio histórico.** (Our boundary with Nicaragua: an historical study.)
Luis Fernando Sibaja Chacón. San José: Comisión Nacional de Conmemoraciones Históricas, 1974. 279p. maps. bibliog.

The present work was the author's doctoral dissertation, completed at the Universidad Complutense de Madrid in 1972. The emphasis is on the colonial period, when the boundaries among Spanish possessions in America were poorly defined, and the book depends on research in Spanish archives. Several of the important colonial documents are reprinted in full. Nevertheless, there is adequate treatment of the geographical basis for the frontier between Costa Rica and Nicaragua and of the 19th-century disputes and agreements on the boundary. Thirteen maps are included.

441 **The deterioration of relations between Costa Rica and the Sandinistas.**
Robert D. Tomasek. Washington, DC: American Enterprise Institute for Public Policy Research, Center for Hemispheric Studies, 1984. 46p. bibliog. (Occasional Papers Series, no. 9).

In this explanation of the causes of the deterioration of relations between Nicaragua and Costa Rica after 1979 Tomasek gives his attention to several factors: ideological differences, border problems centring on the San Juan river, accusations of disinformation, asylum for exiles, and United States policy. The research was carried out in Costa Rica in 1983.

442 **El militarismo en Costa Rica y otros ensayos.** (Militarism in Costa Rica and other essays.)
Fernando Volio Jiménez. San José: Libro Libre, 1985. 245p.

In a country which has had no army since 1949, as is the case in Costa Rica, it is unusual to find a title like this. The truth is that the book is not on militarism but rather on human rights, liberty, democracy, and foreign policy, themes more attractive to a Costa Rican audience and apparently to Volio. The book does include a long essay on militarism, which reviews Costa Rica's 19th-century experience with military leaders, the abolition of the army, and security threats such as those that materialized when invading forces entered Costa Rican soil from Nicaragua in 1948 and 1955. Because of Volio's own involvement in foreign policy in the 1980s (he served as

Minister of Foreign Relations) his most interesting essays are those on Costa Rica–Nicaragua relations and the Contadora group.

With the United States

443 Back from the brink.
Marc Edelman. *Report on the Americas*, vol. 19, no. 6 (Nov.-Dec. 1985), p. 37-48.
The contribution of this article is to tie the economic crisis of the early 1980s suffered by Costa Rica to increased pressure from the United States to draw Costa Rica into its war against the Sandinistas in Nicaragua. Details of the crisis and of economic assistance from the United States (via the Agency for International Development) are presented in graphic form. Edelman also provides details of the effort of the United States to privatize the Costa Rica economy and of the lengthy negotiations between the Costa Rican government and the International Monetary Fund.

444 The United States and Central America, 1944-1949.
Thomas M. Leonard. Tuscaloosa, Alabama: University of Alabama Press, 1984. 215p.
Chapter one (p. 15-46) of this book is the most nearly complete account available of United States relations with Costa Rica in the 1944-49 period. Professor Leonard provides essential information about domestic politics in Costa Rica in this important transition period and concentrates on the reactions of United States diplomatic and consular personnel to events in the period.

445 Costa Rica: democratic model in jeopardy.
Andrew Reding. *World Policy Journal*, vol. 3, no. 2 (Spring 1986), p. 301-15.
After a few comments on the uniqueness of Costa Rica's political system and economic model the author focuses on United States–Costa Rican relations. He is critical of the Ronald Reagan administration and its pressure on various Costa Rican administrations and individual political leaders to take a stronger anti-Nicaragua diplomatic and military stance. President Luis Alberto Monge's Declaration of Neutrality of 17 November 1983 is given attention in the context of United States–Costa Rican relations, as is the presidential campaign of 1986.

446 Domestic politics and foreign policy: Costa Rica's stand on recognition, 1923-1934.
Richard V. Salisbury. *Hispanic American Historical Review*, vol. 54, no. 3 (Aug. 1974), p. 453-78.
In this article, which is based on primary sources, Salisbury explains the origins of the strong support of Costa Rica for non-recognition of revolutionary governments, a position incorporated in the Washington Treaty of Central American Peace and Amity in 1923, and the evolution of Costa Rica's stand on recognition policy until the treaty was abrogated in 1934.

Foreign Relations. With the United States

447 **United States intervention in Nicaragua: the Costa Rican role.**
Richard V. Salisbury.   *Prologue*, vol. 9 (Winter 1977), p. 209-17.
As a neighbour of Nicaragua, Costa Rica could not help but be affected when the
United States intervened militarily in Nicaragua in 1911 and again in 1926. Costa
Rica's reaction to these crises, before and after the actual interventions, is carefully
catalogued in this article, based on archival sources in Washington and San José. The
role of President Ricardo Jiménez Oreamuno of Costa Rica in these matters is
particularly important since two of his presidential terms coincided with the crises. His
ambivalence, Salisbury suggests, mirrors Costa Rica's problems as a small nation in a
region dominated by the United States.

448 **Las alianzas conflictivas: las relaciones de Estados Unidos y Costa Rica
desde la Segunda Guerra Mundial a la guerra fría.** (Conflicting
alliances: the relations of the United States and Costa Rica from the
Second World War to the Cold War.)
Jacobo Schifter.   San José: Libro Libre, 1986. 317p.
This is a translation of the dissertation which gained the author his PhD in 1985 from
Columbia University. Schifter used extensive primary documents both in the National
Archives in Washington and those of Costa Rica. He traces the relationship of the
United States with the Costa Rican administrations of Calderón Guardia and Picado
and with some leaders of the opposing factions from 1940 to 1948. Diplomatic relations
became progressively worse, especially after the defeat of Germany and the beginning
of Cold War fears in the United States. Schifter believes that the United States
embassy pressurized the Picado administration diplomatically but was not involved
militarily in the revolution of 1948 which overthrew Picado's government.

The Costa Rica reader.
See item no. 9.

**Nobel Costa Rica: a timely report on our peaceful pro-Yankee, Central
American neighbor.**
See item no. 15.

The origins of Costa Rican federalism.
See item no. 166.

Woodrow Wilson's use of the non-recognition policy in Costa Rica.
See item no. 202.

Carrillo y Costa Rica ante la federación. (Carrillo and Costa Rica before the
Federation.)
See item no. 208.

Tinoco y los Estados Unidos: génesis y caída de un régimen. (Tinoco and the
United States: genesis and fall of a régime.)
See item no. 217.

La campaña del tránsito, 1856-1857. (The transit campaign, 1856-57.)
See item no. 218.

Costa Rican trade and navigation ties with United States, Germany and Europe: 1840 to 1885.
See item no. 233.

Don Pepe: a political biography of José Figueres of Costa Rica.
See item no. 235.

Costa Rica: a country at the crossroads.
See item no. 308.

Voices from Costa Rica.
See item no. 382.

Costa Rica.
See item no. 385.

Costa Rica's political turmoil: can production support the welfare state?
See item no. 396.

Costa Rica: crisis y desafíos. (Costa Rica: crisis and challenges.)
See item no. 398.

Costa Rica, Honduras, and Panama.
See item no. 411.

Security assistance in Costa Rica.
See item no. 449.

The militarization of Costa Rica.
See item no. 451.

Costa Rica, a study in economic development.
See item no. 492.

Costa Rica, Panama and Central American economic integration.
See item no. 510.

Costa Rica and the Central American Common Market.
See item no. 511.

Materiales para la historia de las relaciones internacionales de Costa Rica: bibliografía, fuentes impresas. (Materials for the history of the international relations of Costa Rica: bibliography, printed sources.)
See item no. 748.

Military

449 Security assistance in Costa Rica.
James M. Bolling, Andras V. Aradi. *DISAM Journal of International Security Assistance Management*, vol. 12, no. 1 (Fall 1989), p. 75-83.

Bolling and Aradi, captains in the United States Army, describe the Costa Rican Public Security Force and their role in managing the United States security assistance programme in Costa Rica. The first part, by Captain Bolling, focuses on the process of helping Costa Rica choose $35 million worth of military equipment and maintaining it. Captain Aradi, in the second part, describes various training programmes, particularly one for the Civil Guard.

450 De nuestra historia patria: hechos militares y políticos. (Our country's history: military and political events.)
Rafael Obregón Loría. Alajuela, Costa Rica: Museo Histórico Cultural Juan Santamaría, 1981. 417p. bibliog.

In view of Costa Rica's peaceful reputation a book on the country's military conflicts seems a rarity, but when this book was first published in 1951 (by *La Nación*, San José), the revolution of 1948 was still fresh in people's memories. Obregón's approach is to provide a brief synopsis of every event in Costa Rican history since independence in which military conflict was involved. He stretches the concept in order to include political conflicts which involved the threat of the use of force, as in the bloodless coup of January 1917, when Federico Tinoco removed President Alfredo González Flores from office. The 1981 edition, updated by students, includes a few events of the 1950-80 period such as conflicts with Nicaragua and strikes.

451 **The militarization of Costa Rica.**
John Saxe-Fernández. *Monthly Review: An Independent Socialist Magazine*, vol. 24, no. 1 (May 1972), p. 61-70.

This article focuses on the efforts of the Costa Rican government, aided and abetted by the United States since the 1960s, to modernize and strengthen Costa Rica's security forces.

Costa Rica, a country study.
See item no. 11.

El militarismo en Costa Rica y otros ensayos. (Militarism in Costa Rica and other essays.)
See item no. 442.

Constitution and Laws

452 **La Constitución de 1949: antecedentes y proyecciones.** (The constitution
of 1949: antecedents and projections.)
Oscar R. Aguilar Bulgarelli. San José: Editorial Costa Rica, 1973.
191p. bibliog.

The special appeal of this book, which has been reprinted many times, is the author's
successful effort to place the constitution in historical perspective. The book covers
political history preceding the constituent assembly of 1949, the debates in the
assembly, and the principal articles of the constitution.

453 **Constitución política de la República de Costa Rica.** (Political
constitution of the republic of Costa Rica.)
Carlos Manuel Arguedas. San José: Editorial Costa Rica, 1981. 407p.

This edition of the constitution of 1949 is valuable for the annotations, concordance,
and comprehensive index. The author, an official of the Technical Services
Department of the National Assembly, in effect provides a handy guide to the
constitution and its modifications up to 1980.

454 **Desarrollo constitucional de Costa Rica.** (The constitutional
development of Costa Rica.)
Mario Alberto Jiménez Quesada. San José: Editorial Juricentro,
1979. 3rd ed. 171p. bibliog.

This is a brief outline of the constitutional history of Costa Rica based on an
admittedly weak basis of legal and historical studies at the time of the first edition,
published in 1951. There is no evidence of updating in the second or third editions
despite many legal and historical studies on the constitution of 1949 published between
1951 and 1979. The author emphasizes the continuity of Costa Rican constitutional
ideas.

455   **Las constituciones de Costa Rica.** (The constitutions of Costa Rica.)
Compiled by Hernán G. Peralta.   Madrid: Instituto de Estudios
Políticos, 1962. 660p. (Las Constituciones Hispanoamericanas, no. 16).
In this volume, which contains the complete texts of all of Costa Rica's constitutions,
Peralta traces the constitutional history of Costa Rica. The strengths of the book are
the authoritative discussions of the origins of public law in Costa Rica and the
insightful interpretations of the relations between constitutional law and political
history. *Las constituciones de Costa Rica* is one of a series on Latin American
constitutions published by the Instituto de Estudios Políticos.

Costa Rica: monumentos históricos y arqueológicos. (Costa Rica: historical
and archaeological monuments.)
See item no. 121.

El puerto de Puntarenas: (algo de su historia.) (The port of Puntarenas: a
little of its history.)
See item no. 179.

Legislación indigenista de Costa Rica. (Indian legislation of Costa Rica.)
See item no. 267.

Los caminos del indigenismo. (The roads of Indianism.)
See item no. 272.

Las luchas por el seguro social en Costa Rica. (The fight for social security in
Costa Rica.)
See item no. 347.

Libertades públicas en Costa Rica. (Public liberties in Costa Rica.)
See item no. 353.

Costa Rica: a meaningful democracy.
See item no. 362.

Notes on Costa Rican democracy.
See item no. 364.

**Génesis del gobierno de Costa Rica: a través de 160 años de vida
independiente.** (The genesis of government in Costa Rica in 160 years of
independent life.)
See item no. 461.

La clase política y el poder judicial en Costa Rica. (Politics and judicial power
in Costa Rica.)
See item no. 467.

A statement of the laws of Costa Rica in matters affecting business.
See item no. 515.

Law and agrarian reform in Costa Rica.
See item no. 549.

Constitution and Laws

Historia agrícola de Costa Rica. (An agricultural history of Costa Rica.)
See item no. 551.

Boceto histórico del ferrocarril nacional. (An historical sketch of the national railway.)
See item no. 571.

Labor law and practice in Costa Rica.
See item no. 585.

Administration and Local Government

456 **Legislative institution building in Brazil, Costa Rica, and Lebanon.**
Abdo I. Baaklini, James J. Heaphey. Beverly Hills, California: Sage
Publications, 1976. 57p. bibliog. (Sage Professional Papers in
Administrative and Policy Studies, series no. 03-027).
The authors, one a political scientist and the other a specialist in public administration,
discuss recent legislative reforms in the three countries and make comparisons of their
legislatures from the perspective of administration. The focus of the study is on the
efforts of the legislatures to professionalize legislative staff.

457 **Municipal government in Costa Rica: its characteristics and functions.**
Christopher E. Baker, Ronald Fernández Pinto, Samuel Z. Stone.
San José: Associate Colleges of the Midwest Central American Field
Program, School of Political Science, University of Costa Rica, 1972.
173p. bibliog.
Baker, Fernández, and Stone headed a team of students who surveyed the literature
on municipalities, read the minutes of municipal council meetings, and interviewed
council members. The basic purpose was to identify characteristics of municipal politics
and contribute to the national debate on municipal reform. Data were gathered from
twenty-five rural municipalities. The authors conclude that municipal government is
badly in need of reform.

458 **An empirical test of "legalism" in administration.**
Charles Goodsell. *Journal of Developing Areas*, vol. 10, no. 4 (July
1976), p. 485-94.
In a direct comparison of postal services in the United States and Costa Rica Goodsell
finds that postal regulations in Costa Rica are less complex, that regulations in Costa
Rica are less rigidly enforced, and that the postal bureaucracy of Costa Rica has
proportionately fewer lawyers than its equivalent in the United States. This work
should be required reading for critics of Latin American legalism and bureaucracy.

459 **Recent public administration literature in Costa Rica.**
George M. Guess. *Latin American Research Review*, vol. 15, no. 3
(1980), p. 273-80.

In a review of four books on Costa Rican economics and social classes, all of which
touch on public administration, Guess points out that the books fail to diagnose and
analyse organizational behaviour. They also fail, according to Guess, to examine the
budgeting and management control process. Guess may be targeting the wrong works,
since none of the books is by a specialist in public administration, but he is correct in
stressing the need for professional studies of public administration in Costa Rica.

460 **Estudio sobre las instituciones autónomas de Costa Rica.** (A study of the
autonomous institutions of Costa Rica.)
Oswaldo Herbster de Gusmao. San José: Instituto Centroamericano
de Administración Pública, 1973. 129p. (Serie Investigación, no. 304).

This study, commissioned by the president of Costa Rica, reviews the constitutional
and legal antecedents of Costa Rica's autonomous agencies (such as the National
Insurance Institute), compares them with similar agencies in Panama, analyses their
practicality, and makes suggestions for improvement.

461 **Génesis del gobierno de Costa Rica: a través de 160 años de vida
independiente.** (The genesis of government in Costa Rica in 160 years
of independent life.)
Wilburg Jiménez Castro. San José: Universidad de Costa Rica, 1986.
2 vols. bibliog.

For the layperson the attractive aspect of this book is likely to be the numerous
organization charts which show how the government of Costa Rica worked at various
times in its history. Students of Costa Rican history will benefit from the detailed
explanations of how specific governmental institutions such as the legislature and
municipalities evolved. Autonomous agencies, the judiciary, and the electoral system
are equally well covered.

462 **La Asamblea Legislativa en Costa Rica.** (The legislative assembly in
Costa Rica.)
Hugo Alfonso Muñoz Q. San José: Editorial Costa Rica, 1977,
2nd ed. 305p. bibliog.

Muñoz, a distinguished Costa Rican lawyer and jurist with a doctorate in constitutional
law from the University of Paris, provides a solid and comprehensive explanation of
how the deputies to the National Assembly are elected and how the Assembly
functions. There is also ample discussion of relations with the executive, the
autonomous agencies, and with the political system in general. He believes that the
Assembly should be reformed; in particular he opposes the one-term limitation for
deputies and favours a more democratic selection of the deputy candidates by the
political parties. The 3rd edition was published in 1988 by the Editorial Costa Rica and
(like the Assembly) has not been updated.

463 San José, Costa Rica local government: demands and decisions.
Herbert Hernando Ortega. PhD dissertation, University of
Oklahoma, 1974. 352p. (Available from University Microfilms, Ann
Arbor, Michigan, order no. 74-21,984).

Despite problems of readability and organization this dissertation offers information on
the structure of municipal government in Costa Rica and details on decisions made by
the Municipal Council of San José. The study provides useful information about the
functioning of the Municipal Development and Advisory Institute, which was created
as an autonomous agency in 1970. One significant conclusion the author reaches is that
the Municipal Council of San José is not properly equipped, administratively or
budgetarily, to handle many of the problems it faces.

464 A multidimensional view of power in San José, Costa Rica.
Ransford Comstock Pyle. PhD dissertation, University of Florida,
1974. 255p. (Available from University Microfilms, Ann Arbor,
Michigan, order no. 75-3521).

A detailed, sophisticated description of San José is the central contribution of this
anthropological study. There is no better account of San José and its *barrios* [districts]
and how *josefinos* [inhabitants of San José] perceive them. The perceptions were
arrived at by means of a lengthy questionnaire submitted to approximately 100
university students, and followed by interviews. Another contribution of the study,
albeit more controversial, is criticism of the 'myths' of Costa Rican history: lack of
class distinctions, the large size of the middle class, and equality of income distribution.
Relying heavily on the works of Samuel Stone, Pyle emphasizes élitist dominance in
politics and commerce.

465 El poder ejecutivo en Costa Rica. (The executive power in Costa Rica.)
Magda Inés Rojas. San José: Editorial Juricentro, 1980. 343p.
bibliog. (Colección Escuela Libre de Derecho).

An exhaustive study of the constitutional bases of executive power in Costa Rica and
its historical use. Despite the fact that the constitution of 1949 limited the president's
powers, the tendency since 1949 has been for the president to extend his powers over
legislation and finances. The author believes that an even further extension of these
powers would be desirable.

**466 Bureaucratic politics and social policy: the emergence of Costa Rica's
welfare state.**
Mark B. Rosenberg. In: *Politics and public policy in Latin America*,
edited by Steven Hughes, Kenneth J. Mijeski. Boulder, Colorado:
Westview Press, 1984, p. 117-33.

In this analysis of policy-making in Costa Rica Professor Rosenberg chooses the
adoption of social security and its subsequent universalization as a case-study. In a
political atmosphere where both the executive and legislature are weak the Social
Security Institute, an autonomous agency, has taken on special importance. Rosenberg
points out that the two principal political parties which have ruled Costa Rica since
1948 have tended to agree on the need for an expansive social welfare system, or, put
in another way, the political élites have been more concerned with mass welfare than

those in other Latin American countries. He praises the Institute as intolerant of corruption, incompetence, and political patronage.

467 **La clase política y el poder judicial en Costa Rica.** (Politics and judicial power in Costa Rica.)
Jorge Rhenán Segura. San José: Editorial Universidad Estatal a Distancia, 1982. 202p. bibliog.

Conventional wisdom in Costa Rica holds that the judicial power is independent and apolitical. Segura's thesis is that while the judicial power is independent it is by no means apolitical, partly because judges belong to the same political class as legislators and executives. After reviewing the historical antecedents and the administrative structure of the judicial system he reviews the careers of all 214 magistrates of the Supreme Court from 1824 to 1981 and finds that nearly fifty per cent also held executive and legislative positions. This does reveal a close political connection, but the study fails to show how this connection affects judicial decisions.

468 **An analysis of rural food distribution in Costa Rica.**
Michael Thomas Weber. PhD dissertation, Michigan State University, 1976. 306p. (Available from University Microfilms, Ann Arbor, Michigan, order no. 75-5913).

The author completed much of the research for this work while working on a marketing project in Costa Rica with Michigan State University and the United States Agency for International Development mission. The study provides detailed information on patterns of retail and wholesale sales in two counties in Costa Rica, Puriscal and Naranjo. Numerous maps and charts are included but, unfortunately, some of the maps are virtually unreadable in the University Microfilms copy. The author's purpose is to evaluate projects proposed by the county governments to expand the public market in their county seats and to propose alternative investments. He concludes that the proposals are of extremely limited benefit.

469 **Recentralization: the budgetary dilemma in the economic development of Mexico, Bolivia, and Costa Rica.**
James W. Wilkie. In: *Fiscal policy for industrialization and development in Latin America*, edited by David T. Geithman. Gainesville, Florida: Center for Latin American Studies, University of Florida, 1974, p. 200-61.

Among the Latin American countries which have experienced revolutionary change and followed this change with an attempt to decentralize public administration, Costa Rica is in the middle ground. That is, Costa Rica's allocation of 48.9 per cent of budgetary power to autonomous agencies after the revolution of 1948 is lower than Bolivia's and higher than Mexico's after their revolutions. Wilkie's contribution is a lucid explanation of the power of Costa Rica's autonomous agencies, made more vivid by comparison with similar agencies in Mexico and Bolivia. He also clearly sets out the administrative problems created by high budgetary allocations to agencies independent of the executive, thus creating a demand for recentralization. The remarks of several commentators on Wilkie's work are appended.

Mensajes presidenciales. (Presidential messages.)
See item no. 215.

Estudio de comunidades indígenas: zonas Boruca-Térraba y China Kichá. (A study of indigenous communities: the Boruca-Térraba and China Kichá.)
See item no. 263.

The structure of leadership and its characteristics in a Costa Rican community.
See item no. 316.

Quién gobierna en Costa Rica?: un estudio del liderazgo formal en Costa Rica. (Who governs in Costa Rica?: a study of the formal leadership of Costa Rica.)
See item no. 356.

Are Latin Americans politically rational?: citizen participation and democracy in Costa Rica.
See item no. 358.

Notes on Costa Rican democracy.
See item no. 364.

Políticas de crecimiento urbano: la experiencia de Costa Rica. (The politics of urban growth: the experience of Costa Rica.)
See item no. 367.

Legislative–executive policy-making: the cases of Chile and Costa Rica.
See item no. 375.

Community power brokers and national political parties in rural Costa Rica.
See item no. 393.

Democracia en Costa Rica?: cinco opiniones polémicas. (Democracy in Costa Rica?: five polemical opinions.)
See item no. 403.

Ricardo Jiménez Oreamuno, "su pensamiento". (Ricardo Jiménez Oreamuno, 'his thought'.)
See item no. 417.

Rafael Yglesias Castro.
See item no. 708.

Lubeck & Lubeck's who's who in Costa Rica, 1979-1980: professions, commerce, government.
See item no. 723.

Proceso de estructuración territorial en Costa Rica: bibliografía sobre la problemática urbana y regional, 1945-81. (The process of territorial structure in Costa Rica: a bibliography of urban and regional problems, 1945-81.)
See item no. 757.

Economics

General

470 **An analysis of inflation in the small, open economy of Costa Rica.**
Victor Brajer.   Albuquerque, New Mexico: Latin American Institute,
University of New Mexico, 1986. 53p. bibliog. (Research Paper series,
no. 18).

The subject of this study is inflation in Costa Rica from 1970 to 1985. The purpose is
threefold: first to discover what caused inflation in this period; second to determine if
the nature of the inflation changed during the period; and third, what role monetary
and non-monetary factors had in determining the rate of inflation. The author finds
that expansionist fiscal policy, rising real wages, and higher import prices all helped to
provoke inflation.

471 **Costa Rica: la economía en 1985.** (Costa Rica: the economy in 1985.)
Víctor Hugo Céspedes S., Alberto di Mare, Ronulfo Jiménez.   San
José: Academia de Centroamérica, 1986. 208p. bibliog.

Provides a detailed look at Costa Rica's economic malaise in one year, 1985, revealing
the depth of the effects of the economic crisis which struck Costa Rica earlier in the
decade. Gross national product (GNP) in 1985 grew by only one per cent, or less than
population growth. Sixty-two tables and ten graphs help the reader grasp the details of
the problem, which the authors see as a failure to promote exports, both traditional
and non-traditional.

472 **Problemas económicos en la década de los ochenta.** (Economic problems in the decade of the eighties.)
Víctor Hugo Céspedes S. (et al.). San José: Editorial Studium, 1983. 203p.

This detailed analysis was prepared by Costa Rican economists affiliated with the Academia de Centroamérica, a conservative institution. Numerous tables present statistical data collected by the Central Bank on all aspects of the economy: economic growth, foreign debt, monetary and credit policy, government income and expenditures, foreign trade, employment, productivity, and energy. The authors attribute the economic crisis to changes in international markets and to government policies based on a protectionist strategy of import substitution and active public sector involvement in the economy.

473 **Recent literature on Costa Rica's economic crisis.**
Marc Edelman. *Latin American Research Review*, vol. 18, no. 2 (1983), p. 166-80.

In this review essay of five books on the economy of Costa Rica the author provides a good overview of the economic crisis of the early 1980s as well as pinpointing the good and bad points of the works reviewed. The analysis centres on the four most commonly held explanations of the crisis: the declining terms of trade, the problem of state intervention in the economy, economic mismanagement, and the limits of the country's productive structure. All five books reviewed are in Spanish and were published in 1980-81.

474 **Obras de Rodrigo Facio.** (The works of Rodrigo Facio.)
Rodrigo Facio Brenes. San José: Editorial Costa Rica, 1972-82. 4 vols. bibliog.

In the first volume (1972, 415p.), which contains two of Facio's major works on the Costa Rican economy and fourteen short articles and reviews on economic questions, Facio touches on the all-important Costa Rican economic issues of the day. His work *Estudio sobre economía costarricense* (Study of the Costa Rican economy) was his law degree thesis at the University of Costa Rica in 1941 and was first published by the Editorial Surco for the Centre for the Study of National Problems in 1942. It was aimed at influencing governmental policy, and many of his suggestions were carried out after the revolution of 1948. The second volume (1973, 340p.) contains a more technical financial study, *La moneda y la banca central* (Money and central banking), originally published by the Fondo de Cultura Económica in Mexico City in 1947. Volume three (1977, 203p.) is entitled *Documentos universitarios* (University documents) and contains several speeches and related university documents written while Facio was rector of the University of Costa Rica (1952-60). In volume four (1982, 541p.), entitled *Obras históricas y políticas* (Political and historical works), the publisher had collected primarily newspaper articles on politics, economics, and finance. Other essays touch on such topics as the Communist Party, international election supervision, and trade unions.

475 **Employment and economic growth in Costa Rica.**
Gary S. Fields. *World Development*, vol. 16, no. 12 (Dec. 1988),
p. 1493-1509. bibliog.

The central issue addressed by this article is the identification of who benefited from
different epochs in Costa Rica's economic growth in the period 1960-85. From 1960 to
1980, according to the author, employment kept up with population growth, the share
of wage-earners in the Costa Rica labour force increased, the largest percentage
increases in employment took place in the highest-paid occupations, the Costa Rican
labour force became markedly better educated, and income inequality declined. The
author clearly explains the reasons for these trends in narrative form and supplies
supportive statistical data. He also provides an analysis of the economic crisis of 1980-
82 and explains the resumption of the earlier favourable trends during the subsequent
recovery. Finally, he makes specific policy recommendations. The economic picture is
rosier than most economists have painted, but the article nevertheless deserves close
attention by anyone interested in Costa Rica's economy.

476 **Fear of adjusting: the social costs of economic policies in the 1970s.**
Claudio González-Vega. In: *Revolution and counter-revolution in
Central America and the Caribbean*, edited by Donald Schulz, Douglas
H. Graham. Boulder, Colorado: Westview Press, 1984, p. 351-83.

The author deals much more with economic policies than with their social costs. He
criticizes the politicians of the 1970s for their fear of making structural changes, such as
a change in the protectionist policy of import substitution or a cut in private and public
spending. The article ends on a very pessimistic note, concluding that if politicians are
unable to make structural changes because of political fears of the high social costs
involved, Costa Rica's democracy may not survive. The chapter contains various charts
of economic conditions from 1950 to 1983.

477 **Costa Rica.**
Lowell Gudmundson. In: *Latin America and Caribbean:
contemporary record*, edited by Jack W. Hopkins. New York: Holmes
and Meier, 1984-85, Vol. IV, p. 454-69. map.

After a sceptical look at President Monge's 'proclaimed victory' over the economic
crisis, the author emphasizes political issues. Monge's administration had to react to
two issues in late 1984 and 1985: the pullout of United Brands from its banana
operations in the South Pacific zone, and the pressure from political opponents and
from the United States to abandon neutrality. The presidential campaign of 1985 is
covered, and although Gudmundson erred in his prediction of the eventual victor (as
did many political analysts), the discussion is full of useful information concerning the
parties and the candidates.

478 **Hacia dónde va Costa Rica?: 56 preguntas y respuestas sobre la crisis.**
(Where is Costa Rica going? 56 questions and answers on the crisis.)
Edited by Miguel Gutiérrez Saxe. San José: Editorial Porvenir, 1985.
158p. bibliog.

The authors of the articles included in this edited volume believe that the
contemporary crisis of Costa Rica is economic, political and moral, but the questions
and answers focus sharply on the economic crisis. Questions on the International

Monetary Fund, multinational corporations, classes benefiting and classes suffering from the economic crisis, tax policies, etc. are answered in a straightforward, non-traditional manner. In essence the book is a primer on current economic problems for the non-specialist.

479 **The economic cycle in Latin American agricultural export economies, 1880-1930: a hypothesis for investigation.**
Héctor Pérez Brignoli. *Latin American Research Review*, vol. 15, no. 2 (1980), p. 3-33.
In this succinct discussion of the theory of export economies the cases of Argentine wheat and Costa Rican coffee in the 1880-1930 period are compared. Pérez Brignoli explains how the expansion of coffee production in Costa Rica did not result in any major land concentration.

480 **Capitalismo y crisis económica en Costa Rica: treinta años de desarrollo.**
(Capitalism and economic crisis in Costa Rica: 30 years of development.)
Sergio Reuben Soto. San José: Editorial Porvenir, 1982. 266p.
bibliog. (Colección Debate).
Backed by numerous sets of statistics on production during the years 1950 to 1980 the author, a demographer trained in Mexico, attempts to account for the economic crisis of Costa Rica in the 1980s. The author makes a special effort to avoid duplicating previous studies of the coffee and banana industries, and instead deals with total agricultural and manufacturing output. He is also concerned with how capitalism dictates the organization of society for production.

481 **El Fondo Monetario Internacional y Costa Rica, 1978-1982: política económica y crisis.** (The International Monetary Fund and Costa Rica, 1978-82: political economy and crisis.)
Eugenio Rivera Urrutia. San José: Departamento Ecuménico de Investigaciones, 1982. 179p. bibliog. (Colección Centroamérica).
This work is a study of economic policies during the Rodrigo Carazo administration, which the author characterizes as a period of crisis. The author gives special attention to the debate over economic policies that took place within the administration and within the business community, particularly over the issue of government intervention in the economy and the steps required by the International Monetary Fund. The crisis culminated in the 1981 decision to suspend payment of the foreign debt.

482 **Costa Rica hoy: la crisis y sus perspectivas.** (Costa Rica today: the crisis and its perspectives.)
Edited by Jorge Rovira Mas. San José: Editorial Universidad Estatal a Distancia, 1983. 248p. bibliog.
The crisis referred to in the title is the economic crisis of 1981-82. Economists, sociologists, and historians contributed papers on various aspects of the crisis at a conference held in Heredia in October 1982, and thirteen of the presentations were chosen for publication in this volume. The principal purpose of the papers is to relate the economic problems of contemporary Costa Rica with the country's historical background.

483 **The Costa Rican laboratory.**
Sol W. Sanders. New York: Priority Press, 1986. 72p.

A clearly written, succinct description of the economic crisis of the 1980s. Historical factors such as the revolution of 1948 and the Central American Common Market form the backdrop as the author weaves together other factors, such as the international debt, pressure from the International Monetary Fund, tax policy, export policy, inflation, devaluation, and financial assistance from the United States Agency for International Development into a coherent whole. Numerous tables provide statistical detail on the crisis.

484 **Historia económica y hacendaria de Costa Rica.** (An economic and financial history of Costa Rica.)
Tomás Soley Güell. San José: Editorial Universitaria, 1947-49.
2 vols. (Sección Ciencias Sociales y Jurídicas, no. 1).

Soley Güell's monumental study of economic and financial history of Costa Rica is over forty years old but still useful. Volume one devotes approximately 100 pages to the colonial period and twice that to the 19th century up to 1890. Volume two covers only as far as the León Cortés administration (1936-40). Before 1940 Soley y Güell published other books on Costa Rica's monetary and financial history but most of his views are available in this book which is both factual and interpretative. He does not hesitate to condemn what he believes to have been unsound policy.

485 **Costa Rica: crisis, adjustment policies and rural development.**
Juan M. Villasuso. *CEPAL Review*, no. 33 (Dec. 1987), p. 107-13.

For a succinct and balanced account of the Costa Rican economic model, the crisis it suffered in the late 1970s and the early 1980s, and policy reaction to the crisis, students of the Costa Rican economy can do no better than search out this article. Villasuso served as minister of planning in the Oscar Arias administration (1986-90).

Economic development

486 **Nuevos rumbos para el desarrollo costarricense.** (New directions for Costa Rican development.)
Oscar Arias Sánchez. Ciudad Universitària Rodrigo Facio, San José: Editorial Universitaria Centroamericana, 1979. 150p. (Colección Seis).

A comprehensive essay on Costa Rica's political economy. It touches on issues of economic development, demography, international relations, planning, and democracy. Written in 1979, it is a reliable guide to the attitudes which the author brought to the presidency, 1986-90.

487 **Los problemas económicos del desarrollo en Costa Rica.** (Economic problems of development in Costa Rica.)
Edited by Oscar Barahona Streber. San José: Editorial Universidad Estatal a Distancia, 1981. 230p. (Cátedra Libre).

The lectures in this volume were presented before a university audience in 1979 by a group of prominent economists, some of them also Costa Rican government officials. The topics covered include social security, inflation, the budget, alternative economic models, and statistical measures of Costa Rican development. Questions from the audience and each speaker's replies are included.

488 **Income distribution and economic development: some intra-country evidence.**
Manuel J. Carvajal, David T. Geithman. *Southern Economic Journal,* vol. 44, no. 4 (April 1978), p. 922-8. bibliog.

This is a technical explanation of how income distribution figures from each of Costa Rica's 335 *distritos* [districts] is affected by variables such as education, age, unemployment, and the economic sector. The figures are taken from the 1963 census.

489 **The limits of reform development in contemporary Costa Rica.**
Juan M. Del Aguila. *Journal of Interamerican Studies and World Affairs,* vol. 24, no. 3 (Aug. 1982), p. 355-74. bibliog.

An overview of the economic and political factors contributing to the economic crisis of the late 1970s and early 1980s. Del Aguila believes that the political and social strain created by the crisis combined with the absolute growth of the electorate has left the government in an extremely difficult position. The article contains a very brief but useful discussion of the 1982 elections, including a focus on the nature of the party system in Costa Rica.

490 **Nicaragua and Costa Rica.**
Lawrence E. Harrison. In: *Underdevelopment is a state of mind: the Latin American case,* Lawrence E. Harrison. Cambridge, Massachusetts: Center for International Affairs, Harvard University, 1985, p. 35-59.

Although comparison of the economic development of Nicaragua and Costa Rica helps to explain the relative failure of the former and the success of the latter, this account is marred by a rather subjective interpretation of regional aspects of the national character of Spain and their presumed affects on the national character of Costa Rica. The author served as director of the United States Agency for International Development (USAID) in both countries.

491 **Exports and economic growth in Costa Rica: past trends and medium-term possibilities.**
Luis Liberman.   PhD dissertation, University of Illinois. 1972. 205p.
bibliog. (Available from University Microfilms, Ann Arbor, Michigan,
order no. 73-17,297).

Two principal purposes shape this work: the first is to analyse the theoretical and
empirical impact of exports on economic development in Costa Rica's past; the second
is to construct a model and forecast the impact of the export sector on Costa Rica's
economy in 1970-80. Although the forecast is obviously out of date, the model is worth
studying in relation to what actually happened in the decade of the 1970s. The general
survey of the significance of exports in the Costa Rican economy is excellent.

492 **Costa Rica, a study in economic development.**
Stacy May (et al.).   New York: Twentieth Century Fund Study Group,
1952. 374p. maps.

Although the statistics are outdated, this book stands out as an early classical economic
study of development at the outset of the so-called development decade. It is based on
the findings of a group of five economists and financial experts sent to Costa Rica in
1950 by the Twentieth Century Fund. The purpose was to establish an economic baseline to serve as a guide for the formulation of foreign aid policy of the United States in
Costa Rica. Policy recommendations on development and fiscal policy are quite
specific. It remains the only English-language survey of all aspects of the Costa Rican
economy and is therefore still useful as an introduction and invaluable as an historical
source.

493 **Equitable growth: the case of Costa Rica.**
Phillip W. Rourk.   Washington, DC: United States Agency for
International Development, 1979. 93p. bibliog.

Rourk argues that Costa Rica is the sole example of a Latin American country which
has successfully pursued a strategy of combining economic development with an
equitable distribution of the benefits. Numerous tables illustrating Costa Rica's record
in comparison with other Latin American countries – on such social measures as
longevity, infant mortality, distribution of income, percentage of the population below
the poverty line, and physical quality of life – substantiate Rourk's interpretation. It is
initial conditions such as scarcity of labour, abundant land, and a democratic system of
government which account for the differences and not, according to Rourk,
administrative decisions.

494 **Costa Rica: two great assets and many problems.**
John Sheahan.   In: *Patterns of development in Latin America: poverty,
repression and economic strategy*, John Sheahan. Princeton, New
Jersey: Princeton University Press, 1987. p. 288-96. bibliog.

Costa Rica's two great assets, according to Sheahan, are 'its open political system and
its relatively inclusive society'. Within a framework of recent political history Sheahan
explains how Costa Rica's democratic system led to a model of greater urban–rural
cooperation and a more reliable welfare state than in most Latin American countries.
A weakening Central American Common Market, failed import substitution projects,

high oil prices, and inflation strained the system in the late 1970s and early 1980s, but Costa Rica recovered and Sheahan makes suggestions on how to build on the recovery.

495 **Hacia una interpretación del desarrollo costarricense: ensayo sociológico.** (Towards an interpretation of Costa Rican development: a sociological essay.)
José Luis Vega Carballo.   San José: Editorial Porvenir, 1983. 4th ed. 420p. bibliog. (Colección Debate).

This collection of essays by a prominent Costa Rican sociologist is arranged chronologically to offer a sociological interpretation of Costa Rican history within the framework of dependency theory. The topics covered include: the colonial transition from the cultivation of cacao to tobacco, and later to coffee; the role of mining; the development of a bourgeoisie dependent on the international economy, first through coffee exports and later through banana exports.

Investigaciones geográficas en la sección oriental de la península de Nicoya, Costa Rica. (Geographical investigations in the eastern section of the Nicoya peninsula, Costa Rica.)
See item no. 35.

El desarrollo nacional en 150 años de vida independiente. (National development during 150 years of independence.)
See item no. 153.

Historia económica del tabaco: época colonial. (The economic history of tobacco: colonial era.)
See item no. 183.

Historia económica de Costa Rica, 1821-1971. (Economic history of Costa Rica, 1821-1971.)
See item no. 199.

Lucha social y guerra civil en Costa Rica, 1940-1948. (The social conflict and civil war in Costa Rica, 1940-48.)
See item no. 228.

Historia económica de Costa Rica, 1950-1970. (The economic history of Costa Rica, 1950-70.)
See item no. 235.

Población, fecundidad y desarrollo en Costa Rica, 1950-1970. (Population, fecundity and development in Costa Rica, 1950-70.)
See item no. 238.

An economic analysis of migration in Costa Rica.
See item no. 240.

Demography and development: the lessons of Costa Rica.
See item no. 243.

Economics

Rural development in Costa Rica.
See item no. 303.

Turrialba: social systems and the introduction of change.
See item no. 306.

Rural electrification and development: social and economic impact in Costa Rica and Colombia.
See item no. 310.

Urban poverty and economic development: a case study of Costa Rica.
See item no. 326.

Situation, principal problems and prospects for the economic and social development of Costa Rica.
See item no. 327.

Liberalismo: veinticinco años de ANFE. (Liberalism: twenty-five years of ANFE.)
See item no. 357.

Costa Rica.
See item no. 373.

Costa Rica.
See item no. 384.

Costa Rica.
See item no. 385.

Democratic stability and economic crisis: Costa Rica, 1978-1983.
See item no. 387.

Costa Rica's political turmoil: can production support the welfare state?
See item no. 396.

Costa Rica: crisis y desafíos. (Costa Rica: crisis and challenges.)
See item no. 398.

Costa Rica: problems of social democracy.
See item no. 400.

One road to democracy with development: José Figueres and the social democratic project after 1948.
See item no. 401.

Ideas políticas elementales. (Elementary political ideas.)
See item no. 420.

Costa Rica.
See item no. 422.

Costa Rica: the end of the fiesta.
See item no. 423.

Costa Rica: Gesellschaft und Kultur eines Staates mit ständiger aktiver und unbewaffneter Neutralität. (Costa Rica: the society and culture of a state practising active and unarmed neutrality.)
See item no. 434.

Back from the brink.
See item no. 443.

The Inter-American Development Bank and political influence, with special reference to Costa Rica.
See item no. 499.

The Inter-American Development Bank and policy making in Costa Rica.
See item no. 500.

Ciento cinco años de vida bancaria en Costa Rica. (150 years of banking in Costa Rica.)
See item no. 501.

Agricultural credit in Costa Rica.
See item no. 506.

Trade structure and linkages in Costa Rica: an input–output approach.
See item no. 508.

Costa Rica, Panama and Central American economic integration.
See item no. 510.

El desarrollo del capital en la industria de Costa Rica, 1950-1970. (The development of capital in the industry of Costa Rica, 1950-70.)
See item no. 512.

Export beef production and development contradictions in Costa Rica.
See item no. 519.

Agricultural choice and change: decision making in a Costa Rican community.
See item no. 537.

Population growth, economic progress, and opportunities on the land: the case of Costa Rica.
See item no. 550.

A case study of response to agricultural prices in Costa Rica.
See item no. 554.

An assessment of the agricultural sector in Costa Rica.
See item no. 555.

La production agricole et la vie rurale au Costa Rica. (Agricultural production and rural life in Costa Rica.)
See item no. 556.

Economics

Bureaucracy and the unmanaged forest commons in Costa Rica, or why development does not grow on trees.
See item no. 562.

Pasture expansion, forestry and development contradictions: the case of Costa Rica.
See item no. 563.

Formación de la fuerza laboral costarricense: una contribución a la historia económica social y administrativa de Costa Rica. (Formation of the Costa Rican labour force: a contribution to the economic, social and administrative history of Costa Rica.)
See item no. 582.

Labor mobility and economic growth: the Central American experience – Costa Rica and El Salvador.
See item no. 586.

Legal minimum wages as an instrument of social policy in Costa Rica.
See item no. 587.

Towards a national employment policy: the case of Costa Rica.
See item no. 588.

Educational problems related to the economic development of Costa Rica.
See item no. 612.

Alfredo González Flores, "su pensamiento." (Alfredo González Flores, 'his thought'.)
See item no. 721.

Rodrigo Facio: el economista. (Rodrigo Facio: the economist.)
See item no. 722.

Bibliography of poverty and related topics in Costa Rica.
See item no. 750.

Bibliografía agrícola de Costa Rica. (Agricultural bibliography of Costa Rica.)
See item no. 751.

Investment, Finance, Banking and Currency

496 Income and export taxation of agriculture in Costa Rica and Honduras.
Donald E. Baer. *Journal of Developing Areas*, vol. 8, no. 1 (Oct. 1973), p. 39-54.

The principal conclusion of Baer's study is that a large proportion of farms in Costa Rica and Honduras are excluded from any significant direct taxation. Neither country relies on a property tax. Indirect taxes on income and exports produce revenue, but in Costa Rica income tax is paid by a relatively few agriculturalists and the tax on exports is low. The study provides statistical data on taxation of agriculture primarily from the 1960s.

497 The retail sales tax in a developing country: Costa Rica and Honduras.
Donald E. Baer. *National Tax Journal*, vol. 24 (1971), p. 465-73.

Honduras was the first Central American country to adopt a sales tax and Costa Rica the second. Because the Central American Common Market of the early 1960s resulted in declining government revenue from import taxes, the Costa Rican legislature instituted a sales tax in July 1967. During 1968, the first full year of operation, the Costa Rican sales tax represented 13 per cent of the central government's tax receipts. This article describes the tax legislation, exemptions, administration of the tax, and results. Comparison with Honduras is helpful in understanding the Costa Rican approach to taxation.

498 British investments in Costa Rica.
Henry C. Bischoff. *Inter-American Economic Affairs*, vol. 7, no. 1 (Summer 1953), p. 37-47.

One learns from this brief article, based mainly on British Stock Exchange yearbooks, that British investments in Costa Rica were not numerous – reaching a peak of about two million pounds in 1900 – and profits not very high.

499 **The Inter-American Development Bank and political influence, with special reference to Costa Rica.**
R. Peter DeWitt, Jr.   New York: Praeger, 1977. 197p. bibliog.
(Praeger Special Studies in International Economics and Development).

Although there is some discussion of the general benefits to economic development in Costa Rica, the principal approach of the book is to consider the Inter-American Development Bank as an instrument of United States policy. According to DeWitt the Bank's loans to Costa Rica favour Central American economic integration, which favours United States investment in Costa Rica and the interests of multinational corporations. Also, instead of supporting social programmes which would bring greater benefits to Costa Rica the Bank has gradually shifted to the support of transport and power projects which force Costa Rica to import goods from the United States. This in turn worsens Costa Rican terms of trade and increases its debt service. The study, which the author expressly places in the dependency school, was originally a dissertation in political science.

500 **The Inter-American Development Bank and policy making in Costa Rica.**
R. Peter DeWitt, Jr.   *Journal of Developing Areas*, vol. 15, no. 1 (Oct. 1980), p. 67-82.

Professor DeWitt shows that the loan policies of the Inter-American Development Bank (IADB) coincide with the Latin American policy of the United States and do not necessarily advance the best interests of the Latin American member countries. His study shows that instead of furthering social programmes, which would benefit Costa Rica, IADB loans fund infrastructure projects. These encourage imports (primarily from the United States), increasing Costa Rican indebtedness and stimulating foreign (primarily United States) investment in Costa Rica. Since IADB policies may also influence other lending agencies, Costa Rica is not in effect in control of its own economic development.

501 **Ciento cinco años de vida bancaria en Costa Rica.** (150 years of banking in Costa Rica.)
Rufino Gil Pacheco.   San José: Editorial Costa Rica, 1975. 3rd ed. 415p. bibliog.

Banking is a controversial subject in Costa Rica. This book sheds light especially on the controversy surrounding the decree of nationalization of the banking system by the Government Junta in June 1949 and subsequent legislation. It also covers the history of private banking from the mid-19th century to the 1940s. Finished in 1958, the first edition was not published until 1962, and for recent important changes in the Costa Rican banking system more recent sources would have to be consulted. The book suffers somewhat from organizational peculiarities and excess of detail but it is a solid reference on Costa Rican banks.

502 **Banco central. (The Central Bank.)**
Carlos Hernández. San José: Editorial Universidad Estatal a Distancia, 1980. 146p. bibliog.

Readers should choose this book for clear answers to the following questions within the Costa Rican context: what does a Central Bank do? how does it affect the money supply? inflation? unemployment? economic development? Hernández, an official of the Costa Rican Central Bank, also reviews the history of banking in Costa Rica and discusses the relation of the Central Bank to other banks in the country and overseas.

503 **Inside Costa Rica: behind the banana curtain.**
Atlanta, Georgia: Guide Publications, 1979. 30p.

The author, who is nowhere identified in the booklet, attempts to debunk the reputation of Costa Rica for democracy and honest, stable government. Presented as a guide to investors, it actually seems to warn prospective investors away by emphasizing excessive bureaucracy, corruption, and illegality. Victor Rasmussen, the presumed author, was killed in a road accident in Atlanta in 1980.

504 **Tax systems of Latin America: Costa Rica.**
Joint Tax Program of the Organization of American States and the Inter-American Development Bank. Washington, DC: Pan American Union, 1966. 76p.

Basic data on the entire tax structure of Costa Rica as of 1966 is contained in this booklet, one of a series on tax structure in the Latin American countries sponsored by the Organization of American States.

505 **Costa Rica: investor's guide.**
Felicia M. Morales. San José: American Chamber of Commerce of Costa Rica, 1979. 65p.

A precise, attractive presentation of background information on Costa Rica, on the business climate, and on general economic conditions. The publication also contains basic information on banks, government agencies, and professional associations.

506 **Agricultural credit in Costa Rica.**
Robert C. Vogel, Claudio González Vega. San José: Associated Colleges of the Midwest, 1969. 157p.

This economic analysis contains the results of extensive interviews of Costa Rican farmers, bankers, officers in cooperatives (and others) on the availability of credit to agriculturalists. The long introduction is a careful study of banking and loan practices and the conclusion offers specific suggestions on how to improve agricultural credit. For example, the authors argue that a low interest rate for agricultural loans, generally favoured by economic development specialists, is in effect a subsidy to the relatively few well-off people who get the available loans. High interest rates, they argue, might be more likely to put loans in the hands of the poorest farmers.

507 **Confronting the coffee oligarchy: the roots of Costa Rica's 'middle road'.**
Anthony Winson. *Canadian Journal of Latin American and Caribbean Studies*, vol. 9, no. 17 (1984), p. 33-50. bibliog.
In this important revisionist article Winson, a sociologist, attempts to account for the success of the National Liberation Party in taming the coffee oligarchy and creating a more diversified economy. The focus is on national budgeting and tax legislation, topics which have generally escaped the attention of other scholars. Winson believes that President José Figueres' political skill in promoting the new tax legislation of 1952 was the principal factor in producing the revenue that enabled Costa Rica to expand public services in the 1950s. The tax legislation marks a clear break between the coffee oligarchy of the past and the political economic model of the future.

The Costa Rican laboratory.
See item no. 353.

One road to democracy with development: José Figueres and the social democratic project after 1948.
See item no. 401.

Obras de Rodrigo Facio. (The works of Rodrigo Facio.)
See item no. 474.

Hacia dónde va Costa Rica?: 56 preguntas y respuestas sobre la crisis. (Where is Costa Rica going? 56 questions and answers on the crisis.)
See item no. 478.

Historia económica y hacendaria de Costa Rica. (An economic and financial history of Costa Rica.)
See item no. 484.

Structural determinants of the location of rural development institutions in Costa Rica.
See item no. 546.

Foreign Trade

508 Trade structure and linkages in Costa Rica: an input–output approach.
Victor Bulmer-Thomas. *Journal of Development Economics*, vol. 5 (March 1978), p. 73-86.
In this brief, technically oriented article Bulmer-Thomas provides the first input–output analysis of Costa Rica's trade performance. Before this, there had been no good measure of Costa Rica's ambitious policy of import-substituting industrialization. The period covered is the 1960s, when the Central American Common Market provided the framework for Costa Rica's industrialization policy. The author concludes that trade with the rest of Central America produced a comparative advantage in consumer durables, particularly metal goods and electrical equipment.

509 Notas introductorias al conocimiento de la sociedad costarricense y de los efectos de la integración centroamericana. (Introductory notes on Costa Rican society and the effects of Central American integration.)
Daniel Camacho. San José: Universidad de Costa Rica, 1978. 126p.
(Avances de Investigación, no. 32).
This article outlines the often-overlooked negative effects of the Central American Common Market movement. It emphasizes the increased dependence of Costa Rican industry on foreign goods.

510 Costa Rica, Panama and Central American economic integration.
James D. Cochrane. *Journal of Inter-American Studies*, vol. 7, no. 3 (July 1965), p. 331-44.
Cochrane first explains the reasons for Costa Rica's hesitancy in joining the Central American Common Market. They centred on fears of losing control of its industrial development policy, its customs, and its social welfare programme, and on nationalist objections to close cooperation with countries with different political and ethnic conditions. Secondly, Cochrane explains why Costa Rica changed its mind and joined the Common Market in 1963. He concludes that changing economic conditions and

foreign policy pressures convinced Costa Rica that staying out of the Common Market promised more disadvantages than did joining. Finally, Cochrane connects Panama's similar dilemma with the above.

511 Costa Rica and the Central American Common Market.
Charles E. Staley. *Economica Internazionale*, vol. 15, no. 1 (Feb. 1962), p. 117-30.

In this article Staley provides a criticial appraisal of the reasons for Costa Rica's original refusal to join the Central American Common Market in 1960. He argues that none of the reasons was convincing. Since Costa Rica soon joined the Common Market he must have been right.

The development of foreign trade and communication in Costa Rica to the construction of the first railway.
See item no. 165.

Modernization and dependency in Costa Rica during the decade of the 1880's.
See item no. 213.

Costa Rican trade and navigation ties with United States, Germany and Europe: 1840 to 1885.
See item no. 233.

Agrarian capitalism and the transformation of peasant society: coffee in Costa Rica.
See item no. 311.

Costa Rica, Honduras, and Panama.
See item no. 411.

Problemas económicos en la década de los ochenta. (Economic problems in the decade of the eighties.)
See item no. 472.

The economic cycle in Latin American agricultural export economies, 1880-1930: a hypothesis for investigation.
See item no. 479.

The Costa Rican laboratory.
See item no. 483.

Exports and economic growth in Costa Rica: past trends and medium-term possibilities.
See item no. 491.

British investments in Costa Rica.
See item no. 498.

The Inter-American Development Bank and political influence, with special reference to Costa Rica.
See item no. 499.

Sobre la evolución de las actividades bananeras en Costa Rica. (The evolution of the banana industry in Costa Rica.)
See item no. 522.

Export subsidies: the case of Costa Rica's banana industry.
See item no. 526.

Industry

General

512 **El desarrollo del capital en la industria de Costa Rica, 1950-1970.**
(The development of capital in the industry of Costa Rica, 1950-70.)
Francisco Esquivel Villegas.   Heredia, Costa Rica: Editorial
Universidad Nacional, 1985. 200p. bibliog.

There is no doubt that Costa Rican industry experienced rapid growth after the
revolution of 1948. However, there is controversy over the issue of who received the
principal benefits of the expansion. According to Esquivel, the benefits fell more to
United States enterprises, which took advantage of Costa Rica's entry into the Central
American Common Market in 1963, than to Costa Rican enterprises. Charts show
precisely what kinds of industry expanded most rapidly and which interests, foreign or
national, dominated.

513 **The case of Costa Rica.**
Lincoln G. Valentine.   Washington, DC: Gibson Brothers, 1919.
109p.

Valentine, a business promoter with petroleum interests in Costa Rica in the early 20th
century, is the author of this inside explanation of politics and commerce during the
Alfredo González Flores administration (1914-17). He pays special attention to
González Flores' fall from power in 1917.

514 **Costa Rican industrial crossroads: final report.**
Chicago, Illinois: Wolf Management Engineering Company, 1962.
162p.

The purpose of this study, contracted by the United States Agency for International
Development, is to assist the government of Costa Rica in planning industrial
development. The report stresses the need for setting up action programmes, planning
councils, broad basic surveys, feasibility studies, and investment credit institutions.

515   **A statement of the laws of Costa Rica in matters affecting business.**
Harry A. Zürcher, Sr., Erick Montoya, Edgar A. Zürcher.
Washington, DC: Organization of American States, 1978. 5th ed. 312p.
bibliog.

Thirty-six chapters in this statement summarize the basic legislation of Costa Rica, especially in the areas of commercial, industrial, and labour law. This revised and enlarged edition supersedes the volume published in 1969. A useful bibliography on codes, court reports, and legal works is appended.

Cattle industry

516   **La élite ganadera en Costa Rica.** (The cattlemen's élite in Costa Rica.)
Irene Aguilar, Manuel Solís.   San José: Editorial de la Universidad de
Costa Rica, 1988. 178p.

With a solid base in the censuses of 1955, 1963, and 1973, and with additional data from newspapers and documents the authors provide a clear picture of the effects of the rapid expansion of cattle production, primarily for export, in the last three decades. They document the concentration of cattle production and export in the hands of relatively few companies and explain how government policies, despite a public commitment to small landowners, helped to bring the concentration about.

517   **Modernization of Costa Rica's beef cattle economy: 1950-1985.**
John P. Augelli. *Journal of Cultural Geography*, vol. 9, no. 2
(Summer 1989), p. 77-90. maps.

The social and ecological costs of modernization in Costa Rica are increasingly being examined. One of the best examples is this article on the beef industry. After an outline of the historical and geographical parameters of the industry, Augelli analyses the factors that brought on the impulse for modernization, documents Costa Rica's change from being a net importer of beef in 1950 to an important exporter of beef in the 1980s, and reports on the positive and negative consequences of the transformation.

518   **Land utilization in Guanacaste Province of Costa Rica.**
Henry F. Becker. *Geographical Review*, vol. 33, no. 1 (Jan. 1943),
p. 74-85. map.

The principal focus here is the cattle industry, but with some attention given to farming and logging. Comments on communication and transport reveal how primitive economic conditions were in the North Pacific zone of Costa Rica in the 1940s.

519 **Export beef production and development contradictions in Costa Rica.**
Susan E. Place. *Tijdschrift voor Economische en Sociale Geografie,*
vol. 76, no. 4 (1985), p. 288-97. bibliog.

The author describes the boom in beef production in Costa Rica since the 1950s. The government's role in promoting beef production for export, on the assumption that it would help to diversify the economy and increase employment, is also described. She concludes that far from developing Costa Rica's economy and contributing to the general welfare, increasing beef production has deepened the country's dependence on foreign markets and caused widespread ecological damage, thus limiting future development options.

Coffee industry

520 **The formation of the coffee estate in nineteenth-century Costa Rica.**
Ciro F. S. Cardoso. In: *Land and labour in Latin America: essays on the development of agrarian capitalism in the nineteenth and twentieth centuries,* edited by Kenneth Duncan, Ian Rutledge, Colin Harding. Cambridge, England: Cambridge University Press, 1977, p. 165-202. (Cambridge Latin American Studies, no. 26).

This is an excellent brief overview of the beginning of the coffee revolution in Costa Rica in the early 19th century. The author concentrates chronologically on the period 1830-60 and geographically on the Central Valley. According to Cardoso, Costa Rica's small population and consequent labour shortage, as compared to the labour surplus in other coffee-growing countries, kept wages up and landed estates relatively small. Although Costa Rica prospered more than some other countries that followed the same development path it still became dependent on outside capital and markets.

521 **Coffee production and processing on a large Costa Rican "finca".**
Paul C. Morrison, Thomas L. Norris. *Papers of the Michigan Academy of Science Arts and Letters,* vol. 39 (1954), p. 309-22.

In this study of the Aquiares coffee *finca* [estate] near Turrialba the emphasis is placed on the different agricultural and administrative practices between coffee production in the Turrialba area and that of the Central Valley.

Banana industry

522 **Sobre la evolución de las actividades bananeras en Costa Rica.** (The
evolution of the banana industry in Costa Rica.)
Reinaldo Carcanholo. *Estudios Sociales Centroamericanos*, vol. 7,
no. 19 (Jan.-April 1978), p. 143-203.
This is first and foremost a statistical study, with twenty-six charts showing banana
exports, value and percentage of exports, exports by different ports, level of
investment by the banana companies, prices compared with other banana-producing
countries, etc. Secondly, it is a narrative of the history of United Fruit Company
operations in Costa Rica. The latter is heavily dependent on out-of-date secondary
sources, and the operations of other banana companies are neglected.

523 **Limón, 1880-1940: un estudio de la industria bananera en Costa Rica.**
(Limón, 1880-1940: a study of the banana industry en Costa Rica.)
Jeffrey Casey Gaspar. San José: Editorial Costa Rica, 1979. 331p.
maps. bibliog.
Most books on the banana industry in Costa Rica take positions strongly in favour of
or strongly against the United Fruit Company. This one, by contrast, is an even-
handed economic and social analysis of the United Fruit Company experience in
Limón Province. One chapter details the Company's contracts with private banana
proprietors and with labourers, subjects not usually treated in banana industry
literature. Casey also carefully assesses the economic impact of the Company in Limón
and on the nation as a whole. The result provides material for the Company's friends
as well as its detractors.

524 **Evolution of the banana industry of Costa Rica.**
Clarence F. Jones, Paul C. Morrison. *Economic Geography*, vol. 28,
no. 1 (Jan. 1952), p. 1-19. maps.
Jones and Morrison approach the banana industry from the point of view of production
and management and give little attention to tax and labour controversies. They provide
a good historical overview of banana production on the Caribbean coast of Costa Rica
in the peak years 1900 to 1930, and adequately cover the efforts of the banana
companies to deal with Panama and sigatoka diseases and with soil exhaustion. The
latter half of the article narrates the operations, begun in the 1930s, of the United Fruit
Company in the Quepos and Golfito regions of the Pacific coast.

525 **Social aspects of the banana industry.**
Charles David Kepner. New York: AMS Press, 1936. 230p. bibliog.
(Studies in History, Economics, and Public Law, no. 414).
Within the broad topic of the banana industry this book focuses on the activities of the
United Fruit Company. Since much of the story of United Fruit unfolds in Costa Rica
the book has a place in this bibliography. Unlike the banana industry accounts which
take the boardroom perspective, this book deals principally with banana workers, their
wages, working conditions, and unionization. Coverage of United Fruit's experience
with workmen's compensation laws in Costa Rica is provided.

171

526 **Export subsidies: the case of Costa Rica's banana industry.**
Jennifer Morsink-Villalobos, James R. Simpson.   *Inter-American Economic Affairs*, vol. 34, no. 3 (Winter 1980), p. 69-86.

The authors focus carefully on the potential of the banana industry in Costa Rica. They conclude that an export subsidy on bananas would not violate the General Agreement on Tariffs and Trade (GATT) and would not be harmful to the world banana industry. It would, however, help Costa Rica keep its share of the banana export market.

527 **Effective agricultural development of former banana lands: the west coast of Costa Rica.**
Pierre A. D. Stouse, Jr.   *Revista Geográfica*, no. 66 (June 1967), p. 153-62. map.

The geographical focus of this article is the Quepos–Parrita banana lands of the Pacific coast of Costa Rica and the theme is the search on the part of the United Fruit Company for agricultural stability, in particular to find crop substitutes for bananas. Disease and soil exhaustion forced the company to abandon banana production and experiment with African oil palm, cacao, and other products. Patterns of settlement, the effects on the labour force, and relations between the United Fruit Company and other producers are also discussed.

528 **Instability of tropical agriculture: the Atlantic lowlands of Costa Rica.**
Pierre A. D. Stouse, Jr.   *Economic Geography*, vol. 46, no. 1 (Jan. 1970), p. 78-97.

Stouse, a geographer, analyses the economic, geographical, and cultural factors that have produced the instability of banana production on the Atlantic side of Costa Rica. Pressures which operate on the large fruit corporations, the independent producers, the cooperatives, and the small owners are also analysed. Stouse notes the revival of banana production on the Atlantic coast since 1958 and predicts (as it turned out, quite correctly) the abandonment of much of the land then in production.

Fishing industry

529 **An investigation into the microbiological quality of fish in Guatemala and Costa Rica.**
Edited by Luis F. Arias.   Kingston, Rhode Island: International Center for Marine Resource Development, University of Rhode Island, 1978. 34p. map. bibliog. (ICMRD Working Paper, no. 3).

After conducting two surveys of fish handling by artisan fishers in Costa Rica, the authors severely criticize insanitary practices. They report high counts of bacteria, coliform, and *Staphylococcus*, which they conclude are the result of contamination by human sources. Inadequate icing and poor handling during transport and display are among the problems mentioned. The study was commissioned by the United States Agency for International Development.

530 **Small scale fisheries in Central America: acquiring information for decision making.**
Edited by Jon G. Sutinen, Richard B. Pollnac. Kingston, Rhode Island: International Center for Marine Resource Development, University of Rhode Island, 1979. 612p.

This book is a multidisciplinary collection of twenty-nine articles dealing with Costa Rica, El Salvador, and Guatemala, with an emphasis on Costa Rica. The idea of the volume is to shed light on the development of the small-scale fishery and on government policies affecting this sector. The articles range in focus from artisan fishermen in the Gulf of Nicoya, to the marketing sector (including the middleman and fish quality), and finally to the administration of official Costa Rican fishery policies.

Costa Rica ayer y hoy, 1800-1939. (Costa Rica yesterday and today, 1800-1939.)
See item no. 13.

Costa Rica: immigration pamphlet with two maps, a guide for the agricultural class coming from other countries to make Costa Rica its home.
See item no. 16.

Costa Rica: a geographical interpretation in historical perspective.
See item no. 22.

Revista Geográfica. (Geographical Review.)
See item no. 31.

The development of foreign trade and communication in Costa Rica to the construction of the first railway.
See item no. 165.

La minería en Costa Rica (1821-1843). (Mining in Costa Rica, 1821-43.)
See item no. 200.

Urbanization and modernization in Costa Rica during the 1880s.
See item no. 212.

Cultural change, social conflict, and changing distributions of authority in the Caribbean lowlands of Costa Rica.
See item no. 266.

The adaptation of West Indian Blacks to North American and Hispanic culture in Costa Rica.
See item no. 268.

Emigrantes a la conquista de la selva: estudio de un caso de colonización en Costa Rica, San Vito de Java. (Emigrants conquering the jungle: case-study of a colonization in Costa Rica, San Vito de Java.)
See item no. 279.

Ethnicity and livelihoods: a social geography of Costa Rica's Atlantic zone.
See item no. 305.

Some aspects of life on a large Costa Rican coffee finca.
See item no. 307.

Agrarian capitalism and the transformation of peasant society: coffee in Costa Rica.
See item no. 311.

Peasants of Costa Rica and the development of agrarian capitalism.
See item no. 312.

Peripheral capitalism and rural–urban migration: a study of population movements in Costa Rica.
See item no. 331.

Costa Rica.
See item no. 477.

The economic cycle in Latin American agricultural export economies, 1880-1930: a hypothesis for investigation.
See item no. 479.

Capitalismo y crisis económica en Costa Rica: treinta años de desarrollo.
(Capitalism and economic crisis in Costa Rica: 30 years of development.)
See item no. 480.

Hacia una interpretación del desarrollo costarricense: ensayo sociológico.
(Towards an interpretation of Costa Rican development: a sociological essay.)
See item no. 495.

Inside Costa Rica: behind the banana curtain.
See item no. 503.

Costa Rica: investor's guide.
See item no. 505.

Confronting the coffee oligarchy: the roots of Costa Rica's 'middle road'.
See item no. 507.

Notas introductorias al conocimiento de la sociedad costarricense y de los efectos de la integración centroamericana. (Introductory notes on Costa Rican society and the effects of Central American integration.)
See item no. 509.

Fertile lands of friendship: the Florida–Costa Rican experiment in international agricultural cooperation.
See item no. 532.

The Tuis archives: cattle ranching on the frontier of colonization in Costa Rica, 1873-1876.
See item no. 543.

Costa Rican agriculture: crop priorities and country policies.
See item no. 547.

Costa Rica, land of the banana.
See item no. 548.

Population growth, economic progress, and opportunities on the land: the case of Costa Rica.
See item no. 550.

La production agricole et la vie rurale au Costa Rica. (Agricultural production and rural life in Costa Rica.)
See item no. 556.

Pasture expansion, forestry and development contradictions: the case of Costa Rica.
See item no. 563.

Boceto histórico del ferrocarril nacional. (An historical sketch of the national railroad.)
See item no. 571.

Rails across Costa Rica: the development of the Costa Rican interoceanic and other railways.
See item no. 574.

La huelga bananera de 1934. (The banana strike of 1934.)
See item no. 577.

Ethnic diversity on a corporate plantation: Guaymí labor on a United Brands subsidiary in Costa Rica and Panana.
See item no. 580.

Decision-making activity sequences in an hacienda community.
See item no. 591.

Ecological upset and recuperation of natural control of insect pests in some Costa Rican banana plantations.
See item no. 602.

"Oiketicus kirbyi" (Lepidoptera: Psychidae): a pest of bananas in Costa Rica.
See item no. 603.

Bananera: a tropical plantation on the Pacific Lowlands of Costa Rica.
See item no. 608.

Hydro and geothermal electricity as an alternative for industrial petroleum consumption in Costa Rica.
See item no. 622.

Carlos Luis Fallas: su época y sus luchas. (Carlos Luis Fallas: his era and his struggles.)
See item no. 697.

Industry

Lubeck & Lubeck's who's who in Costa Rica, 1979-1980: professions, commerce, government.
See item no. 723.

Keith and Costa Rica: a biographical study of Minor Cooper Keith.
See item no. 734.

Agriculture

531 **The dairy situation in Costa Rica.**
Gregorio Alfaro.   San José: Ministerio de Agricultura e Industrias,
Servicio Técnico Interamericano de Cooperación Agrícola, 1960. 23p.
This brief study contains data on dairy herds and on the production and consumption
of dairy products.

532 **Fertile lands of friendship: the Florida–Costa Rican experiment in
international agricultural cooperation.**
Edited by Daniel E. Alleger.   Gainesville, Florida: University of
Florida Press, 1962. 312p. maps. bibliog.
Through a series of studies done during 1954-60 this book provides solid information
on the agricultural situation in Costa Rica. Detailed studies on animal nutrition,
pastures, the cheese, milk, and cattle industries, land use, and farm marketing are
included. The University of Florida, by means of a contract with the United States
Agency for International Development, helped Costa Rica expand its agricultural
extension system during that time.

533 **Alternative actions in Costa Rica: peasants as positive participants.**
Leslie Anderson.   *Journal of Latin American Studies* (Cambridge),
vol. 22, no. 1 (Feb. 1990), p. 89-113.
This article focuses on organized, non-violent action by Costa Rican farmers
attempting to defend their interests. Such action, falling between outright rebellion and
everyday resistance, appears attractive in Costa Rica because of the strength of its
democratic traditions. The author conducted interviews with peasants in three villages
where land conflicts had occurred and where peasants had organized non-violent
resistance. She stresses their sense of dignity, justice, and collectivism over their
individual self-interest. Although the article is successful in presenting the peasants'
point of view it fails to present the view of the bureaucracy who have to deal with the
problem.

534 **Cultivando la tierra: treinta años con plantas y libros.** (Cultivating the land: 30 years with plants and books.)
José María Arias Rodríguez. San José: Librería Trejos, 1976. 2nd ed. 412p. bibliog.

After getting a degree in pharmacy and working as assistant to Clodomiro Picado Twight the author bought land in 1925 near Río Segundo and for thirty years experimented with a wide variety of plants for commercial production. The book collects his thoughts and reports the results of his many experiments concerning irrigation, drainage, pruning, grafting, and fertilizers in connection with particular plants. He also discusses organizations of benefit to agriculture in the early 20th century.

535 **Bananera: a tropical plantation on the Pacific lowlands of Costa Rica.**
John P. Augelli. In: *Focus on geographic activity: a collection of original studies*, edited by Richard S. Thomas, Donald J. Patton. New York: McGraw-Hill, 1964, p. 31-6. maps.

The purpose of the article is to describe the physical layout, cycle of activities, and regional impact of a typical banana plantation. Although not identified precisely, 'Bananera' is located near Palmar Sur near the Río Grande de Térraba in the South Pacific region of Costa Rica. Professor Augelli, a well-known geographer, makes a special contribution by relating the characteristics of Bananera to those of a typical modern tropical plantation.

536 **Reforma agraria y poder político.** (Agrarian reform and political power.)
Francisco Barahona Riera. San José: Editorial Universidad de Costa Rica, 1980. 472p. bibliog.

For anyone interested in understanding the roots of the agrarian problem in Costa Rica and its social and economic dimensions, this is a key study. The facts on land tenure, land use, production of various crops, and agricultural exports are extensively laid out in both narrative and graphic form. Rural class structure, income, and labour union activity in rural areas are also covered in detail. Unlike many books on agrarian reform in Latin America there is ample discussion of the evolution of the position of the various political parties on specific agrarian reform issues. Indeed, as the title indicates, that is the principal objective of the book. In addition, there is some consideration of actions taken by relevant agencies, particularly the Institute of Land and Colonization. The study is well documented. The author, a sociologist, favours structural reform of the agrarian system.

537 **Agricultural choice and change: decision making in a Costa Rican community.**
Peggy F. Barlett. New Brunswick, New Jersey: Rutgers University Press, 1982. 196p. bibliog.

The disciplinary perspective of this excellent study is that of economic anthropology. The setting is the village of Pasos, in Puriscal canton, and the focus is on the strategies of farmers as they use their natural environment to meet their needs. Among the issues raised are ecological adaptations to a changing international and external environment, household production decisions, the pressures of increasing population, and the process of development. It is both a traditional community study, which demonstrates intimate knowledge and sympathy with the subjects of the inquiry, and a sophisticated, methodologically sound analysis of larger national and international pressures on the community. The research was carried out between September 1972 and September 1973.

538 **Labor efficiency and the mechanism of agricultural evolution.**
Peggy F. Barlett. *Journal of Anthropological Research*, vol. 32, no. 2 (Summer 1976), p. 124-40.

In this study of regional Costa Rican agriculture the focus is on farmers' adaptation to rapid population growth and loss of soil fertility. According to the author, farmers in this situation tend to resort to labour-intensive agricultural methods.

539 **The structure of decision-making in Paso.**
Peggy F. Barlett. *American Ethnologist*, vol. 4, no. 2 (May 1977), p. 285-307.

A highly sophisticated and detailed study of agricultural decision-making in the Costa Rican peasant community of Paso. The author, an economic anthropologist, carefully interviewed peasants about their decisions to plant coffee, corn, beans, and pasture. Her purpose was to weigh such factors as family size, land size, risk and labour input in crop decisions, and to test decision-making theory among peasants.

540 **Fact sheets on Costa Rican agriculture.**
Manuel J. Carvajal, James E. Ross. San José: United States Agency for International Development, 1968. 35p. bibliog.

This report contains statistical data on agricultural products, exports and credit, and on land use in the 1950s and 1960s.

541 **Agricultural production and infrastructure in the Río Frío development region of Costa Rica.**
William M. Edwards, D. Craig Anderson. Ames, Iowa: Department of Economics, Iowa State University, 1984. 51p. bibliog. (Monograph no. 17).

In 1975 the Land and Colonization Institute officially designated the Río Frío region as a 'development region' for the purpose of reducing the problem of land invasions by promoting orderly settlement. A decade later, this monograph reports on the general agricultural situation (soils, crops, labour requirements, marketing, and credit) and on the availability of education and social services. In addition to the research by Iowa State University and Universidad de Costa Rica staff and students, the authors base their conclusions on interviews of farmers in the region.

542 **Technical assistance in agriculture to the government of Costa Rica.**
Victor E. Green, Jr. San José: United States Agency for International Development, 1968. 17p.

Unexpected gems of information about a variety of technical assistance projects are found in this brief report. It summarizes the activities of a University of Florida team of agricultural scientists who were contracted to work in Costa Rica during 1965-68. It contains personal sidelights on these activities, and information on a range of topics such as the use of pesticides, the campaign to increase corn yields, home gardening, and attempts to cooperate with banking and research institutions.

543 **The Tuis archives: cattle ranching on the frontier of colonization in Costa Rica, 1873-1876.**
Carolyn Hall. *Revista Geográfica*, nos 86-87 (July 1977-June 1978), p. 101-17.

The discovery of the Tuis archives, two volumes of notes and accounts of a Costa Rican cattle ranch, gave Professor Hall an opportunity in this article to analyse conditions on a specific ranch and to formulate hypotheses about the nature of land use and settlement in the Cartago–San Ramón area. The hypotheses centre on the relationship of cattle production to the urban market and the scarcity of labour.

544 **Agrarian reform in Costa Rica.**
George W. Hill. *Land Economics*, 40, no. 1 (Feb. 1964), p. 41-8.

The author, a rural sociologist with the Land Tenure Center of the University of Wisconsin, discusses the founding of the Instituto de Tierras y Colonización (Land and Colonization Institute), and the government of Costa Rica's effort to address the problems of large-scale land ownership and of squatters.

545 **Un área rural en desarrollo: sus problemas económicos y sociales en Costa Rica.** (A rural area in development: its economic and social problems in Costa Rica.
George W. Hill, Manuel Gollás Quintero, Gregorio Alfaro. San José: Instituto Universitario Centroamericano de Investigaciones Sociales y Económicas, 1964. 56p. maps.

One of the few works on the Coto Brus valley in southwest Costa Rica, this study by agricultural economists covers land tenure, manpower, capital investment, and production.

546 **Structural determinants of the location of rural development institutions in Costa Rica.**
Vernon Eugene Jantzi. Ithaca, New York: Cornell University, 1976. 151p. bibliog. (Dissertation Series, Cornell University, Latin American Studies Program, no. 65).

Institutional tracking is the process of predicting an institution's location, especially at the regional level, through criteria taken into account by administrators. In this dissertation in the field of sociology the location of Costa Rican agricultural extension facilities and rural credit banks over three time periods – 1937-48, 1949-60, and 1961-73 – is examined in the light of institutional tracking theory.

547 **Costa Rican agriculture: crop priorities and country policies.**
Martin Kriesberg, Ervin Bullard, Wendell Becraft. Washington, DC:
Foreign Economic Development Service, United States Department of
Agriculture; United States Agency for International Development,
1970. 55p.

The result of a team effort commissioned by the United States Agency for
International Development (USAID) to provide basic data for recommendations on
commodity programmes to be supported by the USAID mission in San José. After an
analysis of world and domestic market conditions for all crops produced in Costa Rica,
the team recommends that no support be given to the traditional export crops:
bananas, coffee, sugar, and beef. Assistance should rather be given to speciality crops
such as fruit, nuts, and flowers, and to small farmers for increased production of
subsistence crops, specifically corn and beans. Assistance to research and marketing is
also recommended.

548 **Costa Rica, land of the banana.**
Paul B. Popenoe. *National Geographic Magazine*, vol. 41, no. 1
(Jan. 1922), p. 201-20.

Despite the title, the article contains as much material on the coffee industry as the
banana industry. It also covers other agricultural products as well as forestry and
mining, and it contains descriptions of Costa Rica's major cities. In his general remarks
on the uniqueness of Costa Rica, Popenoe attributes 'the superior intelligence and
civilization of the inhabitants' to the predominance of European influence.

549 **Law and agrarian reform in Costa Rica.**
James Rowles. Boulder, Colorado: Westview Press, 1985. 230p.

The present study is an unusual one. It is a detailed account of the struggle of the
Costa Rican legislature to pass the Law of Land and Land Settlements in 1961. It
covers early discussions of agrarian reform legislation in the 1940s, debates in the
National Assembly prior to passage of the law, and subsequent amendments of the
legislation until 1974. Professor Rowles is a lawyer who undertook the research for this
study while he was a visiting professor of law in Costa Rica during 1972-74, and the
approach is legal, not political. There are few accounts of Latin American legislative
battles in English because few English-language legal scholars take Latin American
laws seriously. Professor Rowles shows that efforts to pass reform legislation in Costa
Rica is at the heart of that country's democratic system.

550 **Population growth, economic progress, and opportunities on the land:
the case of Costa Rica.**
Carlos Joaquín Sáenz. Madison, Wisconsin: Land Tenure Center,
University of Wisconsin. (Research Paper, no. 48 (June 1972), p. 1-70).

An abbreviated version of the author's 1969 doctoral dissertation in agricultural
economics at the University of Wisconsin. Although the early historical parts are
sketchy the author makes a significant contribution in explaining how Costa Rican
political leaders, mainly representing coffee interests, responded to the crisis of falling
coffee prices in the 1890s and early 20th century. Using the old-fashioned but useful
approach of political economy, the author then discusses how political decisions
affected economic development to the 1960s. He concludes with some concrete
suggestions on how to promote economic development through agriculture.

551 **Historia agrícola de Costa Rica.** (An agricultural history of Costa Rica.)
Alberto Sáenz Maroto. San José: Universidad de Costa Rica, 1970.
1087p. bibliog. (Publicaciones de la Universidad de Costa Rica, Serie
Agronomía, no. 12).

This publication is a strange, heavy volume, useful because of the abundance of detail,
but practically impossible to use with any efficiency. The emphasis is on government
action in agriculture through the passing of laws. In each chapter the author appears to
summarize facts from the colonial period and laws and decrees from the national
period. Sometimes you cannot tell whether the words are the author's or whether he is
quoting directly from the laws or decrees. There is practically no analysis of any kind,
nor are there any conclusions. As a compendium of agricultural information and
encyclopaedic reference, with chapter headings such as tobacco, wheat, Indian corn,
contraband, agricultural colonization, aviculture, agricultural machinery, agricultural
credit, hunting and fishing, and many more, it could perhaps best belong on the shelves
of research libraries and specialists.

552 **An innovating agrarian policy: the case of Costa Rica.**
José Manuel Salazar, Ennio Rodríguez, José Manuel Salazar, Jr.
Madison, Wisconsin: Land Tenure Center, University of Wisconsin,
1977. 48p. map.

Costa Rica's agrarian policy in the 1960s and 1970s is the subject of this study. It is a
view from the inside, as one of the authors, José Manuel Salazar, was president of the
board of directors of the Land and Colonization Institute at the time the study was
made. The principal contribution is the description of the squatter problems of the
period and the efforts of the Institute to provide a solution to growing land scarcity in
Costa Rica.

553 **Agrarian policies in dependent societies: Costa Rica.**
Mitchell A. Seligson. *Journal of Interamerican Studies and World
Affairs*, vol. 19, no. 2 (May 1977), p. 201-32. bibliog.

This article is a synthesis of the agrarian policy in Costa Rica from the colonial period
to the 1970s. The author identifies four periods of development: the colonial period;
the coffee boom which began after independence; the period that began with the
construction of the railway and the banana plantations; and the present period,
characterized by peasant dissatisfaction and an increase in the number of squatters.
The author relates the agrarian policies carried out in these different periods to the
growth of Costa Rican dependency, and the unequal distribution of land in the
country.

554 **A case study of response to agricultural prices in Costa Rica.**
Charles E. Staley. *Economic Journal*, vol. 71, no. 282 (June 1961),
p. 432-6.

This study explains the reaction, mostly adverse, of the producers of basic food crops
in Costa Rica to prices established by the National Production Council (Consejo
Nacional de Producción).

555 **An assessment of the agricultural sector in Costa Rica.**
San José: United States Agency for International Development, 1977.
This assessment contains a section on the Costa Rican economy; a comprehensive description of the agricultural sector; a section dealing with land tenure, marketing, and other related agricultural problems; and a set of specific suggestions stressing rational utilization of natural resources, diversification, and export promotion.

556 **La production agricole et la vie rurale au Costa Rica.** (Agricultural production and rural life in Costa Rica.)
Alain Vieillard Baron.   Mexico City: Institut Français d'Amérique Latine, 1974. 294p. maps. bibliog.
The theme is agriculture and rural life but the contribution of this book is broader. An extensive introduction on the geographical and cultural basis of Costa Rican agriculture is an admirable synthesis supported by an ample bibliography. There follow two lengthy sections, both solid contributions, on the coffee and banana industries, and the last section deals with remaining agricultural products. The conclusions are somewhat equivocal, as the author recognizes the relative success of Costa Rica's coffee and banana exports but at the same time he sees problems in the future as a result of the instability of export-oriented agriculture and the low income of agricultural workers.

557 **El precarismo rural en Costa Rica, 1960-1980: orígenes y evolución.**
(Rural squatters in Costa Rica, 1960-80: origins and evolution.)
Beatriz Villareal M.   San José: Editorial Papiro, 1983. 189p. maps. bibliog.
Little has been written about the problem of squatters and land invasions in Costa Rica. Villareal's study, although brief and identified by the author herself as preliminary, is therefore important. It focuses on the period 1960-80, when capitalist agriculture expanded rapidly, resulting in displaced *campesinos* [rural people] and more land invasions than before. The ineffectiveness of the Land and Colonization Institute in relation to this problem is revealed in the Institute's own records, the very records Villareal used for this study.

558 **Studying agricultural institutions; a modular approach: A summary report on the agricultural management research and training project MSU-AID.**
Edited by Garland Wood.   East Lansing, Michigan: Michigan State University, 1974. 104p.
The purpose of this multidisciplinary study in agricultural management, funded by the United States Agency for International Development, was to find ways to improve the operations of public institutions in their efforts to assist small farmers. The team used two agricultural projects in Costa Rica as a means of determining the effectiveness of institutions in carrying out small farm development projects.

Agriculture

Costa Rica: immigration pamphlet with two maps, a guide for the agricultural class coming from other countries to make Costa Rica its home.
See item no. 16.

Costa Rica: transition to land hunger and potential instability.
See item no. 17.

Costa Rica: a geographical interpretation in historical perspective.
See item no. 22.

Estudio geográfico regional de la zona atlántico norte de Costa Rica. (A regional geographical study of the north Atlantic zone of Costa Rica.)
See item no. 28.

La colonización agrícola de Costa Rica. (The agricultural colonization of Costa Rica.)
See item no. 34.

La factoría de tabacos de Costa Rica. (The state tobacco agency of Costa Rica.)
See item no. 190.

Costa Rica colonial: la tierra y el hombre. (Colonial Costa Rica: man and the land.)
See item no. 195.

Peasant movements and the transition to agrarian capitalism: freeholding versus hacienda peasantries and agrarian reform in Guanacaste, Costa Rica, 1880-1935.
See item no. 211.

La alborada del capitalismo agrario en Costa Rica. (The dawn of capitalist agriculture in Costa Rica.)
See item no. 216.

Ethnicity and livelihoods: a social geography of Costa Rica's Atlantic zone.
See item no. 305.

Agrarian capitalism and the transformation of peasant society: coffee in Costa Rica.
See item no. 311.

Peasants of Costa Rica and the development of agrarian capitalism.
See item no. 312.

The economic cycle in Latin American agricultural export economies, 1880-1930: a hypothesis for investigation.
See item no. 479.

Capitalismo y crisis económica en Costa Rica: treinta años de desarrollo. (Capitalism and economic crisis in Costa Rica: 30 years of development.)
See item no. 480.

Income and export taxation of agriculture in Costa Rica and Honduras.
See item no. 496.

Agricultural credit in Costa Rica.
See item no. 506.

Confronting the coffee oligarchy: the roots of Costa Rica's 'middle road'.
See item no. 507.

La élite ganadera en Costa Rica. (The cattlemen's élite in Costa Rica.)
See item no. 516.

Modernization of Costa Rica's beef cattle economy: 1950-1985.
See item no. 517.

Land utilization in Guanacaste Province of Costa Rica.
See item no. 518.

Export beef production and development contradictions in Costa Rica.
See item no. 519.

The formation of the coffee estate in nineteenth-century Costa Rica.
See item no. 520.

Coffee production and processing on a large Costa Rican "finca".
See item no. 521.

Evolution of the banana industry of Costa Rica.
See item no. 524.

Effective agricultural development of former banana lands: the west coast of Costa Rica.
See item no. 527.

Instability of tropical agriculture: the Atlantic lowlands of Costa Rica.
See item no. 528.

Organizing through technology: a case from Costa Rica.
See item no. 561.

El componente arbóreo en Acosta y Puriscal. (The forestry component in Acosta and Puriscal.)
See item no. 564.

Labor mobility and economic growth: the Central American experience – Costa Rica and El Salvador.
See item no. 586.

Ecological upset and recuperation of natural control of insect pests in some Costa Rican banana plantations.
See item no. 602.

"Oiketicus kirbyi" (Lepidoptera: Psychidae): a pest of bananas in Costa Rica.
See item no. 603.

Agriculture

Bibliografía agrícola de Costa Rica. (Agricultural bibliography of Costa Rica.)
See item no. 751.

Bibliografías agrícolas de América Central: Costa Rica. (Agricultural bibliographies of Central America: Costa Rica.)
See item no. 754.

Bibliografía retrospectiva sobre política agraria en Costa Rica, 1948-1978. (A retrospective bibliography on agrarian politics in Costa Rica, 1948-78.)
See item no. 755.

Forestry

559 The rain forests of Golfo Dulce.
Paul Hamilton Allen. Stanford, California: Stanford University Press, 1977. 417p. bibliog.

The main part of this book is an alphabetical listing of the trees in the rainforests of Golfo Dulce in the South Pacific region of Costa Rica. A handy utilization list, covering the possible economic uses of the trees mentioned, is also included. Allen lived and worked in the area for five years and is therefore well equipped to describe seasonal changes in the area's forests. The book was originally published in Gainesville in 1956 by the University of Florida Press.

560 Biocultural restoration of a tropical forest.
William H. Allen. *BioScience*, vol. 38 (March 1988), p. 156-61.

Science writer Allen describes a unique ecological restoration project now under way in Costa Rica. The project is to use the Guanacaste National Park as a vehicle for the restoration of 75,000 hectares of the tropical dry forest of Guanacaste to its pre-Spanish state, with its original flora and fauna. Biologist Daniel Janzen, who was interviewed by Allen, is the prime mover, with the cooperation of the Costa Rican government and several international environmental agencies. Education of the local populace to preserve rather than destroy the forest is an integral feature of the plan.

561 Organizing through technology: a case from Costa Rica.
Thomas F. Carroll, Helga Baitenmann. *Grassroots Development*, vol. 11, no. 2 (1987), p. 12-20.

A small, private development organization [called ANAI] has been working in agroforestry on the Caribbean coast of Costa Rica near Panama since 1975. The purpose of the project, which is described in this article, is to develop a diversified agricultural economy while conserving the region's fragile ecosystem. ANAI works with established research institutions to bring in technology and with local farmers to promote innovation.

562 **Bureaucracy and the unmanaged forest commons in Costa Rica, or why development does not grow on trees.**
George M. Guess.   Albuquerque, New Mexico: Latin American Institute, University of New Mexico, 1979. 56p. bibliog. (Working Paper, University of New Mexico, Latin American Institute, no. 1).

There is more to this paper than the title would lead one to believe. Its principal purpose is to explain the failure of the Costa Rican government to include in its development policy a coherent plan for the management of its forestry resources; a second purpose is to recommend a separate forestry development institute. Accompanying data on forest products, land use, and development financing support this explanation. In addition, the author places the forestry issue in the context of a sophisticated discussion of dependency theory, bureaucracy, and Costa Rica's democratic political system. Readers interested in how Costa Rica's system works in a specific case will profit from the combined focus on theory and practice in this paper.

563 **Pasture expansion, forestry and development contradictions: the case of Costa Rica.**
George M. Guess.   *Studies in Comparative International Development*, vol. 14, no. 1 (Spring 1974), p. 42-55. bibliog.

Armed with statistics concerning expanding beef production and declining local beef consumption, Professor Guess presents a well-reasoned article on the mistaken notion that additonal beef production is a solution to Costa Rica's traditional dependency on coffee and banana exports. He argues that since the 1960 establishment of the United States beef quota deforestation has accelerated, rural unemployment has risen, and maldistribution of wealth has intensified. Professor Guess recommends a forest-based industrial strategy as an alternative.

564 **El componente abóreo en Acosta y Puriscal.** (The forestry component in Acosta and Puriscal.)
Edited by Jochen Heuveldop, Leonardo Espinosa.   Turrialba, Costa Rica: Centro Agronómico Tropical de Investigación y Enseñanza, 1983. 122p.

Sponsored by the German Society of Technical Cooperation and several private and public Costa Rican agencies, a team of forestry and development experts concentrate their research and conservation efforts on one deforested area. Because of deforestation, erosion, flooding, and out-migration this area was declared an 'emergency' zone by the Costa Rican government in 1979. The diagnosis provided by the authors of this volume includes a history of agricultural exploitation of the zone, an inventory of native trees, and a discussion of possible conservation measures.

565 **Estudio y actualización de la política forestal de Costa Rica.** (Study and updating of the forestry policies of Costa Rica.)
Francisco Ortuño Medina.   San José: Universidad Estatal a Distancia, 1981. 102p. (Serie Miscelánea, no. 2).

Ortuño was contracted by the Forestry Division of the Costa Rican Ministry of Agriculture to conduct this broad policy study. It includes an overview of the problem of vanishing forests and the conflicting interests of agriculture and other industries dependent on timber. At the same time it contains a plea for a concrete national plan and some specific suggestions on what the plan should do.

566 **The forests of Costa Rica: general report on the forest resources of Costa Rica.**
United States, Department of Agriculture, Forest Service, in cooperation with the Office of the Coordinator of Inter-American Affairs. Washington, DC: Government Printing Office, 1943. 84p. map.

The purpose of this review of forestry resources in Costa Rica was to supply information about available timber which might be useful to the Allied armies during World War II.

567 **Charcoal burners of Costa Rica.**
Ray Witlin. *Americas*, vol. 7, no. 5 (May 1955), p. 28-32.

This is a story of approximately 100 individuals, the *carboneros* [charcoal burners] of the Talamanca region of Costa Rica, who depend for a living on converting the oak forests to charcoal.

568 **Nature's riotous variety.**
Allen M. Young. *Americas*, vol. 37, no. 2 (March-April 1985), p. 22-31.

For the layperson this article by a biologist on the biological diversity and interdependence of the Costa Rican rainforest is an authoritative synthesis. The article, which specifically treats the rainforest of the Caribbean coastal flood-plain, provides both aesthetic and scientific justification for preservation of rainforests in general.

Costa Rican natural history.
See item no. 71.

Guanacaste National Park: tropical ecological and cultural restoration.
See item no. 72.

Clave preliminar de las familias de los árboles en Costa Rica. (Preliminary key to the families of trees in Costa Rica.)
See item no. 73.

Arboles de Costa Rica. (Trees of Costa Rica.)
See item no. 80.

La conservación como instrumento para el desarrollo. (Conservation as an instrument of development.)
See item no. 594.

In the tropics, still rolling back the forest primeval.
See item no. 600.

Bibliografías agrícolas de América Central: Costa Rica. (Agricultural bibliographies of Central America: Costa Rica.)
See item no. 754.

Transport and Communications

569 **Casements and the Costa Rican Pacific road.**
James C. Carey. *Kansas Quarterly*, vol. 2 (Summer 1970), p. 97-101.
In contrast to the building of the Northern Railway by Minor C. Keith and family, the building of the railway from the Central Valley to the Pacific Ocean gets little attention in the Costa Rican historical literature. This study by Carey, a historican, sketches the activities of Dan Casement – who had the contract to build the Pacific railway – and his relatives in Costa Rica from 1897 to 1904, the period when the railway was constructed. It is based primarily on Casement family papers.

570 **El ferrocarril al Atlántico en Costa Rica: 1871-1874.** (The railway to the Atlantic in Costa Rica: 1871-74.)
Jeffrey Casey Gaspar. *Anuario de Estudios Centroamericanos*, no. 2 (1976), p. 291-344.
The railway to the Atlantic coast was completed in 1890. In this article the author concentrates on the early organization of the railway company, the problem of financing, and construction problems in the Central Valley until 1874. There is abundant detail on the salaries of railway workers and about their living and working conditions.

571 **Boceto histórico del ferrocarril nacional.** (An historical sketch of the national railway.)
Joaquín Fernández Montúfar. San José: Imprenta Nacional, 1934.
48p.
In this booklet there are three sections: one dealing with the construction and electrification of the railway from San José to Puntarenas; one focusing on the relation of the railways of Costa Rica to coffee production; and the last giving a list of laws, 1854-1933, pertaining to railway construction.

572 **Historia de la aviación en Costa Rica.** (The history of aviation in Costa Rica.)
Carlos María Jiménez Gutiérrez.   San José: Imprenta Elena, 1962. 187p.

Although lacking in documentation this book delivers its promised synopsis of the history of aviation in Costa Rica, beginning with the arrival of the first aeroplane in the country in 1911. The flying visit of Charles Lindbergh to San José in 1928 was another memorable event, duly recorded by Jiménez, who also gives considerable space to the pioneer aviators and the founders of commercial aviation in Costa Rica.

573 **Costa Rica Railway Company Ltd and Northern Railway Company.**
San José: Northern Pacific Railway Company, 1953. 201p.

The text, which is in English and Spanish, includes data on each of the departments of the railway company. Of principal interest to the historian are details concerning the construction of the railway and accounts of the political and physical obstacles encountered in the construction. It is, of course, an official history and therefore controversial issues are omitted. Many photographs help to capture the atmosphere of the construction era in the late 19th century and of the railway's early operation.

574 **Rails across Costa Rica: the development of the Costa Rican interoceanic and other railways.**
Delmer G. Ross.   Mobile, Alabama: Institute for Research in Latin America, 1976. 153p. map. bibliog.

Although somewhat lacking in interpretation and on the social and political effects of railway concessions and contracts in Costa Rica, this brief book is an excellent narrative about the railway era. It traces the first efforts to build a railway on the Atlantic side, culminating in 1890 in the opening of the Northern Railway Company, which became government property in 1972; and on the Pacific side, which resulted in the completion of the rail service from San José to Puntarenas in 1910. Other railway construction related to the banana industry is also discussed.

575 **The impact of communication on rural development: an investigation in Costa Rica and India.**
Prodipto Roy, Frederick B. Waisanen, Everett M. Rogers.   Paris: UNESCO, 1969. 160p. map. bibliog.

Communications specialists Roy, Waisanen, and Rogers, working under contract with UNESCO, attempt to discover the superior method of introducing innovations to village residents. For the Costa Rican part of the study several villages in the San Isidro del General area, some classified as traditional and some classified as modern, were chosen for the experiment. Of the two methods of introducing innovations, radio forums or literacy readings, radio forums proved to be the more successful.

191

Transport and Communications

The development of foreign trade and communication in Costa Rica to the construction of the first railway.
See item no. 165.

Rural electrification and development: social and economic impact in Costa Rica and Colombia.
See item no. 310.

Labour

576 **Desarrollo del movimiento sindical en Costa Rica.** (Development of the
labour union movement in Costa Rica.)
Carlos Alberto Abarca (et al.). San José: Editorial de la Universidad
de Costa Rica, 1981. 213p. bibliog.
Ten authors, representing the disciplines of history, sociology, and political science,
undertake a panoramic view of the labour movement in Costa Rica. The two historical
articles provide a background for the others which focus on the contemporary period.
Charts and statistics present a picture of the strength of unions and the characteristics
and opinions of union members and leaders. An ample annotated bibliography (p. 195-
211) is an excellent guide to further research.

577 **La huelga bananera de 1934.** (The banana strike of 1934.)
Víctor Hugo Acuña Ortega. San José: Centro Nacional de Acción
Pastoral, Centro de Estudios para la Acción Nacional, 1984. 59p.
Because it contains the essential facts about one of the most important strikes in Costa
Rican history this brief publication is important. However, it lacks documentation and
it appears to be biased in favour of the union and against the foreign banana
companies. The strike itself was important because it marked the entry of the
Communist Party as a force in labour–management disputes.

578 **La Iglesia y el sindicalismo en Costa Rica.** (The Church and syndicalism
in Costa Rica.)
James Backer. San José: Editorial Costa Rica, 1974. 3rd ed. 270p.
bibliog.
This book has a narrow focus – the Church and labour unions – and it deals primarily
with a thirty-year span of history, 1940-70. It is solidly based on a variety of sources,
including interviews with individuals who played a role in the conflicts of the period,
and it allows generalizations about the two institutions covered. Backer concludes that,
except during the archbishopric of Víctor Manuel Sanabria, 1940-52, the Church took a

193

very conservative view of labour union activity. According to Backer, this Church outlook, along with other factors, slowed labour union organization in Costa Rica.

579 **El solidarismo: pensamiento y dinámica social de un movimiento obrero patronal.** (Solidarity: thought and social dynamics of a worker-ownership movement.)
Gustavo Blanco, Orlando Navarro.   San José: Editorial Costa Rica, 1984. 396p. bibliog.
Few English-language studies of Costa Rica give any attention to the Costa Rican solidarity movement. Yet the movement, founded by Alberto Martén in 1947 as an alternative to liberalism and communism, is a significant aspect of labour–capitalist relations. This sophisticated sociological study by Blanco and Navarro, based on a solid and varied foundation of sources, traces the history, ideology, administration, and contemporary condition of the movement. One section is valuable for its discussion of Martén's relations with José Figueres. An extensive set of appendices enables the reader to follow the success of the movement in particular enterprises and its organizational structure. Several interviews with Martén are included.

580 **Ethnic diversity on a corporate plantation: Guaymí labor on a United Brands subsidiary in Costa Rica and Panama.**
Philippe Bourgois.   Cambridge, Massachusetts: Cultural Survival, 1985. 52p. (Occasional Paper, no. 19).
This study is based on nine months of anthropological field research during 1982-83 on the Chiriqui Land Company's Bocas del Toro Division on the Caribbean coast of Costa Rica and Panama. Bourgois accuses the company of systematically exploiting racism and ethnicity and of taking advantage of the lack of sophistication of the indigenous labour force in order to minimize production costs and discourage labour union activity.

581 **Costa Rica: labor force characteristics and evolution 1950-1973.**
Manuel Felipe Calvo C.   In: *Employment and labor force in Latin America: a review at national and regional levels*, edited by Juan J. Buttari. Washington, DC: ECIEL Study, Organization of American States, 1979, vol. 1, p. 231-312.
Relying on data from the censuses of 1950, 1963, and 1973 the author, an economist from the Universidad de Costa Rica, presents detailed characteristics of the working population of Costa Rica. He includes age, sex, region, economic sector, education, and other characteristics in this extract from a two-volume work.

582 **Formación de la fuerza laboral costarricense: una contribución a la historia económica social y administrativa de Costa Rica.** (Formation of the Costa Rican labour force: a contribution to the economic, social and administrative history of Costa Rica.)
Roger Churnside.   San José: Editorial Costa Rica, 1985. 491p. bibliog.
Taking his inspiration from the new economic history school, Churnside brings together social and economic statistics in order to reinterpret Costa Rican economic history. He begins with the colonial period and comes up to the mid-20th century.

Eighty pages of tables and an ample bibliography buttress his arguments. His objective is to link changes in labour force organization (such as *haciendas* [estates] and plantations) and production in Costa Rica to the size and composition of the pool of labour. The reader who stays with the lengthy and tightly knit arguments will be able to judge for himself whether Churnside achieves his objective, but in any case he will doubtless learn along the way a good deal of economic history from the labourer's point of view.

583 **Las luchas sociales en Costa Rica, 1870-1930.** (Social struggles in Costa Rica, 1870-1930.)
Vladimir de la Cruz. San José: Editorial Costa Rica, Editorial Universidad de Costa Rica, 1981. 2nd ed. 304p. bibliog.

This work, based on research in newspapers, pamphlets, and broadsides, is an historical survey of Costa Rican labour movements and the social conflicts that led to the birth of the Costa Rican Communist Party. Beginning with the first artisans' and workers' associations, the author traces the influence of foreign ideologies and links to regional and international organizations in the development of labour organizations in Costa Rica.

584 **El movimiento obrero en Costa Rica, 1830-1902.** (The workers' movement in Costa Rica, 1830-1902.)
Carlos Luis Fallas Monge. San José: Editorial Universidad Estatal a Distancia, 1983. 438p. bibliog.

Fallas Monge takes the broad approach in this important book on labour history. There are lengthy introductory sections on the European background of labour organizations and on general 19th-century Costa Rican history. Interpreting 'workers' broadly, Fallas Monge treats professional groups such as doctors and lawyers (often mentioning the names of members of their organizations), as well as the artisans who organized themselves in mutual assistance societies in the 1870s. Perhaps his most original contribution is the coverage given to Chinese, Italian, Spanish, and Jamaican immigrant workers who were brought to Costa Rica in the late 19th century for specific projects such as the construction of the Northern Railway. In the last third of the book Fallas Monge treats labour–capital conflicts, laws affecting workers, and workers' participation in politics. The book is a well-documented scholarly work of reference.

585 **Labor law and practice in Costa Rica.**
Jessie A. Friedman, Martha R. Lowenstern. Washington, DC: US Department of Labor, Bureau of Labor Statistics, 1962. 43p. bibliog. (BLS Report, no. 220).

Early chapters covering geography, culture, customs, education, and health provide an adequate backdrop for the main purpose of this report: a detailed account of the legal relationships of Costa Rican workers and the conditions of their employment. Under the latter heading topics covered include: hours of work, pay and allowances, safety, insurance, and employment practices. Statistical tables cover population data from 1850 to 1961.

586 **Labor mobility and economic growth: the Central American experience – Costa Rica and El Salvador.**
Jerome B. Gordon. *Economic Development and Cultural Change*, vol. 17, no. 3 (April 1969), p. 319-37.

Focusing on the decade of the 1950s, when Costa Rica had one of the highest annual population increases in the world, Gordon explores the effects of population growth and labour productivity on economic development. He also estimates the rate of growth required in the service and industrial sectors to keep the number of agricultural workers constant. Statistical charts comparing Costa Rica with El Salvador help to highlight Costa Rica's peculiarities.

587 **Legal minimum wages as an instrument of social policy in Costa Rica.**
Peter Gregory. Albuquerque, New Mexico: University of New Mexico, 1981. 41p.

The present article is a sophisticated economic analysis of the impact of minimum wage legislation and policy on overall wages and income distribution in Costa Rica. The period covered is from 1966 to 1975. Gregory concludes that, under conditions of steady and rapid growth, market forces assert more influence on wage levels than minimum-wage policy and that minimum-wage policy has little impact on income distribution. Additional data are provided on regional and sectoral variations in wages and on poverty.

588 **Towards a national employment policy: the case of Costa Rica.**
Eduardo Lizano Fait. *International Labour Review*, vol. 120, no. 3 (May-June 1981), p. 361-74.

An economist's view of the place of labour policy in a national economic development plan, the article focuses on strategies of job creation. Interest in job creation began in Costa Rica in the 1970s when it began to be realized that the country's traditionally low unemployment rate was endangered by rapid industrialization.

589 **The National Wages Board and minimum wage policy in Costa Rica.**
Helen Lom, Eduardo Lizano Fait. *International Labour Review*, vol. 114, no. 1 (July-Aug. 1976), p. 95-106.

In Costa Rica minimum wages have traditionally been determined by a tripartite board composed of representatives of labour, management, and government. This study discusses the changes taking place in the Board by comparing the voting patterns and debate in the Board proceedings in 1962 and 1972. The results point to a polarization of voting patterns in 1972, with the government voting in conjunction with business interests in a large percentage of cases. Although the procedure followed by the Board has changed since the study was written the article is valuable as a case-study.

590 **The Costa Rican labor movement: a study in political unionism.**
Joseph J. McGovern. *Public and International Affairs*, vol. 4, no. 1 (Spring 1966), p. 88-116.

McGovern attempts to illustrate the special problems of labour unions in under-developed countries by focusing on the particular case of Costa Rica. In the first part he explains that in underdeveloped countries the labour movement is less interested in purely economic matters and more concerned with widespread social and political reform. In the second part, which focuses on Costa Rica, he explains that despite the progressive nature of its political, economic, and social structure, Costa Rica's labour union movement more nearly conforms to the model of labour unions in underdeveloped countries. Historically, the two major trade union confederations in Costa Rica have been the Communist central organization and the Rerum Novarum confederation.

591 **Decision-making activity sequences in an hacienda community.**
   Thomas L. Norris. *Human Organization*, vol. 12, no. 3 (Fall 1953), p. 26-30.
This is an anthropological study of the decision-making practices of workers on the coffee farm of Aquiares near Turrialba. The influence of the farm owners and administrators on the workers is shown in the reproduction of the actual dialogue of specific meetings.

592 **Artesanos y obreros costarricenses, 1880-1914.** (Costa Rican workers and artisans, 1880-1914.)
   Mario Oliva Medina. San José: Editorial Costa Rica, 1985. 218p. bibliog.
In this study Olivo emphasizes the political culture of the artisan and worker rather than labour organizations. Making good use of the many ephemeral workers' publications and newspapers of the time he characterizes the changing ideological outlook of the working classes, documents the kind of associations they favoured, describes working and living conditions, and traces the origins of the sentiment of workers' unity. Olivo's goal is to provide a basis for understanding the 'underside' of history, and in this he succeeds.

Los productores directos en el siglo del café. (Direct producers in the century of coffee.)
See item no. 231.

Poverty and labour market in Costa Rica.
See item no. 307.

Sociocultural contrasts in rural and urban settlement types in Costa Rica.
See item no. 315.

Urban poverty and economic development: a case study of Costa Rica.
See item no. 326.

Crisis de 1929 y la fundación del Partido Comunista en Costa Rica. (The crisis of 1929 and the founding of the Communist Party in Costa Rica.)
See item no. 406.

Employment and economic growth in Costa Rica.
See item no. 475.

Social aspects of the banana industry.
See item no. 525.

Labour

Reforma agraria y poder político. (Agrarian reform and political power.)
See item no. 536.

El ferrocarril al Atlántico en Costa Rica: 1871-1874. (The railway to the
Atlantic in Costa Rica: 1871-74.)
See item no. 570.

Carlos Luis Fallas: su época y sus luchas. (Carlos Luis Fallas: his era and his
struggles.)
See item no. 697.

Environment

593 **Costa Rica: model for conservation in Latin America.**
Geoffrey S. Barnard. *Nature Conservancy News*, vol. 32, no. 4 (July-Aug. 1982), p. 6-11.
This brief overview of the Costa Rican National Park system is slightly out of date because the country's parks have expanded since 1982. However, it is useful for the reader who wants a general idea of the situation regarding national parks in that country.

594 **La conservación como instrumento para el desarrollo.** (Conservation as an instrument of development.)
Gerardo Budowski. San José: Editorial Universidad Estatal a Distancia, 1985. 398p.
An anthology of writings on conservation by the noted Costa Rican forester Budowski. The central theme of his writings, as he explains in the introduction, is that far from being inconsistent with development, conservation is a necessity in promoting economic development in countries such as Costa Rica. Most of the thirty-seven articles, which were previously published between 1963 and 1982, touch on the author's experience in Costa Rica, drawing mainly on his expertise in forestry. The subjects treated include: national parks and reserves, agricultural forestry, tourism and conservation, and education and forestry. Separate bibliographies accompany many of the articles.

595 **The Janzen heresy.**
Alston Chase. *Conde Nast Traveler* (Nov. 1989), p. 122-8.
Daniel Janzen, a North American biologist specializing in the tropics, is involved in an experimental national parks effort in Guanacaste, Costa Rica. Rather than focusing on preservation and the exclusion of environment-threatening visitors and nearby

residents, the Janzen approach, which is fully supported by the Costa Rican National Park Service and international environmental agencies, is to encourage human activities that are ecologically sustainable. The article by Chase is a solid, journalistic account of this experiment.

596 **Ecología y desarrollo en Costa Rica: antología.** (Ecology and development in Costa Rica: an anthology.)
Luis Fournier Origgi. San José: Editorial Universidad Estatal a Distancia (EUNED), 1981. 195p. bibliog. (Serie Educación Ambiental, no. 4).

This is the fourth book published by EUNED in a series on education for the environment. In this instance education is taken in the sense of educating the entire citizenry. All sixteen articles in this book touch on problems relating economic development to issues of environmental preservation and population growth. All were written between 1974 and 1981 by Fournier, who holds a PhD degree in botany from the University of California, Berkeley.

597 **Vegetación y clima de Costa Rica**. (Vegetation and climate of Costa Rica.)
Edited by Luis Diego Gómez. San José: Editorial Universidad Estatal a la Distancia, 1986. 2 vols. maps. bibliog.

This two-volume set comes in a box containing twenty large fold-out maps in addition to the maps and illustrations in the books themselves. The first volume, *Vegetación de Costa Rica* (327p.), was written by Gómez, and the second, *Clima de Costa Rica* (118p.), by Wilberth Herrera. Altogether the package contains an enormous amount of geological, geographical, meteorological, and ecological data, presented in graphic and cartographic form and analysed and interpreted in the narrative. It is a technical compilation not meant, as the authors indicate, for the layperson, but the easy-to-read maps and quantities of data about specific regions of Costa Rica make the work not only a valuable reference tool for researchers in a variety of fields but also a dependable information source for prospective investors and explorer-tourists. Not least of the scholarly contributions of this work are the extensive bibliographies in each volume.

598 **Corcovado National Park.**
Dena Kaye. *Connoisseur* (Sept. 1987), p. 133-9.

The author travelled to Corcovado National Park with Prince Bernhard of the Netherlands and spoke to conservationist leaders such as Mario Boza and Alvaro Ugalde. It is a lighthearted, chatty article, but with information on the park system and the World Wildlife Fund's [now, World Wide Fund for Nature] cooperation with Costa Rica in the field of environmental protection. It is illustrated with photographs.

599 **Costa Rica.**
Nature Conservancy News, vol. 34, no. 1 (Jan.-Feb. 1984), p. 4-25.

This issue of *Nature Conservancy News* is dedicated to Costa Rican national parks. It includes an interview with Alvaro Ugalde, one of the pioneers of the park system in Costa Rica, an article by biologist Christopher Vaughan on six endangered feline species in Costa Rica, and an article by biologist Daniel H. Janzen on the importance of the national parks from a researcher's point of view. The exceptional photography matches the optimistic tone of the articles with respect to the current situation and future of the national parks in Costa Rica.

600 In the tropics, still rolling back the forest primeval.
Joanne Omang. *Smithsonian*, vol. 17, no. 12 (March 1987), p. 56-67.

Prospective readers should not be driven away by the title, for those who are interested in the destruction of the forests of Costa Rica would profit from a close look at this article. The author's unusual approach is to attempt to see the process from the point of view of those who profit from the destruction. Through interviews with small farmers, drivers of log-trucks and sawmill workers, Omang makes the point that environmental laws and international agencies concerned with preservation cannot succeed without the understanding and cooperation of these people. Facts and figures on Costa Rican forests, the lumber industry, and forest preservation are presented.

601 Primer Simposio de Parques Nacionales y Reservas Biológicas. (The first symposium on national parks and biological reserves.)
San José: Editorial Universidad Estatal a Distancia, 1982. 168p. maps. bibliog. (Serie Miscelánea, Programa de Educación Ambiental, no. 5).

The first symposium on Costa Rican national parks and biological reserves was held in San José in 1980. Articles published in this book were selected from the oral presentations. The book includes twelve articles by the most prominent specialists on Costa Rican ecology, including Gerardo Budowski, Murray Silberman, Daniel Janzen, Sergio Salas, Carlos Villalobos, and Christopher Vaughan. The most persistent theme evident in the presentations is the need to integrate the concept of environmental preservation with education in general.

602 Ecological upset and recuperation of natural control of insect pests in some Costa Rican banana plantations.
Clyde S. Stephens. *Turrialba*, vol. 34, no. 1 (1984), p. 101-5.

Briefly reviewing the history of insecticide use in banana plantations in southwestern Costa Rica, Stephens concludes that they did more harm than good in the long run. Insect infestation increased with insecticide use. After 1973, according to the author, all insecticide sprays were stopped and within two years a balanced banana ecosystem was established.

603 "Oiketicus kirbyi" (Lepidoptera: Psychidae): a pest of bananas in Costa Rica.
Clyde S. Stephens. *Journal of Economic Entomology*, vol. 55, no. 3 (June 1962), p. 381-6.

Stephens discusses the problem of the appearance of a leaf-eating bagworm in the banana plantations of southern Costa Rica in 1958, and the various natural and chemical methods used to combat the pest.

604 Costa Rica's campaign for conservation.
Marjorie Sun. *Science*, vol. 239, no. 1 (18 March 1988), p. 1366-9. map.

A handy review of Costa Rica's efforts on behalf of environmental conservation and of the significant international assistance received by Costa Rica for conservation.

605 **Pesticides and policies: approaches to pest control dilemmas in Nicaragua and Costa Rica.**
Lori Ann Thrupp. *Latin American Perspectives*, vol. 14, no. 59 (Fall 1988), p. 37-70.

Thrupp analyses and compares pesticide-related policies and programmes in the two countries. She finds that despite strict legal restrictions and the goodwill and intent of the Costa Rican Pesticide Commission and other institutions, little has been accomplished in Costa Rica to contain unwise use of pesticides. According to Thrupp, Nicaragua's more action-oriented policies have achieved more. Research was carried out in Costa Rica and Nicaragua in 1984 and 1985.

606 **Corcovado: meditaciones de un biólogo.** (Corcovado: meditations of a biologist.)
Alvaro Wille Trejos. San José: Editorial Universidad Estatal a Distancia, Universidad de Costa Rica, Consejo Nacional de Investigaciones Científicas y Tecnológicas, 1983. 230p.

This is a personal account of Wille's study-visits to Corcovado Park in the Southern Pacific region of Costa Rica during 1977, 1978, and 1979. Wille, an entomologist, writes in the form of a diary, explaining in detail his arrangements for research in the forests, but at the same time outlining his scientific observations and speculating and theorizing about biology and ecology, and most especially meditating about nature. All this is done in language clearly understandable by the layperson.

607 **Field guide to the natural history of Costa Rica.**
Allen M. Young. San José: Trejos Brothers, 1983. 72p.

Appropriate to Costa Rica's growing fame in scientific tourism, particularly of the biological variety, Young, a zoologist, provides a guide to the country's 'most accessible highlights in the magnificent and diverse flora and fauna'. Following an introduction, the book is divided into sections, each covering one of Costa Rica's three principal regions. There is a short section on the national parks.

Densities of population in Holdridge life zones in Costa Rica: an empirical approach.
See item no. 32.

Recursos naturales. (Natural resources.)
See item no. 43.

The national parks of Costa Rica.
See item no. 53.

Costa Rica: nature, prosperity, and peace on the rich coast.
See item no. 60.

Costa Rican natural history.
See item no. 71.

Guanacaste National Park: tropical ecological and cultural restoration.
See item no. 72.

A naturalist on a tropical farm.
See item no. 74.

A naturalist in Costa Rica.
See item no. 75.

Parque Nacional Corcovado: plan de manejo y desarrollo. (Corcovado National Park: a plan of management and development.)
See item no. 76.

Animales y plantas comunes de las costas de Costa Rica. (Common animals and plants of the coasts of Costa Rica.)
See item no. 77.

Butterflies of Costa Rica and their natural history: Papilionidae, Pieridae, Nymphalidae.
See item no. 90.

The birds of Costa Rica: distribution and ecology.
See item no. 94.

A guide to the birds of Costa Rica.
See item no. 95.

Fruits and the ecology of resplendent quetzals.
See item no. 104.

The population of Costa Rica and its natural resources.
See item no. 253.

Agricultural choice and change: decision making in a Costa Rican community.
See item no. 537.

The rain forests of Golfo Dulce.
See item no. 559.

Biocultural restoration of a tropical forest.
See item no. 560.

El componente arbóreo en Acosta y Puriscal. (The forestry component in Acosta and Puriscal.)
See item no. 564.

Charcoal burners of Costa Rica.
See item no. 567.

Nature's riotous variety.
See item no. 569.

Bibliografía agrícola de Costa Rica. (Agricultural bibliography of Costa Rica.)
See item no. 751.

Education

608　**El viejo liceo: la democracia como consecuencia de la educación pública.**
(The old public school: democracy as a consequence of public
education.)
Isaac Felipe Azofeifa.　San José: Ministerio de Cultura, Juventud y
Deportes, 1973. 103p.

The school referred to is the Liceo de Costa Rica, founded in 1887 as the principal
secondary school in the country. Originally published in 1937, this essay deals generally
with the role of the Liceo in the formation of professionals and the promotion of
science and the humanities. The author also deals with the role of education in forming
Costa Rica's democratic character.

609　**La Universidad de Costa Rica, 1940-1973.** (The University of Costa
Rica, 1940-73.)
Luis Barahona Jiménez.　San José: Editorial Universidad de Costa
Rica, 1976. 408p. bibliog.

The University of Costa Rica is the country's largest and most important institution of
higher learning and the leading university of Central America, modelled in many
respects on North American universities. This detailed and informative history is based
on internal documents and published reports, some of the most important of which are
quoted extensively. Chapters cover the development of the teaching programme,
curriculum reform, the teaching staff, the student body, the university's organization
into schools, departments and affiliated research centres, administrative and gover-
nance structures, and regional campuses and extension programmes. The author taught
at the University from 1948 to 1974.

610 **Influencia de las ideas del doctor Valeriano Fernández Ferraz en la vida cultural de Costa Rica.** (The influence of the ideas of Dr Valeriano Fernández Ferraz in the cultural life of Costa Rica.)
Eduardo Chacón Casares. San José: Editorial Universidad Estatal a Distancia, 1984. 248p. bibliog.

In 1869 Valeriano Fernández Ferraz, a teacher and philosopher from Spain, was contracted to direct the Colegio San Luis Gonzaga in Cartago. Thus began a controversial career as educator, adviser to the government of Costa Rica in educational and cultural matters, library director and moulder of opinion – the controversy lasted until his death in Costa Rica in 1925. This book covers the Costa Rican part of his career (he also taught in Spain, Cuba, and Guatemala) and at the same time illuminates various aspects of educational reform in the 1860-1920 period. Chacón provides material on Fernández Ferraz' philosophy and background on educational thought in Spain and Costa Rica in the late 19th century. A few essays and editorials from Fernández Ferraz' pen are appended (p. 179-236).

611 **Consenso y represión: una interpretación socio-política de educación costarricense.** (Consensus and repression: a sociopolitical interpretation of Costa Rican education.)
Astrid Fischel. San José: Editorial Costa Rica, 1987. 304p. bibliog.

The focus of this book is the educational reform of 1885-90, which the author believes profoundly affected the political system of Costa Rica. Applying Antonio Gramsci's theory of class domination through ideology, the author interprets Costa Rica's educational reform as a means of using the country's entire educational apparatus in order to create national consensus, or the people's acceptance of the political system. Thus, unlike in much of the rest of Latin America, governmental repression was unnecessary. Readers may well question the theory but the book cannot be dismissed; it is well researched, well documented, and carefully presented. Fischel succeeds in her objective of elucidating unexpected connections between Costa Rica's educational system on the one hand and, on the other, liberalism, militarism, and the country's political system.

612 **Educational problems related to the economic development of Costa Rica.**
Gerald W. Fry. *Public and International Affairs*, vol. 4, no. 1 (Spring 1966), p. 66-87.

On the basis of a survey of secondary materials and interviews of education officials, the author highlights specific problems in Costa Rican education at all levels and goes on to make recommendations. He suggests that with a higher rate of student promotion, more emphasis on vocational education, and year-round operation of the school system, more rapid economic development would take place.

613 **Educación en una sociedad libre: fundamentos y ejemplario.** (Education in a free society: foundations and examples.)
Emma Gamboa. San José: Editorial Costa Rica, 1976. 168p. bibliog.

Since education is so important to Costa Rica it is not surprising that Emma Gamboa, who was dean of the School of Education at the Universidad de Costa Rica from 1948 to 1964, has strong views about her speciality, primary education. In this book of essays she reflects on the importance of John Dewey, Omar Dengo, and Roberto Brenes Mesén to Costa Rican education, but she tarries longest on the history of primary education in Costa Rica. She believes that in order to promote democracy in the country it must first be promoted in the primary classroom.

614 **The educational system of Costa Rica.**
Clark C. Gill. Washington, DC: United States Department of Education, 1980. 30p. map. bibliog. (Education around the World, Publication no. E-80-14005).

Education is a particularly high priority in Costa Rican society and this pamphlet is a succinct description of how the Costa Rican educational system came to have such high status. A description of all the institutions of higher education is included. The educational statistics come mainly from the Ministry of Education report of 1977.

615 **The intellectual evolution of Costa Rica.**
Luis Felipe González. *Inter-América*, vol. 6, no. 4, 5 (April-June 1923), p. 250-63, 267-78.

A translation of an article which appeared in the *Revista de Filosofía* of Buenos Aires in November 1922, the present study is an erudite commentary on the European intellectual influences on Latin America in general and Costa Rica in particular. González gives heavy emphasis to education, including higher education. It is a summary of his longer and accurately titled study, *Historia de la influencia extranjera en el desenvolvimiento educacional y científico de Costa Rica* (History of foreign influence in the educational and scientific development of Costa Rica). Although that work was first published by the Imprenta Nacional in 1921, it is still of importance.

616 **Una universidad en una ciudad de maestros.** (A university in a city of teachers.)
Edwin León. Heredia, Costa Rica: Universidad Nacional, 1982. 232p. bibliog. (Colección Barva, Serie Pensamiento, Subserie Ensayo).

This is a history of the development of educational thought in Costa Rica as seen through events leading up to the founding of the Universidad Nacional, Costa Rica's second university, in Heredia in 1973. The author focuses on the role the secondary schools of Heredia played in the development of the national educational system. The Escuela Normal de Costa Rica, Costa Rica's first public teacher-training school, founded in 1914 by Alfredo and Luis Felipe González Flores, was particularly influential.

617 **La educación, fragua de nuestra democracia.** (Education, the forge of our democracy.)
Carlos Monge Alfaro, Francisco Rivas Ríos. San José: Editorial Universidad de Costa Rica, 1978. 2nd ed. 202p.

The first edition of this book was published by the Editorial Universidad de Costa Rica in 1978, under Monge's name alone. Monge, author of Costa Rica's most widely used textbook history of Costa Rica and long-time rector of the Universidad de Costa Rica, and Rivas trace the increasingly heavy commitment of Costa Rican authorities to education. Obviously proud of their country's reputation in education they call for continuing effort and focus on education. They conclude that industrialization and increasing population, among other things, put a strain on Costa Rica's educational resources.

618 **La universidad en el desarrollo histórico nacional.** (The University in national historical development.)
Carlos Monge Alfaro. San José: Ministerio de Cultura, Juventud y Deportes, 1978. 229p. bibliog. (Serie de la Cultura, no. 1).

As a historian and rector of the Universidad de Costa Rica from 1961 to 1970 the author is in an excellent position to place the development of the university in the context of the history of the country, and he succeeds in doing that. Besides his successful treatment of the founding of the Universidad de Santo Tomás in 1844 and its refounding as the Universidad de Costa Rica in 1940, Monge also covers the so-called interregnum of 1888 to 1940 when no university existed. The emphasis falls on the post-1940 period.

619 **Costa Rica's Universidad Estatal a Distancia: a case study.**
Greville Rumble. Milton Keynes, England: Distance Education Research Group, Open University, 1981. 44p. map. bibliog. (Distance Education Research Group Papers, no. 4).

After a brief introduction to the country and to higher education the author, who identifies himself as a consultant to the university, focuses on the Universidad Estatal a Distancia (State Extension University) which was founded in 1979. He provides a statistical profile of students of the university and describes the university's organization, the study programmes available, and the twenty-two academic centres. Although Rumble believes that the university is an essentially healthy institution, he is critical of the quality of instruction, the high dropout rate, and the over-centralization of administration.

620 **La Universidad de Costa Rica: trayectoria de su creación.**
(The University of Costa Rica: the path of its creation.)
Luis Demetrio Tinoco. San José: Editorial Costa Rica, 1983. 508p.

This is a compilation of separately published documents – speeches, letters, newspaper articles, editorial cartoons – on the debate surrounding the establishment of the Universidad de Costa Rica in 1941. The author was the Calderón Guardia administration's Secretary of Public Education at that time; later he became rector of the Universidad de Costa Rica. Tinoco also provides extensive excerpts from his private diary.

Costa Rican life.
See item no. 4.

Los costarricenses. (The Costa Ricans.)
See item no. 5.

The Costa Ricans.
See item no. 6.

Education

El desarrollo nacional en 150 años de vida independiente. (National development during 150 years of independence.)
See item no. 153.

Desarrollo de las ideas filosóficas en Costa Rica. (The development of philosophical ideas in Costa Rica.)
See item no. 167.

Obras de Rodrigo Facio. (The works of Rodrigo Facio.)
See item no. 474.

Baratijas de antaño. (Musings from the past.)
See item no. 625.

Science and Technology

621 **La ingeniería en Costa Rica, 1502-1903: ensayo histórico.** (Engineering in Costa Rica, 1502-1903: an historical essay.)
Hernán Gutiérrez Braun.   Cartago, Costa Rica: Editorial Tecnológica de Costa Rica, 1981. 163p. bibliog.
Contains essential facts about the construction of churches, mines, roads, railways, docks, and public buildings in Costa Rica and about the engineers who designed them.

622 **Hydro and geothermal electricity as an alternative for industrial petroleum consumption in Costa Rica.**
Washington, DC: Inter-American Development Bank, 1982. 141p. map. bibliog.
Costa Rica has no petroleum resources but petroleum products account for approximately seventy per cent of the total commercial energy consumed. Recognizing these facts and realizing the financial advantage of locally produced energy, the Inter-American Development Bank commissioned this detailed study of potential hydro and geothermal electricity production. The study includes an analysis of the economic costs and concludes that there are substantial opportunities for the substitution of hydro and geothermal electricity for petroleum in industrial applications.

623 **Serpientes venenosas de Costa Rica.** (Poisonous snakes of Costa Rica.)
Clodomiro Picado Twight.   San José: Editorial Costa Rica, 1976. 2nd ed. 241p.
Clodomiro Picado was one of Costa Rica's best-known scientists of the early 20th century. In this book Picado, a microbiologist, discusses the poisonous snakes of Costa Rica, their poison, and the medical treatment of snakebite victims. A bibliography of 111 of Picado's publications is appended to this edition. The first edition of *Serpientes venenosas* was published in 1931 by Imprenta Alsina of San José.

209

624 **Costa Rica.**
Christopher Roper, Jorge Silva. In: *Science and technology in Latin America*, edited by Christopher Roper, Jorge Silva. London: Longman, 1983, p. 92-9. (Longman Guide to World Science and Technology).

All Costa Rican organizations involved in research on scientific and technological topics are described in the chapter on Costa Rica in this book. It includes governmental as well as private agencies. Following an introduction to Costa Rica, there are additional sections on the financing of research and on the National Council for Scientific and Technological Research.

625 **Baratijas de antaño.** (Musings from the past.)
José Fidel Tristán. San José: Editorial Costa Rica, 1966. 185p.

This is a mostly autobiographical account by one of Costa Rica's earliest students of natural science. Tristán, who was born in 1874 and who died in 1932, comments in this memoir on prominent educators like Mauro Fernández (Tristán's uncle), scientists like Paul Biolley, and on institutional support for research and teaching in the sciences. The memoir was put together from diaries, notes, and documents from the 1920s.

626 **Ensayos e ideas científicos.** (Scientific ideas and essays.)
Rodrigo Zeledón. San José: Editorial Costa Rica, 1976. 198p.

Zeledón is a microbiologist with many years of service in public education and the promotion of scientific research in Costa Rica as director of the National Council on Scientific and Technological Research. These essays were published in newspapers in the 1970s. They contain Zeledón's views on specific topics such as toxoplasmosis and encephalitis, broader topics such as nutrition and vaccination, and general issues of scientific education, scientific research, and the promotion of science. Also included is a biographical sketch of Clodomiro Picado Twight, pioneer Costa Rican scientist.

Costa Rican natural history.
See item no. 71.

Vidy y obra del doctor Clodomiro Picado T. (Life and works of doctor Clodomiro Picado T.)
See item no. 730.

Literature

627 Franciso y los caminos. (Francisco and his journeys.)
Francisco Amighetti. San José: Editorial Costa Rica, 1980. 188p.
'I write about things of no importance', says Amighetti in the preface. But Amighetti is one of Costa Rica's greatest artists and cultural heroes and therefore his autobiographical comments on places that he has visited and word-pictures of scenes he has painted have more than casual interest.

628 Costa Rica en seis espejos. (Costa Rica in six mirrors.)
Stefan Baciu. San José: Ministerio de Cultura, Juventud y Deportes, 1974. 139p. bibliog. (Serie Nos Ven, no. 7).
A literary study of six Costa Rican poets: Asdrubal Villalobos, Max Jiménez, César Vallejo, Francisco Amighetti, Jorge Debravo, and Eunice Odio Boix.

629 Evolución en la poesía costarricense, 1574-1977. (Evolution of Costa Rican poetry, 1574-1977.)
Alberto Baeza Flores. San José: Editorial Costa Rica, 1978. 412p. bibliog.
In this somewhat anecdotal volume of poetry criticism Baeza Flores discusses every major poet of Costa Rica, including one from the colonial period. In addition to basic biographical information about all poets Baeza Flores provides criticism of major poets such as Roberto Brenes Mesén (1874-1947), Alfredo Cardona Peña (1917-), Isaac Felipe Azofeifa (1912-), Eunice Odio (1922-75), Jorge Debravo (1938-67), Carmen Naranjo (1931-), and Laureano Albán (1942-).

630 **Contemporary Costa Rican literature in translation: a sampler of poetry, fiction and drama.**
Edited by Ervin Beck, Wilbur Birky.   Goshen, Indiana: Pinchpenny Press, 1975. 119p.

Selections of poetry, drama, and short stories by Costa Ricans make up this anthology. Because few Costa Rican writers have been translated into English this translation project by a group of Goshen College faculty and students is a unique contribution, enabling English readers to get a taste of Costa Rican *belles-lettres*. Among the writers represented are Carmen Naranjo, Quince Duncan, and José León Sánchez. Jézer González, a professor of Costa Rican literature, offers a brief introductory commentary (also translated into English) on the writers selected.

631 **Historia y antología de la literatura costarricense.** (History and anthology of Costa Rican literature.)
Abelardo Bonilla.   San José: Universidad de Costa Rica, 1957-61.
2 vols. (Sección de Literatura y Artes, no. 3).

The great value of this history and anthology by one of the best-known literary critics of Costa Rica is that it is both detailed and comprehensive. No major cultural figure – including poets, historians, novelists, lawyers, and educators – is left out. The first volume, which covers the history of Costa Rican literature, has chapters on such movements as positivism and modernism, and includes a chapter on journalism. The anthology itself (volume two) contains excerpts from sixty-two Costa Rican authors and short biographical sketches of each. The fourth edition of volume one, slightly altered, was published by Editorial Studium of San José in 1981.

632 **Historia del teatro en Costa Rica.** (History of the theatre in Costa Rica.)
Fernando Borges Pérez.   San José: Editorial Costa Rica, 1980. 116p.

This is a brief, informal history of theatres and the principal theatrical performances in Costa Rica from 1837 onwards. Despite lack of documentation it contains considerable detail about personalities and about the finances involved in the business of constructing theatres and operating them. It was originally published as *Historia del teatro en Costa Rica* by Imprenta Española in San José in 1942.

633 **El costumbrismo en Costa Rica.** (The 'costumbrismo' movement in Costa Rica.)
Margarita Castro Rawson.   San José: Imprenta Lehmann, 1971. 2nd ed. 478p. bibliog.

Margaret Castro Rawson, known as Margarita de Méndez in the English-speaking world, explains Costa Rican 'cuadros de costumbres', or short stories based on local legend and local speech. Approximately two-thirds of the book is made up of an anthology of selected stories. Many of the stories were printed anonymously in newspapers in the 19th century, but at the beginning of the 20th century the genre was well established and considered sufficiently respectable for writers to be identified with it. Writers such as Manuel González Zeledón and Pío Víquez were popular 'costrumbistas'.

634 **Narrativa contemporánea de Costa Rica.** (Contemporary narrative in Costa Rica.)
Edited by Alfonso Chase. San José: Ministerio de Cultura, Juventud y Deportes, 1975. 2 vols. (Serie Estudios Literarios, no. 1).

After a lengthy critical introduction (p. 19-152) Chase offers short biographies and bibliographies of twenty-four Costa Rican short-story writers of the 20th century. None of the selected writers had published before 1925. Recognizing that few Costa Rican writers have gained international stature Chase suggests that Costa Rican literature is more valuable for what it says than the form in which it is said.

635 **El negro en la literatura costarricense.** (Blacks in Costa Rican literature.)
Selected by Quince Duncan. San José: Editorial Costa Rica, 1975. 190p.

This book contains twenty-two short stories or excerpts selected from the writings of authors who are linked to two regions of Costa Rica: the Central Valley and Limón. All selections, however, treat characters who are black. The purpose of the dichotomy is to illuminate the contrasting images of blacks held by those from the centre of Hispanic power and those from the periphery. Quince Duncan, who made the selection, provides in the introduction a short commentary on the black population of Limón.

636 **Revista Iberoamericana: número especial dedicado a la literatura de Costa Rica.** (The *Iberoamerican Journal*: special edition dedicated to Costa Rican literature.)
Edited by Juan Duran Luzio. Pittsburgh, Pennsylvania: Instituto Internacional de Literatura Iberoamericana, 1987. 492p.

The appearance of this issue of the *Revista Iberoamericana* is a major event in Costa Rican literary criticism. That thirty-one articles on a variety of genres of Costa Rican literature, primarily contemporary, could be published at one time is itself an indication of the maturity of Costa Rica as a publishing centre. This is especially so as the editor says it is his intention merely to provide a sample of Costa Rican literature. The articles in this collection deal mainly with Costa Rican novelists – Carlos Luis Fallas, Yolanda Oreamuno, Carlos Gagini, Joaquín Gutiérrez, and others – but poets and dramatists are also covered.

637 **Poesía contemporánea de Costa Rica: antología.** (Contemporary poetry of Costa Rica: an anthology.)
Selected by Carlos Rafael Duverrán. San José: Editorial Costa Rica, 1978. 2nd ed. 443p.

Duverrán explains in the introduction that this book is an anthology representative of 20th-century Costa Rican poetry. Beginning with the work of Roberto Brenes Mesén (1874-1947) the book includes fifty-three poets, divided into seven generational groupings, and 225 poems. Succinct biographical sketches accompany the selected poems. The editor notes a steady progression from the excessive individualism and parochialism of the early 20th-century poetry to the universalism of the poetry of the 1960s and 1970s.

638 **Narrativa de Carlos Luis Fallas.** (Narrative of Carlos Luis Fallas.)
Carlos Luis Fallas. San José: Studium Generale Costarricense, 1984.
2 vols. (Clásicos Costarricenses).

The two novels *Mamita Yunai* and *Gentes y gentecillas* are included in the first volume (589p.), along with an introduction by Manuel Picado. Volume two (499p.) contains two additional novels, *Mi madrina* and *Marcos Ramírez*, as well as *Tres cuentos*. Fallas is the best-known Costa Rican novelist and *Mamita Yunai*, which is about the United Fruit Company, is perhaps the best-known novel with a Costa Rican setting.

639 **Los caminos del teatro en Costa Rica.** (The paths of the Costa Rican theatre.)
Guido Fernández. San José: Editorial Universitaria Centroamericana, 1977. 186p. bibliog. (Colección Aula).

As one would expect from a collection of newspaper articles and speeches, this book suffers to some extent from repetition and lack of continuity. Nevertheless, Fernández, Costa Rica's leading theatre critic, offers a sophisticated running commentary on Costa Rican dramatists, directors, theatres, actors, and the various public and private institutions that support them. The period covered is 1968-76.

640 **'Cuentos ticos': short stories of Costa Rica.**
Ricardo Fernández Guardia, translated by Gray Casement.
Cleveland, Ohio: Burrows Brothers, 1905. 293p.

Casement selects and translates eleven of Fernández Guardia's best-known stories taken from Costa Rica's past. In addition to the stories themselves, which are well translated and give the reader the flavour of the colonial period and early independence period, Casement provides a seventy-two-page introduction on Costa Rica at the beginning of the 20th century. A remarkable set of photographs of Costa Rica assists in recreating the past.

641 **Ensayistas costarricenses.** (Costa Rican essayists.)
Luis Ferrero. San José: Lehmann Editores, 1979. 3rd ed. 418p.
bibliog. (Biblioteca Patria, no. 7).

Much has been written in essay form in Latin American literature as a whole, and much about the essay as a literary form, but about the essay in Costa Rica there is little except this book. Ferrero thus makes a contribution when he, after carefully defining his terms, discusses the Costa Rican essay and selects eighteen representative essays for inclusion in the anthology section of the book (beginning on p. 101). Many of the essays selected touch on the theme of the Costa Rican national character. An ample biographical sketch of each essayist is included. The first edition of this book was published by the same publisher in 1971.

642 **Resumen de literatura costarricense.** (A review of Costa Rican literature.)
Virginia Sandoval de Fonseca. San José: Editorial Costa Rica, 1978. 190p.

Compressed in this small volume the reader will find biographical sketches and short commentaries of literary criticism about approximately 140 Costa Rican authors. Interspersed among the treatments of individuals are general comments on the evolution of the various genres of literature in Costa Rica.

643 **Obras escogidas.** (Selected works.)
Joaquín García Monge, selected by Eugenio García Carillo. San José: Editorial Universitaria Centroamericana, 1974. 632p. (Colección Séptimo Día).

An anthology of over a hundred essays on a wide range of political and literary subjects by the distinguished writer and editor of *El Repertorio Americano*, a well-known literary magazine published in San José. García was born in 1881 and died in 1958. The selection of essays was made by his son, Eugenio García Carillo.

644 **Antología femenina del ensayo costarricense.** (Anthology of Costa Rican women essayists.)
Edited by Leonor Garnier. San José: Ministerio de Cultura, Juventud y Deportes, 1976. 442p. bibliog. (Estudios Literarios, no. 3).

This volume contains essential biographical information about each of the eleven women essayists whose writings were selected. It includes selected essays by anthropologists such as María Eugenia Bózzoli and educators such as Emma Gamboa as well as literary criticism by writers such as Margarita Castro Rawson and María Rosa Picado. Many of the essays treat Costa Rican subjects.

645 **Social rebellion as represented in Costa Rican fiction, 1940-50.**
Charles L. Kargleder. *Annals*, Southeastern Conference on Latin American Studies, vol. 15 (March 1984), p. 54-60.

The author believes that Costa Rican fiction reached its maturity during the decade of the 1940s and that the primary theme of the novels of this period was social protest. He illustrates his point by providing synopses of *Mamita Yunai* by Carlos Luis Fallas, *Puerto Limón* by Joaquín Gutiérrez, *El sitio de las abras* by Fabián Dobles, and *Pedro Arnaez* by José Marín Cañas.

646 **Relatos escogidos.** (Selected stories.)
Carmen Lyra (pseudonym for María Isabel Carvajal), selected by Alfonso Chase. San José: Editorial Costa Rica, 1977. 534p. bibliog. (Colección Nuestros Clásicos, no. 12).

This collection of the works of Carmen Lyra (1888-1949), an essayist and novelist noted for her work as an educator and for her Communist Part affiliation, includes prose fiction, essays, and some of her well-known children's stories. Alfonso Chase, who made the selection, contributes an excellent commentary on her work as both writer and political figure.

647 **El cuento costarricense: estudio, antología y bibliografía.** (The Costa
Rican short story: study, anthology and bibliography.)
Seymour Menton.   Mexico City: Ediciones de Andrea; Lawrence,
Kansas: University of Kansas Press, 1964. 184p. (Antologías Studium,
no. 8).

Twenty-two Costa Rican short-story writers, among them the leading literary figures of
the 1890-1960 period, are represented in this anthology. Professor Menton, for his
part, offers a short biographical sketch of each author, and in the thoughtful and
thorough introduction, provides an analysis of Costa Rican literature in the light of the
country's history and social conditions.

648 **Novel and context in Costa Rica and Nicaragua.**
Raymond D. Souza.   *Romance Quarterly*, vol. 34, no. 4 (Nov. 1986),
p. 453-62.

Souza's approach in this article is to contrast the recent works of two Costa Rican
novelists and two Nicaraguan novelists, keeping in mind the revolutionary context of
Nicaragua and the democratic capitalist context of Costa Rica. He chooses several
prize-winning novels of Carmen Naranjo and one novel of Samuel Rovinski as
representative of Costa Rica. Souza notes a greater emphasis on prose fiction in Costa
Rica than in Nicaragua, and a larger reading public in Costa Rica.

649 **El Teatro Nacional: (apuntes para la biografía de un coliseo).**
(The National Theatre: (notes for a biography of a theatre).)
Alfonso Ulloa Zamora.   San José: Editorial Costa Rica, 1972. 147p.
bibliog.

Costa Rica's National Theatre, which was inaugurated in 1898, is the subject of this
brief study. Photographs of the building, inside and outside, help the reader
understand why this is the first building on tourists' lists.

650 **Five women writers of Costa Rica.**
Edited by Victoria Urbano.   Beaumont, Texas: Asociación de
Literatura Femenina Hispánica, 1978. 131p.

Short stories of five Costa Rican women writers (Carmen Naranjo, Yolanda
Oreamuno, Eunice Odio, Rima Vallbona, and Victoria Urbano) are collected in this
volume, along with short biographical sketches and critical essays about their work.

651 **El soneto en la poesía costarricense.** (The sonnet in Costa Rican
poetry.)
Francisco Zuñiga Díaz.   San José: Editorial Universidad de Costa
Rica, 1979. 247p. bibliog.

The introduction is brief, leaving unanswered some questions about poetry in Costa
Rica, but the basic contribution is substantial in that it lists twenty-four of the principal
Costa Rican poets who have composed sonnets and gives details of their publications.

La patria esencial. (The essence of the country.)
See item no. 2.

El desarrollo nacional en 150 años de vida independiente. (National development during 150 years of independence.)
See item no. 153.

El negro en Costa Rica: antología. (The negro in Costa Rica: anthology.)
See item no. 260.

Cultural policy in Costa Rica.
See item no. 674.

Libros y folletos publicados en Costa Rica durante los años 1830-1849. (Books and pamphlets published in Costa Rica during the years 1830-49.)
See item no. 689.

Carlos Luis Fallas: su época y sus luchas. (Carlos Luis Fallas: his era and his struggles.)
See item no. 697.

Ideas, ensayos y paisajes. (Ideas, essays and landscapes.)
See item no. 703.

Moisés Vincenzi.
See item no. 711.

Roberto Brenes Mesén.
See item no. 712.

La clara voz de Joaquín García Monge. (The clear voice of Joaquín García Monge.)
See item no. 716.

Anastasio Alfaro.
See item no. 718.

Joaquín García Monge.
See item no. 719.

A tentative bibliography of the *belles-lettres* of the republics of Central America.
See item no. 745.

Bibliografía selectiva de la literatura costarricense. (A selected bibliography of Costa Rican literature.)
See item no. 756.

Language

652 **El español de América y Costa Rica.** (The Spanish of America and
   Costa Rica.)
   Arturo Agüero Cháves.   San José: Lehmann, 1962. 286p. bibliog.

The serious student of linguistics will find here material on the history of changes in the
Spanish language during the period of Spanish migration to America. Spanish spoken
in Costa Rica is given special treatment. Language students in quest of local Costa
Rican expressions will find a thorough list, with explanations. The author also touches
on the history of language study in Costa Rica.

653 **El habla popular en la literatura costarricense.** (Popular speech in Costa
   Rican literature.)
   Víctor Manuel Arroyo Soto.   San José: Universidad de Costa Rica,
   1971. 320p. bibliog. (Publicaciones de la Universidad de Costa Rica,
   Serie Tesis de Grado, no. 18).

The author makes an important contribution to the scarce literature on Costa Rican
speech, but this rigorous study of the phonetic, lexical, and semantic aspects is limited
to literary texts. It was originally presented as the author's thesis in Madrid in 1969.

654 **Lenguas indígenas costarricenses.** (Indigenous Costa Rican languages.)
   Víctor Manuel Arroyo Soto.   San José: Editorial Universitaria
   Centroamericana, 1972. 2nd ed. 286p. bibliog. (Colección Aula).

A comparison is made of five of the principal languages of Costa Rica – Bribri,
Cabécar, Térraba, Brunka, and Guatuso. Vocabularies were collected while the author
served as a teacher in Buenos Aires, Costa Rica in 1948-49. The study was presented
as a thesis for the licentiate degree in 1951 and first published in 1966 by the Editorial
Costa Rica. The volume consists primarily of vocabulary lists.

655　**The phonological correlates of social stratification in the Spanish of Costa Rica.**
Susan Berk-Seligson, Mitchell A. Seligson. *Lingua*, vol. 46, no. 1 (Sept. 1978), p. 1-28. bibliog.

Forty-eight adult males from Sabanilla were interviewed during 1973 for the purpose of determining the relation of linguistic variation to socio-economic status. Unlike many other linguistic scholars, the authors determined socio-economic status individually and only after the interview was conducted. The authors found that a particular subset of socio-economic variables – consisting of household artefacts, house construction materials and education – was the strongest measure of linguistic performance, and that as the level of formality increases, the use of prestige phonological forms increases.

656　**Estudios de lingüística chibcha.** (Studies of Chibcha linguistics.)
Edited by Adolfo Constenla Umaña, Enrique Margery Peña. San José: Departamento de Lingüística, Universidad de Costa Rica, 1982-85. 4 vols. bibliog. (Estudios Varios sobre las Lenguas Chibchas de Costa Rica. Serie 1).

The series of studies on the Chibcha language is the result of a research programme by the Department of Linguistics of the University of Costa Rica. The eighteen articles, some in English, deal with various technical aspects of the Chibcha language, especially among the Bribri, Cabécar, Guatuso, and Guaymí language groups in Costa Rica. One article summarizes the history of the study of Chibcha in Costa Rica. Many of the articles in these four volumes are by Enrique Margery Peña and Adolfo Constenla Umaña, two prominent professors of linguistics at the University of Costa Rica who are directors of the Chibcha language study project.

657　**Diccionario de costarriqueñismos.** (Dictionary of Costa Ricanisms.)
Carlos Gagini. San José: Editorial Costa Rica, 1979. 4th ed. 243p. (Biblioteca Patria, no. 20).

Gagini, who was born in 1865, was a writer and teacher who took a special interest in linguistics. This book is the first important linguistic publication on Costa Rica; its purpose is to provide a guide to the peculiarities of Costa Rican speech. The *Diccionario* was first published in 1893; the fourth edition (1979) is a reprint of the third edition, which was corrected and enlarged before being published by the Editorial Costa Rica in 1975. As the frequent editions suggest, it is a work fundamental to the study of Costa Rican speech.

658　**Refranes y dichos populares usuales en Costa Rica.** (Proverbs and customary popular expressions in Costa Rica.)
Hermógenes Hernández. San José: Imprenta-Litografía San Martín, 1976. 2nd ed. 166p.

This book is a compilation of refrains and popular sayings found in Costa Rica. A succinct explanation of the meaning of each entry is included, but the introduction offers little information about regional usage or origin. The first edition (San José: Imprenta Elena, 1969), contains the refrains and sayings without the explanations.

659 **The creoles of Costa Rica and Panama.**
Anita Herzfeld. In: *Central American English*, edited by John Holm.
Heidelberg, Germany: Groos, 1983, p. 131-49. bibliog.
The pages listed cover the origin of the black population on the Caribbean coast of
Costa Rica and how Limonese creole emerged as the dominant language of Limón. (A
separate section on Panama follows the article in the Holm book.) The varieties of
speech, along a continuum of standard English and Limonese creole, and sociolinguis-
tic influences on speech patterns are discussed, and examples of speech varieties are
provided. The six-page bibliography is annotated.

660 **English creole speakers in Costa Rica and Panama: a case study of
attitude variation.**
Anita Herzfeld. In: *Vergleichbarkeit von Sprachkontakten*
(Comparability of language contacts), edited by P. H. Nelde. Bonn,
Germany: Dümmler, 1983, p. 43-55. bibliog.
Professor Herzfeld explains the linguistic differences between Limonese creole and
Panamanian creole, the languages spoken by the predominantly black population on
the Caribbean coast of both countries. Jamaican creole is the origin of both languages,
but the Panamanian variety is more influenced by standard English and Spanish.
Sociocultural contrasts, in particular the greater pride taken in language and cultural
differences in Limón, are also taken into account.

661 **Second language acrolect replacement in Limón creole.**
Anita Herzfeld. *Vínculos*, vol. 5, nos 1-2 (1979), p. 19-33.
The purpose of this article is to show the relation of Limonese creole, the language of
Costa Rican blacks in the Limón area, to Spanish. Specifically, the article explains how
Spanish influences the lexicon, semantic range, and syntactic structures of Limonese
creole. The author provides introductory material on the black population and explains
the social and political pressures on Limón creole speakers.

662 **The study of Limón English Creole.**
Anita Herzfeld. In: *Methoden der Kontaktlinguistik* (Methods in
contact linguistic research), edited by P. H. Nelde. Bonn, Germany:
Dümmler, 1985, p. 75-86. bibliog.
The aim of the study is to describe the sociocultural processes that have prompted the
configurations of speech use and speech variation among speakers of English in
Limón. The discussion includes some data on the sociocultural backgrounds of
Limonese. A random sample of 50 individuals was interviewed.

663 **Towards the description of a creole.**
Anita Herzfeld. *Vínculos*, vol. 3, nos 1-2 (1977), p. 105-15.
This is a technical linguistics study which examines the speech of the black population
from the Limón area. The language spoken, Limonese creole, is a derivative of
Jamaican creole, as most Costa Rican blacks came from Jamaica. Through analysis of
the use of the negative the author identifies three kinds of Limonese creole speakers.

664   **Diccionario bribri–español, español–bribri.** (A Bribri–Spanish, Spanish–
      Bribri dictionary.)
      Enrique Margery Peña.   San José: Editorial Universidad de Costa
      Rica, 1982. 160p.

The Bribri language is the most important indigenous language in Costa Rica. It is
spoken by approximately 4,000 persons who live primarily on the Atlantic coast near
Panama but including some who live in the Talamanca Mountains. This dictionary,
which contains an eighty-four-page explanatory introduction by the author, is a result
of a team effort of several Costa Rican linguists and anthropologists starting in the
mid-1970s. The vocabulary comes from two of the three known dialects of Bribri: that
spoken in Salitre, on the Atlantic coast, and that spoken in the towns of Katsi and
Amubre in the Talamanca Mountains.

665   **Las lenguas indígenas de Centro América: con especial referencia a los
      idiomas aborígenes de Costa Rica.** (The indigenous languages of Central
      America: with special reference to the aboriginal languages of Costa
      Rica.)
      Rodolfo R. Schuller.   San José: Imprenta Nacional, 1928. 132p.
      bibliog.

The present work, according to the author's introduction, is a critical examination of
Walter Lehmann's work on Central American Indian languages. But it is more; it is a
thorough, well-documented updating of Lehmann's work. Schuller gives special
attention to Maya, Chibcha, and other influences on Costa Rican indigenous
languages.

666   **The voseo in Costa Rican Spanish.**
      Francisco Villegas.   *Hispania*, vol. 46, no. 3 (Sept. 1963), p. 612-15.

Contradicting previous authors who doubted the wide usage of 'vos' in Costa Rica,
Villegas maintains that it is used throughout Costa Rica without regard to social class,
economic position, geographical distribution, or educational level. It is also found
widely in Costa Rican literature.

667   **El anglicismo en el habla costarricense.** (Anglicism in Costa Rican
      speech.)
      Virginia Zúñiga Tristán.   San José: Editorial Costa Rica, 1976. 166p.
      bibliog.

Alarmed at the invasion of the English language in Costa Rican Spanish, Professor
Zúñiga has done something about it; she has documented it. In a short narrative
section (p. 11-30) she reviews the literature on the subject and offers an explanation
for the penetration of English. The author believes that immigration from Jamaica, the
United States, and the United Kingdom, as well as pressures from education and
business, are primarily responsible. The heart of the book is a dictionary of anglicisms
with definitions, etymology, citations of use, and geographical distribution. Appendices
document English place-names in Costa Rica and the numbers of English-language
immigrants to Costa Rica.

Language

Leyendas y tradiciones borucas. (Boruca legends and traditions.)
See item no. 281.

Central American Spanish: a bibliography, (1940-1953).
See item no. 747.

Art and Architecture

668 **Historia crítica del arte costarricense.** (Critical history of Costa Rican art.)
Carlos Francisco Echeverría.   San José: Editorial Universidad Estatal a Distancia, 1986. 168p.
The physical appearance of this book – the print, the cover, the layout, the photographs, the index – is highly professional, an indication perhaps of the growing sophistication of Costa Rican art. Fortunately, the contents of the book are worthy of the package. While concentrating on a history of Costa Rican art, Echeverría weaves in local social and political history and international influences that affect artistic trends in Costa Rica. He recognizes the significance of indigenous art but chooses to leave that aside for this publication in order to concentrate on painting and sculpture in Costa Rica since about 1850. He focuses of course on the luminaries like Francisco Amighetti but he does not neglect any deserving artists. It is one of the few truly professional books of art criticism published in Costa Rica.

669 **Ocho artistas costarricenses y una tradición.** (Eight Costa Rican artists and a tradition.)
Carlos Francisco Echeverría.   San José: Ministerio de Cultura, Juventud y Deportes, 1977, 181p. (Serie del Creador Analizado, no. 6).
Echeverría makes the interesting case that Costa Rican art is different from that of most other nations partly because it has evolved without the benefit (and influences) of national collectors and critics. The result, according to Echeverría, is that Costa Rican artists have been free to let their own inclinations and talent take them where they want. After a ten-page introduction on such matters Echeverría dedicates separate chapters to eight painters (Teodoro Quirós, Francisco Amighetti, Margarita Bertheau, Fausto Pacheco, Luisa González de Sáenz, Juan Luis Rodríguez, Fabio Herrera, and Virginia Vargas). Black-and-white illustrations accompany each chapter.

223

670   **Cinco artistas costarricenses: pintores y escultores.** (Five Costa Rican artists: painters and sculptors.)
Luis Ferrero.   San José: Editorial Universidad Estatal a Distancia, 1985. 145p.

The format of the book – text on one side, reproductions of paintings or sculptures on the other – is appealing and helps Ferrero achieve his purpose of acquainting readers with five of Costa Rica's leading artists. The chosen ones are Enrique Echandi, Juan Rafael Chacón, Luisa González de Sáenz, Hernán Pérez, and Aquilés Chacón. Ferrero provides ample biographical background and fully discusses the artists' works, but his approach is informal, personal, supportive, as he is writing about friends. It is hard to be an art critic when the art circle, as in Costa Rica, is so small.

671   **La escultura en Costa Rica.** (Sculpture in Costa Rica.)
Luis Ferrero.   San José: Editorial Costa Rica, 1982. 3rd ed. 272p. bibliog.

First published in 1972 by the Editorial Costa Rica, this is the most authoritative book available on the subject of sculpture. It is divided into two sections. The first is a chronological treatment of the history of sculpture in Costa Rica, and the second contains biographies of sixteen Costa Rican sculptors. Both sections are profusely illustrated. Although the focus is sharply on sculpture the author is successful in relating the Costa Rican artistic tradition to events in Costa Rica and to outside influences.

672   **Sociedad y arte en la Costa Rica del siglo 19.** (Society and art in 19th-century Costa Rica.)
Luis Ferrero.   San José: Editorial Universidad Estatal a Distancia, 1986. 213p.

Ferrero says in his introduction that he conceives of history as a complex totality. Therefore, in contrast to his previous works on specific artistic topics, he concentrates in this book on the linkages between art and society in order to recreate 19th-century Costa Rica. The focus is on how four artists – Achiles Bigot, José María Figueroa, Enrique Echandi, and Ezequiel Jiménez Rojas – were received in Costa Rica. He finds that they had to fight against isolation and scorn while the country admired foreign artists. Short biographies of eleven Costa Rican artists of the 19th century are given in an appendix.

673   **Art as a source for the study of Central America: 1945-1975, an exploratory essay.**
Vera Blinn Reber.   *Latin American Research Review*, vol. 13, no. 1 (1978), p. 39-64. bibliog.

The purpose of this essay is to show that art is a source for understanding the uniqueness of nations. In the case of Costa Rica this is certainly achieved.

674   **Cultural policy in Costa Rica.**
Samuel Rovinski.   Paris: UNESCO, 1977. 61p. bibliog.

This publication is one of an international series sponsored by the United Nations Educational, Scientific and Cultural Organization. The author, a short-story writer and playwright, describes the organization and cultural activities of Costa Rica's Ministry of

Culture, Youth and Sports, which was founded in 1970. Additional information is provided on newspapers, radio, television, education, science, libraries, films, and historic preservation.

675 **The precolumbian art of Costa Rica.**
Michael J. Snarskis. *Archaeology*, vol. 35, no. 1 (Jan.-Feb. 1982), p. 54-8.

In this survey of precolumbian art Snarskis, an archaeologist, provides an admirable synthesis of Indian civilizations in Costa Rica before the Spanish conquest. The division of Costa Rica into three archaeological zones – Guanacaste–Nicoya, Central Highlands–Atlantic watershed, and the Diquís Delta (Southeast Pacific area) – provides a framework for the discussion of Mesoamerican and Southern influences on precolumbian Costa Rica. Snarskis provides data on artistic influences from the north and south in support of his view that Costa Rica in precolumbian times was a cultural frontier zone. He also explains the absence of large cities and monuments like those found among the Maya and Aztecs.

676 **Costa Rica.**
Doris Z. Stone, Francisco Amighetti. In: *Encyclopedia of world art*, editor-in-chief Massimo Pallottino. New York: McGraw-Hill, 1961, vol. 4, p. 7-11. bibliog.

This brief survey of Costa Rican art was written by Doris Stone, an archaeologist, and Francisco Amighetti, an artist. The section on the precolonial period, which is the longer of the two, is a systematic account of the artistic styles of the Indian regions of Costa Rica.

677 **Pintores de Costa Rica.** (Painters of Costa Rica.)
Ricardo Ulloa Barrenechea. San José: Editorial Costa Rica, 1982. 5th ed. 288p. bibliog.

Ulloa's approach is comprehensive: to provide a panorama of every aspect of painting in Costa Rica. He discusses groups of painters, painters by the type of painting, institutional support for painters, and finally, individual Costa Rican painters and foreign painters working in Costa Rica and their work. The history of painting in Costa Rica is relatively short; Ulloa states that modern Costa Rican painting begins in 1897 with the founding of the National School of Fine Arts. The book is generously illustrated with black-and-white and colour photographs. The fifth edition is considerably amplified as compared with the first edition, which was published by the Editorial Costa Rica in 1974.

The Costa Ricans.
See item no. 6.

Colección de objetos indígenas de oro del Banco Central de Costa Rica. (A collection of indigenous gold objects of the Central Bank of Costa Rica.)
See item no. 108.

Costa Rica precolombina: arqueología, etnología, tecnología, arte. (Precolumbian Costa Rica: archaeology, ethnology, technology, art.)
See item no. 116.

Art and Architecture

Costa Rica: monumentos históricos y arqueológicos. (Costa Rica: historical and archaeological monuments.)
See item no. 121.

Aboriginal metalwork in lower Central America.
See item no. 124.

Precolombian art of Costa Rica.
See item no. 126.

Some Costa Rica jade motifs.
See item no. 129.

El desarrollo nacional en 150 años de vida independiente. (National development during 150 years of independence.)
See item no. 153.

Notes on present-day pottery making and its economy in the ancient Chorotegan area.
See item no. 275.

Francisco y los caminos. (Francisco and his journeys.)
See item no. 627.

El Teatro Nacional: (apuntes para la biografía de un coliseo). (The National Theatre: (notes for a biography of a theatre).)
See item no. 649.

Fadrique Gutiérrez: hidalgo extravagante de muchas andanzas. (Fadrique Gutiérrez: extravagant *hidalgo* of many deeds.)
See item no. 713.

Music and Dance

678 **La música en Guanacaste.** (The music of Guanacaste.)
Jorge Luis Acevedo. San José: Editorial Universidad de Costa Rica, 1980. 199p. bibliog.

This book is much more than the title suggests. It covers Guanacastecan musical history from the precolonial period; it contains information on the dances of Guanacaste; it includes the music and lyrics from Guanacastecan songs. In addition the book includes articles on Costa Rican music by authors such as Bernal Flores, Guido Sáenz, and Julio Fonseca. Finally, numerous illustrations enhance the narrative.

679 **Vida musical de Costa Rica.** (The musical life of Costa Rica.)
José Rafael Araya Rojas. San José: Imprenta Nacional, 1957. 143p. bibliog.

Contains data on prominent Costa Rican musicians, schools of music, music associations, orchestras, bands, and musical instruments, including indigenous instruments.

680 **Julio Fonseca: datos sobre su vida y análisis de su obra.** (Julio Fonseca: data on his life and analysis of his work.)
Bernal Flores. San José: Ministerio de Cultura, Juventud y Deportes, 1973. 318p. (Serie del Creador Analizado, no. 1).

This book contains biographical notes on Fonseca, an analysis of each of his musical compositions (p. 37-197), a catalogue of his works, and some of his writings. Fonseca was a prolific Costa Rican composer who was born in 1885 and died in 1950.

681 **La música en Costa Rica.** (Music in Costa Rica.)
Bernal Flores.   San José: Editorial Costa Rica, 1978. 141p. bibliog. ˙

A detailed, scholarly history and commentary on Costa Rican music. The work is
divided into three chronological parts: colonial period, 19th century, and 20th century.
Each part contains details on instruments, composers, singers, bands and orchestras,
theatres, and teaching institutions. It is a reliable and well-illustrated volume by Costa
Rica's leading musical scholar.

682 **Para qué tractores sin violines: la revolución musical en Costa Rica.**
(What is the use of tractors without violins: the musical revolution in
Costa Rica.)
Guido Sáenz.   San José: Editorial Costa Rica, 1982. 137p. bibliog.

This book treats two Costa Rican musical organizations, the National Symphony
Orchestra and the Youth Symphony Orchestra, both of which flourished while the
author was Viceminister and Minister of Culture, 1970-78. The two organizations were
rather controversial at the time because of Sáenz' plan, strongly supported by
President José Figueres, to invigorate the orchestras by hiring foreign musicians.

683 **Melico.**
Manuel Segura Méndez.   San José: Editorial Costa Rica, 1965. 173p.

This is an authoritative biography of the famous Costa Rican operatic tenor Manuel
Salazar Melico who was born in 1887 and died in 1950. Documentary materials
concerning Salazar's career are scarce but the author was able to put together the main
story of his performances through newspaper accounts from the United States,
Europe, and Mexico. The text is in Spanish.

Don Manuel María Gutiérrez.

See item no. 725.

Recreation and Leisure

684 **Historia del deporte en Costa Rica.** (The history of sport in Costa Rica.)
Augustín Salas Madrigal. San José: Imprenta Universal, 1951. 80p.
Sports history is not a subject of great scholarly interest in Costa Rica and publications like this booklet are rare. It collects historical articles on Costa Rican sport that Salas previously published in the newspaper *Diario de Costa Rica*. The emphasis falls on the early years of the 20th century and on individual pioneers of specific sports, including instructors of physical education.

Los costarricenses. (The Costa Ricans.)
See item no. 5.

Sociocultural contrasts in rural and urban settlement types in Costa Rica.
See item no. 315.

Cultural policy in Costa Rica.
See item no. 674.

Libraries, Archives and Museums

685 **Don Miguel Obregón Lizano, fundador y organizador de bibliotecas públicas.** (Don Miguel Obregón Lizano, founder and organizer of public libraries.)

Emanuel Aguilar J. (pseudonym for Rafael Obregón Loría). San José: Talleres Gráficos 'La Tribuna', 1935. 52p.

As minister of public instruction in the 1920s Miguel Obregón was known for his promotion of public libraries. Not so well known is the fact that, in 1883, when he was 23, Obregón became the librarian of the University of Santo Tomás. These and other efforts by Obregón to establish a public library system in Costa Rica are treated in this brief but important booklet.

686 **Historical sources in Costa Rica.**

Richard J. Junkins. *Latin American Research Review*, vol. 23, no. 3 (1988), p. 117-27.

Junkins surveys the holdings of Costa Rican libraries and archival depositories and provides basic information about locations and policies. The National Archives properly gets the most attention; Junkins describes the eight major record groups of the Archives. He also describes the rather under-utilized archive of the Catholic Church, now more accessible than before because of the availability of new finding aids. Brief descriptions of the collections of the National Library and the libraries of Costa Rica's two major universities are included.

687 **National Museum of Costa Rica: one hundred years of history.**

Christian Kandler. San José: Ministerio de Cultura, Juventud y Deportes, 1987. 141p. maps. bibliog.

The main contribution of this book is the review of the history of the National Museum. Not only is it satisfactory as an administrative history, it also describes the Museum's relations with other important national institutions such as the National Geographical Institute, and the role played in the Museum's development by scientists and scholars. Historical photographs of museum facilities and administrators and numerous contemporary colour photographs provide an excellent orientation to the Museum.

688   **Costa Rica.**
    Charles L. Stansifer, Richard V. Salisbury.   In: *Research guide to Central America and the Caribbean*, edited by Kenneth Grieb.
    Madison, Wisconsin: University of Wisconsin Press, 1985, p. 134-9.
For those interested in doing research on Costa Rica this chapter in *Research guide to Central America and the Caribbean* provides a description of the principal libraries and archival depositories in Costa Rica. Public and private collections are included.

Cultural policy in Costa Rica.
See item no. 674.

Bibliografía anotada de obras de referencia sobre Centroamérica y Panamá en el campo de las ciencias sociales. (Annotated bibliography of works of reference on Central America and Panama in the social sciences.)
See item no. 746.

Books and Publishing

689 **Libros y folletos publicados en Costa Rica durante los años 1830-1849.**
(Books and pamphlets published in Costa Rica during the years
1830-49.)
Jorge A. Lines.   San José: Universidad de Costa Rica, 1944. 151p.
bibliog.
Of interest primarily to historians and bibliophiles, this list of 102 publications was
compiled by the indefatigable Costa Rican anthropologist and book collector Jorge
Lines. In the introduction he discusses the arrival of the first printing press in 1830, the
publication of the first newspapers, and the first government publications.

690 **Costa Rica.**
Charles L. Stansifer, John P. Bell.   In: *Research guide to Central
America and the Caribbean*, edited by Kenneth Grieb. Madison,
Wisconsin: University of Wisconsin Press, 1985, p. 64-76.
This chapter in *Research guide to Central America and the Caribbean* surveys in broad
terms what historical studies have been completed on Costa Rican history and points
out lacunae. It contains many recommendations useful for anyone proposing to do
research on Costa Rica.

691 **Historians and history writing in Costa Rica.**
Watt Stewart.   *Hispanic American Historial Review*, vol. 27, no. 4
(Aug. 1947), p. 599-601.
Although brief, this pioneering historiographical article points clearly to the growth of
professional history writing in Costa Rica in the 1940s and to the need for more writing
on 20th-century history.

Costa Rican interpretations of Costa Rican politics.
See item no. 374.

Recent public administration literature in Costa Rica.
See item no. 459.

Recent literature on Costa Rica's economic crisis.
See item no. 473.

Mass Media

692 **El hombre que no quiso la guerra: una revolución en el periodismo de
Costa Rica.** (The man who did not want war: a revolution in journalism
in Costa Rica.)
Carlos Morales.   San José: Ariel/Seix Barral, 1981. 270p. bibliog.

Despite the curious title, this work is a serious study by a practising journalist of the
origins of modern journalism in Costa Rica. Early weekly and ephemeral newspapers
are covered but the focus is on the first daily newspapers of the late 19th century. The
revolution in the title refers to the outburst of competitive journalism at the time of the
election of 1889. An appendix lists all Costa Rican newspapers according to the year of
their first appearance.

693 **Periódicos y periodistas.** (Newspapers and journalists.)
Francisco María Núñez.   San José: Editorial Costa Rica, 1980. 113p.
bibliog.

This brief history of journalism in Costa Rica takes the form of short biographical
sketches of prominent journalists, accompanied by information on the newspapers for
which they wrote. Núñez was himself a journalist and popular writer in the middle of
the 20th century.

694 **La desinformación de la prensa en Costa Rica: un grave peligro para la
paz.** (Disinformation in the Costa Rican press: a grave danger for
peace.)
Mario Zeledón Cambronero.   San José: Instituto Costarricense de
Estudios Sociales, 1987. 282p. bibliog.

By means of several specific cases of news stories Zeledón attempts to highlight the
dependency of the Costa Rican press on foreign news services.

El desarrollo nacional en 150 años de vida independiente. (National development during 150 years of independence.)
See item no. 153.

Imagen de la mujer que proyectan los medios de comunicación de masas en Costa Rica. (The image of women projected by the mass media in Costa Rica.)
See item no. 329.

Historia y antología de la literatura costarricense. (History and anthology of Costa Rican literature.)
See item no. 631.

Biographies

695 La mujer costarricense a través de cuatro siglos. (The Costa Rican woman over four centuries.)
Angela Acuña de Chacón.   San José: Imprenta Nacional, 1969-70. 2 vols. 446, 668p. bibliog.

Few Latin American countries have as complete a record of their prominent women as Costa Rica does as a result of these volumes. In addition to the biographical accounts of individual women, they also contain valuable information about women in specific occupations, women's organizations, and legislation affecting women. The author received her law degree from the Universidad de Costa Rica in 1925.

696 José Santos Lombardo.
Oscar R. Aguilar Bulgarelli.   San José: Ministerio de Cultura, Juventud y Deportes, 1973. 162p. bibliog. (Serie ¿Quién Fue y Qué Hizo?, no. 13).

In this brief sketch of the life and career of José Santos Lombardo, who played important political roles in the late colonial period and in the days of independence, Aguilar defends Lombardo against the charges of many Costa Rican historians that he was a monarchist not truly interested in independence. The text is in Spanish.

697 Carlos Luis Fallas: su época y sus luchas. (Carlos Luis Fallas: his era and his struggles.)
Marielos Aguilar.   San José: Editorial Porvenir, 1983. 272p. bibliog. (Colección Debate).

This study is not a complete biography but an account of the public life of Carlos Luis Fallas, one of Costa Rica's best-known writers of the 20th century and one of its most successful union organizers. The focus is heavily on the role of Fallas as a Communist Party member and union organizer in the period of the 1930s, especially at the time of the banana strike of 1934. Because his literary works deal so extensively with his political causes these works are also discussed. Newspapers, Communist Party archives, public records, and secondary sources provide a solid, authentic base for the author's narrative and interpretation.

698 **Don Pepe: a political biography of José Figueres of Costa Rica.**
Charles D. Ameringer. Albuquerque, New Mexico: University of New Mexico Press, 1978. 324p. maps. bibliog.

As head of the Revolutionary Junta (1948-49) and president twice (1954-58, 1970-74), José Figueres played a central role in Costa Rica's modernization and in the international politics of the Central American region. Ameringer's treatment of Figueres in those years is admirably thorough and based on primary source material. The author had access to Figueres' correspondence file for 1950-70. The book is stronger on Figueres' role in international politics than on domestic politics.

699 **El pensamiento político-social de monseñor Sanabria.** (The sociopolitical thought of Monsignor Sanabria.)
Santiago Arrieta Quesada. San José: Editorial Universitaria Centroamericana, 1982. 2nd ed. 334p. bibliog. (Colección Aula).

Archbishop Víctor Sanabria (1899-1952) was a vital figure in the controversial period of the 1940s and the revolution of 1948. He took possession of the archbishopric in 1940 within a few days of the accession to political power of Rafael Calderón Guardia. This book provides basic biographical data but concentrates on his political and social thought, especially his views on social justice and labour relations. It includes some of the Archbishop's public declarations and part of his correspondence with Manuel Mora, leader of the Communist Party.

700 **Autobiografías campesinas.** (Rural autobiographies.)
Heredia, Costa Rica: Editorial Universidad Nacional, 1979-83. 5 vols. (Colección Barva, Serie Sociedad, Subserie Autobiografía).

If one is interested in the underside of social history this remarkable set of *campesino* autobiographies will provide many hours of happy and profitable reading. From 815 autobiographies submitted in the National Contest of Campesino Autobiographies during 1976-78 twenty-seven were selected for publication in this five-volume set. Twenty-two were written by men and five by women. Information on education, social life, leisure time, agricultural and work practices, attitudes towards women and children, and a host of other topics is made available in this set in narrative form. The original unedited manuscripts, consisting of 13,500 pages, will be open to researchers in the year 2003. No country in Latin America has such a rich source of information on rural life.

701 **Francisco Amighetti.**
Stefan Baciu. Heredia, Costa Rica: Editorial de la Universidad Nacional, 1985. 261p. (Colección Barva, Serie Pensamiento, Subserie Ensayo).

Baciu, a literary critic who is a personal friend of Amighetti and thoroughly acquainted with Costa Rican letters, captures in this Spanish text the cultural life of Costa Rica during the last forty years through this personal and balanced portrait of his friend. Since Amighetti is a painter, critic, storyteller, and poet, his life and works provide the reader with insights into contemporary Costa Rican arts and letters. The book, which is more anecdotal than critical, is appropriately illustrated with copies of forty-eight of Amighetti's engravings.

702 **La lucha sin fin: Costa Rica, una democracia que habla español.** (The battle without end: Costa Rica, a Spanish-speaking democracy.)
Alberto Baeza Flores.   Mexico City: Costa-Amic, 1969. 432p. bibliog.

Alberto Baeza Flores, a Chilean poet, essayist, and journalist, wrote this biography of José Figueres after his first visit to Costa Rica. In it he attempts to describe the times and the country as well as the man. It does indeed capture the flavour of the period but uncritically accepts the 'creative democratic ideology' of Figueres and other like-minded Latin American leaders of the time. 'La lucha sin fin' is the name of Figueres' estate.

703 **Ideas, ensayos y paisajes.** (Ideas, essays and landscapes.)
Luis Barahona Jiménez.   San José: Editorial Costa Rica, 1972. 227p.

Among the essays on Spanish and Latin American philosophers in this collection are essays on three of the best-known Costa Rican writers from Cartago: Pío Víquez (1848-99), Mario Sancho (1899-1948), and Víctor Manuel Sanabria (1899-1952). Not surprisingly, Barahona himself is from Cartago.

704 **Monseñor Sanabria: apuntes biográficos.** (Monsignor Sanabria: biographical notes.)
Ricardo Blanco Segura.   San José: Editorial Costa Rica, 1971. 2nd rev. ed. 371p. bibliog. (Serie 'La Propia').

Blanco Segura, Costa Rica's foremost Church historian, passes over Sanabria's personal life and his career as a priest in order to concentrate on his tenure as archbishop (1940-52). Sanabria's role in President Calderón Guardia's social policy, the President's accord with the Communist Party, and the revolution of 1948 are all discussed at length. Taking advantage of access to Church archives Blanco Segura quotes Sanabria's writings and correspondence in support of his narrative. The first edition was published by the Editorial Costa Rica in 1962.

705 **Obispos, arzobispos y representantes de la santa sede en Costa Rica.**
(Bishops, archbishops and representatives of the Papacy in Costa Rica.)
Ricardo Blanco Segura.   San José: Editorial Universidad Estatal a Distancia, 1984. 153p.

The author, a noted Costa Rican religious historian, provides in this book an explanation of the Catholic Church organization in the country and a directory of the most important religious figures in the history of Costa Rica. He begins with the colonial period when Costa Rica was attached to Nicaragua in religious jurisdiction – it became an independent diocese in 1850. In the introduction the author makes candid comments on religious figures he has known.

706 **Figueres and Costa Rica: an unauthorized political biography.**
Harold H. Bonilla.   San José: Editorial Texto, 1975. 214p. bibliog.

Harold Bonilla, a Costa Rican newspaperman and freelance writer who held minor government posts during the 1940s and 1950s, wrote this book with the purpose of giving both sides of José Figueres. The following quotation from the introduction indicates the result: 'José Figueres is an honest man. But he will go down in history in the opinion of many, as a man totally bereft of the most elemental sense of ethics.' It is a rambling, opinionated, personalistic account, but it has the appeal of an insider's version of the major political events of Costa Rica from 1941 to 1974.

707 **Los presidentes.** (The presidents.)
Harold H. Bonilla. San José: Editorial Texto, 1985. 3rd ed. 750p. bibliog.

Originally published in 1942 under the title *Nuestros presidentes* (Our presidents), this work had a second edition in 1979. Bonilla's short, factual accounts of each president are not analytical, but nevertheless they are extremely useful introductions to the lives of all Costa Rican presidents. An excellent, varied collection of photographs adds interest to the volume.

708 **Rafael Yglesias Castro.**
Carlos Calvo Gamboa. San José: Ministerio de Cultura, Juventud y Deportes, 1980. 234p. bibliog. (Serie ¿Quién Fue y Qué Hizo?, no. 27).

Rafael Yglesias Castro (1861-1924) played an important role in Costa Rican politics from the 1880s to 1914. He was president from 1894 to 1902. This book is a documented account of his political career, with emphasis on his role in the formation of the Civil Party, his opposition to the Catholic Union Party, his presidency, and his presidential campaigns of 1910 and 1914. Calvo Gamboa in this Spanish text portrays Yglesias as an authoritarian figure. An introductory chapter describes social and economic conditions in Costa Rica at the end of the 19th century.

709 **Laude, evocación de Mora: el hombre, el estadista, el héroe, el mártir.**
(Praise, evocation of Mora: the man, the statesman, the hero, the martyr.)
Octavio Castro Saborio. San José: Academia Costarricense de la Historia, 1956. 2nd ed. 78p.

It is brief, and, as the title suggests, it is laudatory, but it is also one of the few essays on the life and political career of Juan Rafael Mora (1814-60), president of Costa Rica at the time of the war against the filibusters in Nicaragua (1856-57).

710 **Henri Pittier.**
Adina Conejo Guevara. San José: Ministerio de Cultura, Juventud y Deportes, 1975, 162p. bibliog. (Serie ¿Quién Fue y Qué Hizo?, no. 20).

Henri Pittier was a Swiss naturalist and geographer who worked in Costa Rica from 1887 to 1904 as director of various research institutes. This brief biographical sketch (in Spanish) is based on secondary works. It includes a biography of Pittier's writings, some appraisals of his work by scientists, and excerpts from his best-known publications.

Biographies

711 Moisés Vincenzi.

Rodrigo Cordero. San José: Ministerio de Cultura, Juventud y Deportes, 1975. 307p. bibliog. (Serie del Creador Analizado, no. 3).

Moisés Vincenzi (1895-1964) was a self-trained, slightly eccentric Costa Rican philosopher, teacher, critic, novelist, and poet who published some fifty books and articles between 1917 and 1961. Cordero provides the bare essentials of Vincenzi's life and a bibliography of his publications in this Spanish-language series on Costa Rican thinkers. However, the principal part of the book (p. 73-293) is an anthology of his varied writings.

712 Roberto Brenes Mesén.

María Eugenia Dengo de Vargas. San José: Ministerio de Cultura, Juventud y Deportes, 1974. 437p. bibliog. (Serie ¿Quién Fue y Qué Hizo?, no. 21).

Brenes Mesén, who was born in 1874 and died in 1947, was one of Costa Rica's greatest poets and educators. He also wrote studies on language and spiritualism. He served in the Costa Rican Ministry of Public Instruction and was a professor of Spanish literature at Syracuse and Northwestern universities in the United States from 1920 to 1939. This book (written in Spanish) contains a biography, an anthology of Brenes Mesén's writings (p. 179-410), a chronology of his life, a bibliography of his publications, and a bibliography of works on Brenes and his writings.

713 Fadrique Gutiérrez: hidalgo extravagante de muchas andanzas.

(Fadrique Gutiérrez: extravagant *hidalgo* [gentleman] of many deeds.) Luis Dobles Segreda. San José: Editorial Costa Rica, 1979. 2nd ed. 167p. (Colección 'Nuestros Clásicos', no. 5).

Gutiérrez (1841-97) was a sculptor from Heredia who specialized in monumental stone sculptures. The first edition of this book, which helped rescue the sculptor from neglect, was published in 1954 by Imprenta Trejos in 1954.

714 Who shall ascend; the life of R. Kenneth Strachan: of Costa Rica.

Elizabeth Elliot. New York: Harper & Row, 1968. 171p. map.

This biography of Kenneth Strachan is not strictly about Costa Rica but Costa Rica was the base of Strachan's Latin American Mission and he and his family lived in San José. One can, therefore, learn much about the evangelical Protestant movement in Costa Rica and Central America by reading this book. Strachan's father and mother, Harry and Susan, founded the Latin American Evangelical Campaign in San José in the 1920s and when Kenneth Strachan began his own missionary endeavours in the 1940s he built upon his parents' work. He died in 1965. The biography has neither notes nor bibliography but is based on reading of the extensive Strachan family archive.

715 **Alfredo González Flores.**
Carlos Luis Fallas Monge.   San José: Ministerio de Cultura, Juventud y Deportes, 1976 [1977]. 377p. bibliog. (Serie ¿Quién Fue y Qué Hizo?, no. 24).

Lacking in personal information about González Flores, this is essentially a political biography. Fallas Monge bases his study of the presidency of González Flores (1914-17) on government documents, newspaper reports, and secondary accounts. The focus is heavily on financial and economic matters, which were critical at the time. One chapter contains a description of the educational situation in the 1914-17 period. The text is in Spanish.

716 **La clara voz de Joaquín García Monge.** (The clear voice of Joaquín García Monge.)
Luis Ferrero.   San José: Editorial Costa Rica, 1978. 2nd ed. 143p. bibliog.

Rather than a standard biography this is an essay on the thought of García Monge, one of Costa Rica's leading literary figures of the 1920s and 1930s – he was founding editor of the review *Repertorio Americano* in 1919. As a friend of the subject of the essay Ferrero is familiar with his writings and his activities but he confesses that he did not have access to García Monge's vast correspondence with eminent figures of his time. Separate chapters deal with García Monge's views on America, politics, the arts, and education. The first edition of this book was published by the Editorial Don Quijote in San José in 1963.

717 **Juan Manuel de Cañas.**
Elizabeth Fonseca Corrales.   San José: Ministerio de Cultura, Juventud y Deportes, 1975. 194p. bibliog. (Serie ¿Quién Fue y Qué Hizo?, no. 23).

As a monarchist and as the last Spanish governor of Costa Rica Juan Manuel de Cañas has not attracted the attention of many Costa Rican historians. Elizabeth Fonseca found little information about Cañas' personal life, but in this biographical study she does offer a lucid account of his leadership in suppressing a rebellion in western Costa Rica and Nicaragua in 1812 and of his activity as governor, 1819-21. The study is solidly based on documents in the National Archives of Costa Rica. The text is in Spanish.

718 **Anastasio Alfaro.**
Victoria Garrón de Doryan.   San José: Ministerio de Cultura, Juventud y Deportes, 1974. 189p. bibliog. (Serie ¿Quién Fue y Qué Hizo?, no. 17).

Anastasio Alfaro González (1865-1951) was a scientist, writer, and teacher who founded the National Museum and also directed the National Archives. This book (written in Spanish) provides a sketch of his life and work, including a selection of his correspondence, and contains a small portion of his writings.

719 **Joaquín García Monge.**
Victoria Garrón de Doryan.   San José: Ministerio de Cultura,
Juventud y Deportes, 1971. 166p. bibliog. (Serie ¿Quién Fue y Qué
Hizo? no. 1).

A biography and anthology of one of Costa Rica's best-known novelists and essayists.
García Monge, who was born in 1881 and died in 1958, was particularly well known for
the literary magazine, *Repertorio Americano*, which he founded in 1919 and continued
to edit until his death. The anthology contains only a few of his essays. The text is in
Spanish.

720 **Juan Mora Fernández.**
Carmen Lila Gómez.   San José: Ministerio de Cultura, Juventud y
Deportes, 1973. 145p. bibliog. (Serie ¿Quién Fue y Qué Hizo?,
no. 14).

Mora (1784-1854) was the first chief of state of independent Costa Rica. This brief
biography, written in Spanish and based on original sources in the National Archives
and on secondary sources, accounts for his activities as chief of state (1824-34) and in
subsequent responsibilities as justice, deputy, and senator. The annex (p. 111-34)
contains excerpts from a few of his presidential messages.

721 **Alfredo González Flores, "su pensamiento".** (Alfredo González Flores,
'his thought'.)
Alfredo González Flores, selected by Alberto Cañas.   San José:
Editorial Costa Rica, 1980. 355p. bibliog. (Biblioteca Patria, no. 15).

In the introduction Alberto Cañas describes González Flores (president of Costa Rica,
1914-17) as the first social democrat of the country. In this book, which collects all of
his messages to the National Assembly, two of his publications (one on politics and
petroleum and the other on the economic crisis of the 1930s), and a few of his letters,
there is considerable evidence to justify Cañas' claim.

722 **Rodrigo Facio: el economista.** (Rodrigo Facio: the economist.)
Raúl Estrada Hess.   San José: Universidad de Costa Rica, 1972. 223p.
(Publicaciones de la Universidad de Costa Rica, Serie Economía y
Estadística, no. 36).

Rodrigo Facio Brenes was an indefatigable researcher and political and academic
activist. This biography, essentially an intellectual biography, captures the broad range
of his thinking, especially on the economic problems of his country. In addition to
analysing Facio's intellectual contributions Hess discusses Facio's role as advocate for
the constitution of 1949, as director of the Banco Central, as deputy in the National
Assembly, and as professor and rector of the University of Costa Rica.

723 **Lubeck & Lubeck's who's who in Costa Rica, 1979-1980: professions, commerce, government.**
Edited by Allan E. Hüper. San José: Lubeck, 1979. 892p.
A directory of prominent Costa Ricans primarily in the fields of business and government. Besides the section on individuals (comprising approximately two-thirds of the book) there is a section consisting of short articles on major business enterprises and government agencies. Entries are in English and Spanish.

724 **Dr. Moreno Cañas: a symbolic bridge to the demedicalization of healing.**
Setha M. Low. *Social Science and Medicine*, vol. 16, no. 5 (May 1982), p. 527-31.
Dr Ricardo Moreno Cañas was a famous Costa Rican surgeon who was murdered in 1938. Subsequently, a healing cult developed around him. Through interviews with patients and physicians, the author examines this cult in the light of increasing sophistication and professionalization of medical care in Costa Rica.

725 **Don Manuel María Gutiérrez.**
Carlos Meléndez Chaverri. San José: Ministerio de Cultura, Juventud y Deportes, 1979. 194p. bibliog. (Serie ¿Quién Fue y Qué Hizo?, no. 26).
Unlike the usual superficial, overly patriotic accounts of national-anthem composers this biography of the composer of Costa Rica's national anthem is a sensible, documented study. The author has also added significant data about military band history, music education, and the development of patriotic celebrations in 19th-century Costa Rica. Gutiérrez was born in 1829 and died in 1887. The text is in Spanish.

726 **Dr. José María Montealegre: contribución al estudio de un hombre y una época poco conocida de nuestra historia.** (Dr José María Montealegre: a contribution to the study of a man and an era little known in our history.)
Carlos Meléndez Chaverri. San José: Academia de Geografía e Historia de Costa Rica, 1968. 207p.
This is a well-written, thoroughly documented biography of Montealegre, who was president of Costa Rica 1859-63. The account covers Montealegre's early adventures travelling to Europe (including Scotland where he acquired medical training), as well as his experiences as a coffee *finquero* [estate owner], politician, and president. Montealegre left Costa Rica when Tomás Guardia took over as president in 1870 and died in California in 1887. The study was Melendez' 1951 thesis at the University of Costa Rica.

727 **Juan Vázquez de Coronado: conquistador y fundador de Costa Rica.**
(Juan Vázquez de Coronado: conqueror and founder of Costa Rica.)
Carlos Meléndez Chaverri. San José: Editorial Costa Rica, 1972. 2nd ed. 196p. maps. bibliog.
In this biography of the conqueror of Costa Rica Meléndez places Juan Vásquez de Coronado closer to the ideology of Bartolomé de Las Casas and the idea of peaceful conquest than to the approach of Cortés and Pizarro. His recognition of Indians as

persons and his concern for justice give him a special stature among Spanish conquerors and lead Meléndez to conclude that Vásquez de Coronado was the true founder of ' the Costa Rican nation. Meléndez' interpretation rests on secondary sources and a few published documents.

728 **Otilio Ulate and the traditional response to contemporary political change in Costa Rica.**
Judy Oliver Milner.   PhD dissertation, Louisiana State University. 1977. 241p. bibliog. (Available from University Microfilms, Ann Arbor, Michigan, order no. 77-28,692).

This study focuses on the life and political career of the often overlooked Otilio Ulate Blanco, president of Costa Rica from 1949 to 1953. As an analysis of a conservative political figure operating from traditional Costa Rican political patterns in a time of upheaval the study is a welcome counterbalance to the more controversial and popular treatment of politicians Rafael Calderón Guardia and José Figueres. The watchwords of his administration, according to Milner, were 'pragmatism, conciliation and democracy'.

729 **Rogelio Fernández Güell: escritor, poeta y caballero andante.** (Rogelio Fernández Güell: writer, poet and knight-errant.)
Eduardo Oconitrillo García.   San José: Editorial Costa Rica, 1981. 2nd ed. 132p. bibliog.

Fernández Güell, a journalist and political figure born in 1883, was executed in 1918 because of his armed opposition to the Tinoco government. Oconitrillo, who has written critically of Federico Tinoco, is highly sympathetic with Tinoco's opponent. The story of Fernández Güell's opposition to Tinoco is reconstructed from newspaper accounts and interviews. The first edition of this first biography of Fernández Güell was published by the Editorial Costa Rica in 1980.

730 **Vidy y obra del doctor Clodomiro Picado T.** (Life and works of Doctor Clodomiro Picado T.)
Manuel Picado Chacón.   San José: Editorial Universidad de Costa Rica, 1980. 2nd ed. 286p. (Biblioteca de Autores Costarricenses).

Clodomiro Picado Twight was one of Costa Rica's best-known scientists of the early 20th century. He received his doctorate from the University of Paris in 1913 and continued research in biology and microbiology as Director of the Laboratory at the San Juan de Dios Hospital in San José. This book lacks documentation but is an authoritative account of Picado's education and scientific work. A list of 112 of his scientific publications is appended. Also included in the appendix are fragments from Picado's political commentary, gleaned from private correspondence and newspaper articles. The first edition of this book was published in 1964 in San José by the Editorial Costa Rica.

731 **Calderón Guardia.**
Jorge Mario Salazar Mora. San José: Ministerio de Cultura, Juventud y Deportes, 1980. 240p. bibliog.

There are many books on the politics of the Rafael Angel Calderón Guardia presidency (1940-48), but this one gives a more comprehensive view than most (if not all) of the others. The first chapter offers a short sketch of Calderón Guardia's personal life. The second deals with his political thought, the third achievements of his presidency, and the fifth his participation in political campaigns from 1948 to 1970. The fourth chapter covers his relations with political parties inside Costa Rica, with the Catholic Church (one of the most controversial aspects of his presidency), and his foreign policy as president, particularly his policy toward Panama. Calderón Guardia was born in 1900 and died in 1970. The text is in Spanish.

732 **Máximo Fernández.**
Orlando Salazar Mora. San José: Ministerio de Cultura, Juventud y Deportes, 1975. 345p. bibliog. (Serie ¿Quién Fue y Qué Hizo?, no. 22).

Máximo Fernández (1858-1933) was a powerful political leader who was often a presidential candidate but who never attained the presidency. He served, however, in numerous capacities: as minister, deputy in the National Assembly, and leader of the Republican Party. In this detailed, documented account of his political career, Salazar ascribes Fernández' political successes to a combination of his *campesino* outlook and his legal and oratorical abilities. His failure to win his country's highest political office was due, according to Salazar, to Fernández' inconsistency, as he fluctuated from supporting the masses to supporting the interests of the oligarchy. The text is in Spanish.

733 **Bernardo Augusto Thiel, segundo obispo de Costa Rica: apuntamientos históricos.** (Bernardo Augusto Thiel, second Bishop of Costa Rica: historical notes.)
Víctor Sanabria Martínez. San José: Editorial Costa Rica, 1982. 2nd ed. 812p. bibliog.

Originally published in 1941, this biography is still the most thorough and authoritative biography of Bishop Thiel, who was born in Elberfeld, Germany in 1850 and died in Costa Rica in 1901. Taking advantage of his access to the ecclesiastical archive in San José, Sanabria provides details of the Liberal–Catholic controversy, which led to the expulsion of Bishop Thiel from Costa Rica (1884-86), and in general of the conflict between the Church and the government at a time of secularization. Although the focus of the book is on Bishop Thiel and his role in Church–state relations, the author does devote a chapter to Thiel's efforts to stimulate Church periodicals and to Thiel's own historical writings. The book is extensively documented.

734 **Keith and Costa Rica: a biographical study of Minor Cooper Keith.**
Watt Stewart. Albuquerque, New Mexico: University of New Mexico Press, 1964. 210p. bibliog.

Although partially based on Costa Rican archival research in the 1950s this book has serious deficiencies: it does not separate the important from the trivial; its perspective is Keith's, not Costa Rica's; and it gives little attention to Keith's life before and after his railway-building experience in Costa Rica. It is, however, the most complete account available of the financing and construction of the railway from the Central Valley to the Atlantic coast. Stewart concludes that Keith's principal interest was in making money but that he stopped short of being a robber baron. A Spanish translation was published by the Editorial Costa Rica in San José in 1967.

735 **Juan Vázquez de Coronado y su ética en la conquista de Costa Rica.**
(Juan Vázquez de Coronado and his ethics in the conquest of Costa Rica.)
Victoria Urbano. Madrid: Ediciones Cultura Hispánica, 1968. 317p. bibliog.

This is a scholarly, comprehensive biography of the conqueror of Costa Rica. After giving considerable space to Vázquez de Coronado's lineage and formation in Spain, the author concentrates on his activities while leading an expedition into Costa Rica in 1562. An underlying purpose, as indicated in the title and explained by the author, is to demonstrate that the conquest and pacification of Costa Rica were exemplary and relatively humane. It is, in effect, an effort to contradict the Black Legend of Spanish cruelty and perfidy at the time of the conquest. The research for this work was done in the Archive of the Indies and presented as a doctoral thesis at the Univesity of Madrid.

736 **Jorge Volio y el Partido Reformista.** (Jorgo Volio and the Reform Party.)
Marina Volio. San José: Editorial Universidad Estatal a Distancia, 1983. 4th ed. 277p. bibliog.

To understand fully the pulse of Costa Rican politics in the first third of the twentieth century, one must come to grips with the arresting figure of Jorge Volio: priest, teacher, revolutionary, general, politician, and archivist. This biography suffers somewhat from filial devotion – the author is Volio's daughter – but at the same time it benefits from her intimate knowledge of the Volio personality and from insights gained from his personal papers. Born in Cartago in 1882, Jorgo Volio Jiménez studied for the priesthood in Belgium and returned to Costa Rica as a priest in 1910. After having fought with the Nicaraguans against the United States he left the priesthood and began a career as a politician. During the 1920s, as founder and leader of the Partido Reformista, Volio had considerable impact on Costa Rican politics although he never attained the presidency. This biography by his daughter Marina, a historian, is based on Volio's personal correspondence and secondary material on Costa Rican politics. The first edition was published by the Editorial Costa Rica in 1973.

737 **Apuntes de don Rafael Yglesias Castro sobre su vida privada y actuaciones públicas.** (Notes of Rafael Yglesias Castro on his public activities and private life.)
Rafael Yglesias Castro. San José: Lehmann, 1961. 48p.

These are autobiographical notes, written in 1917, by Rafael Yglesias, who was president of Costa Rica from 1894 to 1902. Although brief, his comments on the Church–state issue, the Northern Railway, boundary problems, and revolts against his government are helpful in understanding the political history of Costa Rica in the late 19th and early 20th centuries.

738 **Rafael Francisco Osejo.**
Chester Zelaya. San José: Ministerio de Cultura, Juventud y
Deportes, 1973. 179p. (Serie ¿Quién Fue y Qué Hizo?, no. 15).
A condensation of the author's two-volume, definitive, documented biography of
Osejo published in San José by the Editorial Costa Rica in 1971. Zelaya effectively lays
to rest much of the controversy surrounding Osejo's political career in the 1821-34
period. Osejo emerges as an influential liberal thinker and a hard-working legislator
who paid particular attention to organizational details in his legislative work. Little
(except that he died in 1848) is known about Osejo after he left Costa Rica in 1834 for
El Salvador. The text is in Spanish.

Don Diego de la Haya Fernández.
See item no. 158.

El poder legislativo en Costa Rica. (Legislative power in Costa Rica.)
See item no. 170.

Monografía de Cartago. (A monograph of Cartago.)
See item no. 181.

La Costa Rica de don Tomás de Acosta. (The Costa Rica of Tomás de
Acosta.)
See item no. 189.

De nuestra historia patria: los gobernadores de la colonia. (Our country's
history: the colonial governors.)
See item no. 197.

Morazán en Costa Rica. (Morazán in Costa Rica.)
See item no. 207.

Alfredo González Flores, estadista incomprendido. (Alfredo González Flores,
a misunderstood statesman.)
See item no. 221.

Los Tinoco, 1917-1919. (The Tinocos, 1917-19.)
See item no. 223.

The anti-imperialist career of Alejandro Alvarado Quirós.
See item no. 230.

**Influencia de las ideas del doctor Valeriano Fernández Ferraz en la vida
cultural de Costa Rica.** (The influence of the ideas of Dr Valeriano
Fernández Ferraz in the cultural life of Costa Rica.)
See item no. 610.

Evolución en la poesía costarricense, 1574-1977. (Evolution of Costa Rican
poetry, 1574-1977.)
See item no. 629.

Narrativa contemporánea de Costa Rica. (Contemporary narrative in Costa
Rica.)
See item no. 634.

Biographies

Ocho artistas costarricenses y una tradición. (Eight Costa Rican artists and a tradition.)
See item no. 669.

Pintores de Costa Rica. (Painters of Costa Rica.)
See item no. 677.

Julio Fonseca: datos sobre su vida y análisis de su obra. (Julio Fonseca: data on his life and analysis of his work.)
See item no. 680.

Don Miguel Obregón Lizano, fundador y organizador de biblotecas públicas. (Don Miguel Obregón Lizano, founder and organizer of public libraries.)
See item no. 685.

Periódicos y periodistas. (Newspapers and journalists.)
See item no. 693.

Directories

739 Historical dictionary of Costa Rica.
Theodore S. Creedman. Metuchen, New Jersey: Scarecrow Press, 1977. 251p. bibliog. (Latin American Historical Dictionaries, no. 16.)

For a handy reference to persons, places, and institutions of historical importance the *Historical dictionary of Costa Rica* is a good place to start. Entries tend to be brief, basic, and to the point. They tend to be political rather than social, economic, or cultural. The annotated bibliography, which is divided into historical periods, is thirty pages in length.

740 Research guide to Costa Rica.
Carlos L. Elizondo, Juan B. González, Luis F. Martínez. Mexico City: Pan American Institute of Geography and History, 1977. 138p. maps. bibliog.

Over half of the guide deals with a variety of maps and their location. The remaining part is an excellent bibliography by Miguel Morales Alvarez concerning the geographical aspects of Costa Rica and its planning problems. Unfortunately, it does not discuss archival depositories and research institutions. The book is a translation of the original Spanish version, also published by the Pan American Institute of Geography and History in 1977.

741 Datos y cifras de Costa Rica. (Facts and statistics about Costa Rica.)
San José: Export and Investment Promotion Centre, 1978. 173p.

The following general headings give an idea of the coverage of this handbook: territory and climate, population, education, health and social security, tourism, agriculture and livestock, industry, domestic trade and services, foreign trade, transport and services, currency, credit and banking, public finances, balance of payments and domestic accounts, incentives, taxes, tax office, and organization of the public administration. Headings and explanations are in English as well as in Spanish. A slightly smaller, updated edition with the same title was published by the Centre in 1985.

Bibliographies

General

742 **A guide to the official publications of the other American republics, VI Costa Rica.**
Compiled by Henry V. Besso. Washington, DC: Library of Congress, 1947. 92p. (Latin American Series, no. 24).
Although somewhat out of date, this volume is still a good basic guide to Costa Rican government publications from 1821 to 1946. Unfortunately, no new guide of this sort exists. Essential information about government ministries and agencies is included, but users must realize that the many autonomous agencies, such as the Costa Rican Electrical Institute, began their institutional lives just after the publication of this guide.

743 **Bibliografía costarricense de ciencias sociales, no. 2.** (A Costa Rican social science bibliography, no. 2.)
María Eugenia Bózzoli de Wille. San José: Universidad de Costa Rica, Facultad de Ciencias y Letras, 1968. 89p. bibliog.
The first part of the bibliography is a list of 103 titles published between 1964 and 1968. The second part, which is extensively annotated and covers items published before 1964, includes 100 of the most important publications in demography, social mobility, personality characteristics, family studies, and social assistance agencies.

744 **Indice bibliográfico de Costa Rica.** (Bibliographical index of Costa Rica.)
Luis Dobles Segreda. San José: Lehmann, 1927-68. 11 vols. bibliog.
An exceptionally thorough bibliography compiled by one of Costa Rica's best-known men of letters. The first nine volumes were published between 1927 and 1936 and the last two were published posthumously in 1968 by the Asociación Costarricense de Bibliotecarios. Although the work is a treasury of information it is a little difficult to

use since the entries are listed chronologically rather than alphabetically, in sections according to topics. The entries themselves are thorough; most are annotated and some contain the entire table of contents of the volume in question. The set should be on the shelf of every Costa Rican bibliophile.

745 **A tentative bibliography of the belles-lettres of the republics of Central America.**
Henry Grattan Doyle. Cambridge, Massachusetts: Harvard University Press, 1935. 136p. bibliog. (Bibliographies of Spanish-American Literature).

Pages 1-59 of this bibliography contain an extensive list, with explanatory notes, of Costa Rican fiction. Although compiled at the point at which Costa Rican literature began to surge, the volume is still a good place to begin a study of precursors of Costa Rican literature in all its genres.

746 **Bibliografía anotada de obras de referencia sobre Centroamérica y Panamá en el campo de las ciencias sociales.** (Annotated bibliography of works of reference on Central America and Panama in the social sciences.)
Rachel Garst. San José: Friends World College, 1983. 2 vols. bibliog.

A large part of volume one (p. 137-218) of this extensive bibliography is on Costa Rica. In addition to published bibliographies this work contains reference works compiled by specific institutions such as the National Geographical Institute and associations such as the Costa Rican Demographic Association. It also contains indexes of Costa Rican periodicals and lists of theses presented at the University of Costa Rica and the Interamerican Institute of Agricultural Sciences at Turrialba. In volume two (p. 643-5) there is an annotated list of libraries and research institutes in Costa Rica.

747 **Central American Spanish: a bibliography, (1940-1953).**
Hensley C. Woodbridge. *Revista Interamericana de Bibliografía*, vol. 6, no. 2 (April-June 1956), p. 103-15.

This annotated bibliography covers several items – books, articles, and one dissertation – dealing with Costa Rican Spanish. All of the items were published between 1940 and 1953.

Topical

748 **Materiales para la historia de las relaciones internacionales de Costa Rica: bibliografía, fuentes impresas.** (Materials for the history of the international relations of Costa Rica: bibliography, printed sources.) Manuel E. Araya Incera. San José: Universidad de Costa Rica, Centro de Investigaciones Históricas, 1980. 91p. bibliog. (Bibliografías y Documentación, no. 1).

Contains 533 items conveniently grouped under six categories: general works on Central America and the Caribbean, international relations and the foreign policy of Costa Rica, relations of Costa Rica with other countries of Central America, relations of Costa Rica with the United States, relations of Costa Rica with European countries, and relations of Costa Rica with international organisms.

749 **Bibliografía antropológica de Costa Rica.** (Anthropological bibliography of Costa Rica.) María Eugenia Bózzoli de Wille. *Boletín Bibliográfico de Antropología Americana*, vol. 38, no. 47 (1976), p. 63-82. bibliog.

Includes books, articles, theses, and scholarly papers presented between 1969 and 1975. Some unpublished papers are included.

750 **Bibliography of poverty and related topics in Costa Rica.** Manuel J. Carvajal. Washington, DC: Rural Development Division, Bureau for Latin America and the Caribbean, United States Agency for International Development, 1979. 329p. bibliog. (Working Document Series Costa Rica, General Working Document, no. 1).

Includes 2,056 bibliographical entries, mostly in Spanish and English, about poverty and its ramifications in Costa Rica. Only a few items are annotated. The strength of the bibliography is the inclusion of PhD dissertations from land grant universities in the United States, theses from the Interamerican Institute of Agricultural Sciences at Turrialba and the University of Costa Rica, publications of the United States Agency for International Development, and reports from various agencies of the Costa Rican government. The volume is well indexed.

751 **Bibliografía agrícola de Costa Rica** (Agricultural bibliography of Costa Rica.) Margarita Castillo, María José Galrao. San José: Instituto Interamericano de Ciencias Agrícolas, Centro Interamericano de Documentación e Informacion Agrícola: SEPSA, Centro Nacional de Información Agropecuaria, 1980. 431p. (Serie Documentación e Información Agrícola, 0301-438, no. 83).

This comprehensive bibliography of 8,100 items published between 1945 and 1980 goes much beyond agriculture. It is divided into the following seventeen sections: agricultural sciences; geography and history; education and extension; administration and legislation; economics, development, and rural sociology; vegetable production; plant protection; forestry; animal husbandry; fishing; machinery and construction;

natural resources; bromatology; home economics; human nutrition; environmental protection; and related areas.

752 **Bibliografía de la geología de Costa Rica.** (A bibliography of Costa Rican geology.)
Compiled by Gabriel Dengo. Ciudad Universitaria: Universidad de Costa Rica, 1962. 67p. bibliog. (Publicaciones de la Universidad de Costa Rica, Serie Ciencias Naturales, no. 3).

In addition to titles on Costa Rican geology taken from the book *Bibliografía geológica y paleontológica de América Central* by Manuel Maldonado-Koerdell (Mexico City: Pan American Institute of Geography and History, 1958), this bibliography contains the titles of geology theses presented at the Universidad de Costa Rica.

753 **Reseña crítica de algunos libros y estudios sobre Guanacaste.** (Critical review of some books and studies on Guanacaste.)
Mireya Hernández de Jaén. *Revista de Costa Rica*, no. 38 (1974), p. 127-62. bibliog.

Although many people complain of the scarcity of information about the Province of Guanacaste, Hernández de Jaén has found hundreds of items, especially archaeological and historical ones, and she lists them in this annotated bibliography. Her critical comments tend to be positive no matter how unprofessional the item under review,but she has nonetheless performed a valuable research service in ferreting out studies otherwise likely to be overlooked.

754 **Bibliografías agrícolas de América Central: Costa Rica.** (Agricultural bibliographies of Central America: Costa Rica.)
Maritza Huertas. Turrialba, Costa Rica: Instituto Interamericano de Documentación e Información Agrícola, 1972. 166p. bibliog. (Bibliografías, Centro Interamericano de Documentación e Información Agrícola, no. 8).

In addition to numerous entries under separate crops and food products, there are sections in this bibliography dedicated to soils, fertilizers, forestry, agricultural economics, rural sociology, entomology, phytography, agricultural engineering, and animal husbandry. Costa Rican government reports are included, as well as theses from the Interamerican Institute of Agricultural Sciences.

755 **Bibliografía retrospectiva sobra política agraria en Costa Rica, 1948-1978.** (A retrospective bibliography on agrarian politics in Costa Rica, 1948-78.)
Dina Jiménez. San José: Universidad de Costa Rica, Vicerrectoría de Investigación, Instituto de Investigaciones Sociales, Centro de Documentación: Consejo Nacional de Investigaciones Científicas y Tecnológicas, 1981. 528p. bibliog.

This work is not easy to use because it is over-indexed, but it offers so many advantages that no researcher in the general area of agrarian politics should fail to consult it. The main advantage is that it is comprehensive, and includes published works and articles, government publications, and even newspaper articles.

756 **Bibliografía selectiva de la literatura costarricense.** (A selected bibliography of Costa Rican literature.)
Charles L. Kargleder, Warren H. Mory. San José: Editorial Costa Rica, 1978. 109p. bibliog.
Literary publications from 1869 to 1976 are included in this bibliography, a useful beginning point for anyone interested in Costa Rican literature. Biographies of literary figures, anthologies, and works of literary criticism are included but most historical works are not.

757 **Proceso de estructuración territorial en Costa Rica: bibliografía sobre la problemática urbana y regional, 1945-81.** (The process of territorial structure in Costa Rica: a bibliography of urban and regional problems, 1945-81.)
Allan Michael Lavall, Miguel Morales, Jorge Arriaga. San José: Instituto Geográfico Nacional, 1981. 410p. bibliog.
The great advantage of this bibliography is the broad coverage of publications of Costa Rican government agencies. Anyone who has worked in Costa Rica or who has done research there knows how difficult it is to identify and locate such studies. It is even more difficult outside Costa Rica because often these items never leave the country. Here is a list of over 3,000 titles of studies and reports on topics such as housing and urbanization, national and regional planning, autonomous agencies, and municipalities – precisely the kind of items lacking in academic libraries, and usually left out of the bibliographies based on the academic library collections. This bibliography does not solve the problem of access, but just knowing that these items exist is a help.

758 **Bibliografía antropológica aborigen de Costa Rica.** (Anthropological bibliography of the Indians of Costa Rica.)
Jorge A. Lines. San José: Universidad de Costa Rica, 1943. 270p. bibliog.
This bibliography is a partially annotated list of 1,262 items. Lines takes a broad view of the discipline of anthropology, and therefore items from cartography, geography, and history appear as well as items from archaeology and linguistics.

759 **Bibliografía antropológica aborigen de Costa Rica.** (An anthropological bibliography of aboriginal Costa Rica.)
Jorge A. Lines, Edwin M. Shook, Michael D. Olien. San José: Tropical Science Center, 1967. 196p. bibliog. (Occasional Papers, no. 7).
This bibliography, one of a series on the Central American republics, contains an extensive list of publications, including archaeological items, on the Indians of Costa Rica. It covers publications up to and including 1964.

760 **A report on folklore research in Costa Rica.**
Doris Z. Stone. *Journal of American Folklore*, vol. 64, no. 251
(Jan.-March 1951), p. 97-103, 113-20.

Some one hundred titles are listed in this survey of research on folklore. A brief introduction to the bibliography is included.

Maps of Costa Rica: an annotated cartobibliography.
See item no. 51.

Revista de Costa Rica en el siglo XIX. (Journal of Costa Rica in the 19th century.)
See item no. 226.

Libros y folletos publicados en Costa Rica durante los años 1830-1849. (Books and pamphlets published in Costa Rica during the years 1830-49.)
See item no. 689.

Costa Rica.
See item no. 690.

Research guide to Costa Rica.
See item no. 740.

Indexes

There follow three separate indexes: authors (personal and corporate); titles; and subjects. Title entries are italicized and refer either to the main titles, or to other works cited in the annotations. The numbers refer to bibliographical entries, not to pages. Individual index entries are arranged in alphabetical sequence.

Index of Authors

Index of Titles

Index of Subjects

Battle of Santa Rosa 205
Bay of Honduras 63
Beaches 33
Beans 539, 547
Beef 517, 519, 547, 563
Belgium 736
Belly, Felix 64
Bernhard, Prince of the
  Netherlands 598
Bertheau, Margarita 669
Bibliographies 742-60
Biblioteca Pâtria series 214
Bigot, Achiles 672
Biographies 160, 170, 181,
  189, 197, 260, 394,
  629, 631, 634, 637,
  641-2, 644, 647, 650,
  671-2, 693, 695-738,
  756
  see also individuals by
  name
Biolley, Paul 625
Biological diversity 568
Biological reserves 57
Birds 71, 74-5, 93-5, 103-6
  fruit-eating 104-5
Birth rate 242-3, 247, 333
Black Legend 194, 735
Blacks 260, 264-5, 269-71,
  635
  see also Afro-Costa
  Ricans; Creoles
Bolivia 469
Borders 214, 440-1
  see also Boundary
  disputes
Boruca 118
Boruca Indians 274, 281,
  289
Boruca-Térraba people 263
Botany see Flora and fauna
Boundary disputes 435-7,
  737
Bourgeoisie 495
Boza, Mario 598
Brazil 456
Brenes, Alberto M. 67
Brenes Mesén, Roberto
  613, 629, 637
  biography 712
Bribri people 257-8, 266,
  276, 289, 292
  language 654, 656, 664
Brunka Indians

language 654
Bryan–Chamorro Treaty
  421
Bryology see Mosses
Bureaucracy 311, 396, 458,
  503, 562
Burials 127, 133-4, 148-9
Buried treasure see Cocos
  Island
Business firms 13
  see also Commerce;
  Investment
Butterflies 90

C

Cabécar Indians 276, 289
  language 654, 656
Cacao 144, 495, 527
Caecilians 101
Cahuita 286
Calderón Guardia, Rafael
  Angel [President] 171,
  198, 227, 229, 232,
  298, 347-8, 371, 409,
  448, 620, 699, 704, 728
  biography 731
Calvert, Amelia 70
Calvert, Philip 67, 70
Calvo, Francisco 295
Camacho, Daniel 236
Campesinos [rural
  population] 231
  autobiographies 700
Canal Treaty 421
Cañas 106
Cañas, Juan Manuel de
  717
Cannabis 332
Capitalism 216, 313, 406,
  480
Carazo, Rodrigo
  [President] 382, 481
Cardona Peña, Alfredo
  629
Caribbean region 23, 265,
  268-71, 286, 524, 561,
  568
Caribbean Sea 62
Carnegie Museum,
  Pittsburgh 123, 148
Carrillo, Braulio 157, 208

Cartago 66, 145, 168, 181,
  224
  earthquake (1910) 44, 46
  genealogies 248
  refounded (1572) 194
  shrine 297
  social classes 188
Cartago–San Ramón area
  543
Cartography see Maps
Casement, Dan 569
Castes see Class
Castro, Fernando 377
Castro Madriz, José María
  [President] 427
Catholic anti-liberalism 415
Catholic Church see
  Roman Catholic
  Church
Catholic Union Party 708
Catholic–Protestant
  relations 293
Cattle ranching 31, 516-19,
  532, 543
  for export 331
Censuses 8, 50, 210, 240-2,
  250-2, 301, 325, 333,
  514, 581
Central America 237, 242,
  396, 398, 408, 499,
  673, 698, 714, 748, 759
Central America, ties with
  1, 166, 215, 427-8,
  431-42, 748
  see also countries by
  name
Central American
  Common Market 235,
  483, 494, 497, 508-12
Central American Mission
  [Protestant] 299
Central Bank of Costa
  Rica 472, 502, 722
  gold museum 108
Central place theory 29
Central Valley 27, 38, 48,
  168, 195, 288, 331,
  520-1, 569-70, 635, 734
  prehistory 118
Centre for the Study of
  National Problems
  198, 419
Ceramics 125, 130-1, 139,
  149

Housing 5, 38, 303, 307, 324, 333, 757
   market 367
Huetar Altántica 26
Huetar Indians 289
Hull, John 15
Human rights 1, 352-3, 442
   violations 3
Hummingbirds 106
Hydro-electricity 622

I

IADB *see* Inter-American Development Bank
Iconography 149
Ideology 408, 415-20, 441, 579, 583
Illegitimacy 334
Illiteracy 324
IMF *see* International Monetary Fund
Immigrants 8, 584
   see also Jamaican; Jewish *(etc) by name*
Immigration 209, 213, 265, 667
Imports 233, 422, 500, 517
   prices 470
   substitution 472, 476, 494, 508
   tax 497
Income distribution 324, 398, 464, 475, 488, 493, 587
   see also Poverty; Wealth
Independence 160, 174-5
   achieved (1821) 159
   150th anniversary (1971) 153
Independence of Guatemala (1821) 220
Independence of Mexico (1821) 220, 224
Indian art 108, 136, 676
   see also Precolumbian period; Prehistory and archaeology
Indian culture 113, 122
   changing patterns 266
   see also Anthropology; Ethnography

Indian languages 255, 261, 281, 654, 656, 664-5
Indian life 255, 263, 759
   social change 256
   see also specific groups by name
Indians and Spanish colonists 191
Indigenous art *see* Indian art
Individual liberty 223
Individualism 1
Industrialists 396
Industrialization 27, 231, 508, 510, 588, 617
Industry 13, 20, 22-3, 237, 367, 480, 509, 512-30, 622, 741
Inequality 3
   see also Income distribution; Land tenure
Infant mortality 243, 345, 493
Inflation 470, 483, 487, 494, 502
Infrastructure 367, 500
Insecticides 602-3
Insects 70-1
Instability *see* Economic instability; Political instability
Institute of Interamerican Agricultural Sciences 182
Institute of Land and Colonization *see* Land and Colonization Institute
Institute of Municipal Development and Assistance 303
Institutional tracking theory 546
Institutions 11, 14
   respect for 1
Instituto de Tierras y Colonización *see* Land and Colonization Institute
Instituto Indigenista Interamericano *see* Interamerican Indigenous Institute

Intellectuals 167
Intendency reforms 166
Inter-American Development Bank 499-500, 622
Interamerican Economic and Social Council 327
Interamerican Indigenous Institute 255, 267
Interamerican Institute of Agricultural Sciences 306, 746, 750, 754
Intergenerational relationships 314
Intergovernmental Committee on Migration 279
Internal migration 17, 31, 36, 278, 324
International boundaries 13
   see also Borders; Boundary disputes
International capitalism dependency on 157
International market conditions 312, 472
International Monetary Fund 373, 382, 443, 478, 481, 483
International relations 10, 214, 396, 486, 748
Investment 233, 496-507, 545
   see also Foreign investment
Investors 8, 49, 55-6, 503, 597
Iowa State University 541
Irrigation 534
Israel 262
Isthmus of Rivas 113
Italian immigrants 279, 584
Italy 229
ITCO *see* Land and Colonization Institute
Iturbide, Agustín de 224

J

Jade 109-11, 115, 119, 129, 137

Map of Costa Rica

This map shows the more important towns and other features.